THE GREAT INDIAN RELIGIONS

THE GREAT INDIAN RELIGIONS

BEING A POPULAR ACCOUNT OF

BRAHMANISM, HINDUISM, BUDDHISM, AND ZOROASTRIANISM

WITH ACCOUNTS OF THE VEDAS AND OTHER INDIAN SACRED BOOKS, THE BUDDHIST SACRED BOOKS, THE ZENDABESTA, SIKHISM, JAINISM, MITHRAISM, ETC

G. T. BETTANY

GYAN

Published by

GYAN

Gyan Publishing House
5, Ansari Road
Daryaganj, New Delhi-110002
Phone: 011-47034999, 9811692060
E-mail: books@gyanbooks.com

Distribution Network
gyanbooks.com
India, USA, Canada, UK, Australia

ISBN: 978-93-6780-650-0 (HB)

First Published, 1802

2nd Impression 2024

Printed at: Gyan Press, Delhi.

THE GREAT INDIAN RELIGIONS
Author: G. T. BETTANY

THE GREAT INDIAN RELIGIONS.

"The World's Religions" Series.

THE GREAT INDIAN RELIGIONS

BEING A POPULAR ACCOUNT OF

BRAHMANISM, HINDUISM, BUDDHISM, AND ZOROASTRIANISM.

With Accounts of the Vedas and other Indian Sacred Books, the Buddhist Sacred Books, the Zendavesta, Sikhism, Jainism, Mithraism, etc.

BY

G. T. BETTANY, M.A., B.Sc.,

Author of "The World's Inhabitants," "Life of Charles Darwin," etc.

WITH NUMEROUS ILLUSTRATIONS.

WARD, LOCK, BOWDEN AND CO.,
LONDON: WARWICK HOUSE, SALISBURY SQUARE, E.C.
NEW YORK: BOND STREET.
MELBOURNE: ST. JAMES'S STREET. SYDNEY: YORK STREET.
1892

PREFACE.

In recent years there has been an enormous amount of study of the religions of India and the allied people of ancient Bactria and Persia; and we may now form definite opinions as to many questions which in previous ages were not understood. There can be little doubt of the great antiquity of the religious ideas represented by the Vedas, extending probably to a thousand years before Christ. We see in them that the early belief in numerous spirits superintending departments of nature had become crystallised into poetry of a high order in the hands of a series of religious poets; and we realise too the common origin of numerous ideas about religion and the gods which both the early Aryan Hindus and the Greeks had. We find in them a worship of the Powers of Nature personified, which was in many ways of an elevating nature. Ideas of immortality and a future life are by no means absent. Later on, we find expressions pointing to the existence of ancestor worship and the tendency to deification of departed heroes.

In still later times the remarkable attainments of many Hindus, both in philosophy and in legislation, were displayed in such books as the Brahmanas, the Upanishads, and the laws of Manu; and by this time the Brahmans had made themselves of vital importance as a religious caste, without whom the Hindus could not attain or keep ceremonial and religious purity. Henceforward the Hindu system presents a remarkable combination of degeneration into polytheism with degrading rites, and of movements aiming at elevation and reform. The later of these have been Sikhism and the Brahmo Somaj, to which considerable reference will be made in the following pages.

Buddhism is really an offshoot of early Brahmanism, and was in part a revolt against the iron tyranny of the Brahmans, in part a revolt against polytheism and a reaction towards unbelief in any knowledge of the gods or certainty of immortality. The idea of seeking absorption in the Infinite was however conjoined with a practical moral discipline that long gave Buddhism an enormous vitality and power of increase. Later, like most religions, it became degraded, practically polytheistic, and full of meaningless or superstitious rites. In power to develop and influence people for good it appears now to be far inferior to Hinduism.

Zoroastrianism was a simpler yet a kindred system, reversing early Vedism in some curious features. In its simple worship of God by the symbol of fire it had a lofty side. In its conception of a dual government of the universe by good and evil powers it contributed most importantly to world-philosophy. It never appears to have degenerated like Hinduism, for Mohammedanism violently expelled it, and was manifestly a higher religion. Until modern days its few surviving representatives were sunk in ignorance even of their own religion; but a revival of learning has taken place among the Parsees, which bids fair to keep their religion alive in its purer aspects for a long time.

CONTENTS.

BRAHMA (FROM A NATIVE PICTURE).

CHAPTER I.

The Early Vedic Religion.

Analogies to Greek and Roman Religion—Date of the Rig-Veda, anterior to writing—Language of Rig-Veda—Religious basis—The earliest hymns—Worship of powers of Nature personified—Dyaus and Prithivi (heaven and earth)—The origin of things—Mitra and Varuna—Indra, the god of the clear blue sky—The Maruts, or storm-gods—The sun-gods, Surya and Savitri—Pushan—Soma, the Indian Bacchus or Dionysus—Ushas, the dawn goddess—Agni, the god of fire—Tvashtri—The Asvins—Brahmanaspati—Vishnu—Yama, and a future life—Virtues rewarded by heaven—Future punishment—Transition to monotheism and pantheism—Visvakarman—Absence of later Hindu doctrines—Organisation of early Hindus—Morals—The other Vedas—The Brahmanas—Human sacrifice—Animal sacrifice—Tradition of a flood—Immortality—Idea of the sun's course—Origin of caste—Self-assertion of Brahmans—Nature of the Brahmanas—Household sacrifices—Purification—Fasting—Establishment of sacrificial fires—The Upanishads—The syllable Om—The origin of the world in ether—The Atman, or self-existent—The Svetas-vatara—Transmigration of souls—Purpose of the Upanishads.

WHATEVER may have been the history of the Aryans, by whom the Vedas were produced, previous to their entering India, it is certain that when they did so, long before Buddhism took its rise, in the sixth century B.C., they had developed religious ideas and conceptions which present singular analogies and similarities to those which appear to be most primitive among the Greeks; and which suggest, if they do not prove, that the European and Hindu Aryans sprang from a common stock. When we find their divinities termed "devas," or "the shining ones," and recognise the same word in the Latin Deus, divinity; when we compare the Dyaushpitar (Heaven-Father) of Sanskrit, with Jupiter or Diespiter of Rome, and the Zeus of Greece; Varuna, the encompassing sky in Sanskrit, with Ouranos Uranus in Greek; and many other like words, we cannot help realising that, strange as it might seem at first, Brahmanism and Greek and Latin religion sprang from a similar source. And it is not very important which is the older. We know that the Hindu sacred books, the Vedas,—at any rate some of them,—are among the oldest of extant human compositions, and exhibit to us some of the earliest human ideas that were handed down by writing.[1]

Analogies to Greek and Roman religion.

The best opinions place the date of the Rig-Veda somewhere between 800 and 1200 B.C. The collection consists of ten books, containing altogether 1,017 hymns; eight out of ten books begin with hymns addressed to Agni, and others addressed to Indra follow. It appears probable that at least two distinct generations or series of authors composed them, the later being more imitative and reflective; and it is probable that some of the hymns date from a period earlier even than 1200 B.C. In the whole series there is no reference to anything connected with writing, and this suggests that they are relatively anterior to the Book of Exodus, where "books" and writing are distinctly mentioned. Even long after the period of the Rig-Veda, writing

Date of the Rig-Veda.

Anterior to writing.

[1] See Muir, "Original Sanskrit Texts" (M.); Max Müller, "History of Ancient Sanskrit Literature," "Lectures on the Origin and Growth of Religion," "Sacred Books of the East" (M. M.); Sir Monier Williams, "Indian Wisdom," "Hinduism" (M. W.); Sir W. W. Hunter, "India;" H. H. Wilson's works.

is never mentioned. Thus we must ascribe the preservation of these wonderful collections entirely to memory, which is, no doubt, equal to the task. Many years, we know, are still regularly spent by Brahmans in the slow, methodical learning and repetition of their sacred literature; and there is every sign of this habit having been handed down from a period when no other means of preserving the Vedas existed. In ancient compositions, later than the Rig-Veda, we are told in detail every event in the life of a Brahman, but there is no mention of his learning to write. It is not till we come to the Laws of Manu that writing is spoken of.

Language of Rig-Veda.

The very language of the Rig-Veda is a further confirmation of its antiquity. The words are so difficult of explanation as to have given rise to extensive commentaries ever since. When the words are known, great differences of opinion arise as to how they are to be connected together, or what idea they represent. Often the most puerile or irrelevant things (to us) are interspersed among the loftiest sentiments, and great verbosity alternates with the most terse and pregnant aphorisms. This precludes the idea of single authorship of any considerable portions. In fact, early Hindu literature was not concerned about authorship in the modern sense. The word Veda, meaning "knowledge," clearly refers to Divine knowledge, imagined as proceeding like breath from the self-existent Spirit, and inspiring a class of sages called Rishis; and thus it is held to this day to be absolutely infallible.

Religious basis.

The general form of the Vedas is that of the simplest lyrical poetry, with a not very regular metrical flow; and the matter is almost exclusively religious. This fact is regarded as due largely to the character of the people. "No great people, surely," said Prof. Whitney, "ever presented the spectacle of a development more predominantly religious; none ever grounded its whole fabric of social and political life more absolutely on a religious basis; none ever meditated more deeply and exclusively on things supernatural; none ever rose, on the one hand, higher into the airy regions of a purely speculative creed, or sank, on the other, deeper into degrading superstitions—the two extremes to which such a tendency naturally leads."

The earliest hymns.

Although the earliest Vedic hymns are so ancient, they must have been preceded by an indefinitely long period of growth and development of the race, for the language is fixed, complex, full-grown; the idea of gods was fully developed, indeed their number seems to have been fixed as thirty-three, who are described as all great and old, and are besought not to lead their votaries far from the paths of their fathers. It may be said generally that in the earliest hymns each god that is manifested is for the time being contemplated as supreme and absolute, and not limited by the powers of the rest. Max Müller says, "Each god is to the mind of the suppliant as good as all the gods. He is felt at the time as a real divinity, as supreme and absolute, in spite of the necessary limitations which, to our mind, a plurality of gods must entail on every single god." In fact the early Hindu of the Vedas was a worshipper of the powers of Nature personified, and capable of being influenced by his praises, prayers, and actions. Their qualities are not precisely limited or distinguished from one another. While the gods are termed immortal, they are mostly not regarded as uncreated or self-existent, but are often described as the offspring of heaven and earth. There is no uniformity, however, on this point. But there are numerous passages reconcilable with the view that some of these gods represent deified ancestors, as where they are said to have acquired immortality by their acts, or their virtues, or by gift of Agni; and it is even implied that the gods named were the successors of others previously existing. Thus we find Indra thus invoked, "Who made thy mother a widow? What god was present in the fray, when thou didst slay thy father, seizing him by the foot?" and there is no doubt that at times the gods are represented as being at war with one another. As to the powers and prerogatives of the gods, they are above all mortals, who can by no means frustrate their decrees,

Worship of powers of Nature personified.

they will reward dutiful worshippers, and punish the negligent.

Heaven and Earth, the progenitors of the gods, are represented by Dyaus and Prithivi. Hymns addressed to them include the following, "At the festivals (I worship)

VARUNA (FROM A NATIVE PICTURE).

with offerings, and celebrate the praises of Heaven and Earth, the promoters of righteousness, the great, the wise, the energetic, who, having gods for their offspring, thus lavish, with the gods, the choicest blessings, in consequence of our hymn. With my invocations I adore the thought of the beneficent

Dyaus and Prithivi (Heaven and earth).

Father, and that mighty inherent power of the Mother. The prolific Parents have made all creatures, and through their favours (have conferred) wide immortality on their offspring." . . . So closely did the old Hindus approach the Greeks and Romans in their conceptions of Mother Earth and Father Heaven. In various passages, however, they are themselves spoken of as created, especially by Indra, who formed them out of his own body, and to whom they do homage. How then was the origin of things imagined? The following extract is from Sir Monier Williams's metrical rendering of one of the most remarkable Vedic hymns.

The origin of things.

"In the beginning there was neither nought nor aught,
Then there was neither sky nor atmosphere above.
What then enshrouded all this teeming universe?
In the receptacle of what was it contained?
Was it enveloped in the gulf profound of water?
Then there was neither death nor immortality,
Then there was neither day nor night, nor light nor darkness,
Only the Existent One breathed calmly, self-contained.
Then first came darkness hid in darkness, gloom in gloom.
Next all was water, all a chaos indiscrete
In which the One lay void, shrouded in nothingness."

But Dr. Muir's literal translation gives a better notion of the original: "There was then neither nonentity nor entity; there was no atmosphere nor sky above. What enveloped (all)? Where, in the receptacle of what (was it contained)? Was it water, the profound abyss? Death was not then, nor immortality; there was no distinction of day or night. That One breathed calmly, self-supported; there was nothing different from, or above it. In the beginning darkness existed, enveloped in Darkness. All this was undistinguishable water. That One which lay void, and wrapped in nothingness, was developed by the power of fervour. . . . Who knows, who here can declare, whence has sprung, whence, this creation? The gods are subsequent to the development of this (universe); who then knows whence it arose? From what this creation arose, and whether (any one) made it or not,—he who in the highest heaven is its ruler, he verily knows, or (even) he does not know." From this we see that man in the ancient Vedic times had progressed almost, if not quite, as far in speculation as to the origin of things as the latest and most advanced of men, and with as little definite result.

Mitra and Varuna.

Leaving aside Aditi, apparently a personification of universal Nature or Being, the mother of the gods (Adityas), and capable of setting people free from sin, but confessedly a difficult personification to explain, we pass to consider the characters of Mitra and Varuna, sons of Aditi, frequently associated, and often interpretable as day and night. Varuna is sometimes represented as visible; and the two deities are said to mount on a car drawn by horses, and soar to the highest empyrean, and behold all things in heaven and earth. Sometimes the sun is called the eye of Mitra and Varuna; and both jointly and separately they are termed king of all and universal monarch. Varuna has attributes like those of the Greek Ouranos, Latinised as Uranus. He made the sun to shine; the wind is his breath; river courses are hollowed out by his command, and the rivers pour their water into the one ocean, but never fill it. He knows the flight of birds in the sky, the path of ships on the ocean, the course of the far-travelling wind, and beholds all the sacred things that have been or shall be done. He beholds as if he were close at hand. Whatever two persons sitting together, devise, Varuna the king knows it, as a third. He has unlimited control of men, and is said to have a thousand remedies; hence he is besought to show his deep and wide benevolence, and drive away evil and sin. Muir's verse translation, almost literal, is so attractive that it demands quotation.

"The mighty Lord on high, our deeds as if at hand, espies;
The gods know all men do, though men would fain their deeds disguise.
Whoever stands, whoever moves, or steals from place to place,
Or hides him in his secret cell—the gods his movements trace.
Wherever two together plot, and deem they are alone,
King Varuna is there, a third, and all their schemes are known.
This earth is his, to him belong those vast and boundless skies;
Both seas within him rest, and yet in that small pool he lies.

Whoever far beyond the sky should think his way to wing,
He could not there elude the grasp of Varuna the King.
His spies descending from the skies glide all the world around,
Their thousand eyes all-scanning sweep to earth's remotest bound.
Whate'er exists in heaven and earth, whate'er beyond the skies,
Before the eyes of Varuna, the King, unfolded lies.
The ceaseless winkings all he counts of every mortal's eyes;
He wields this universal frame, as gamester throws his dice.
Those knotted nooses which thou fling'st, O God, the bad to snare,
All liars let them overtake, but all the truthful spare."

INDRA (FROM A NATIVE PICTURE).

In this and in many other passages Varuna appears as a moral Being of high elevation. His forgiveness is implored by the Rishi or sacred bard; and it is urged that wine, anger, dice, or thoughtlessness have led him astray. Very much the same attributes are ascribed to Mitra and Varuna together as to the latter alone. It will be seen later how closely the Zoroastrian Mithra resembles the Indian Mitra; and there cannot be much doubt that this conception of the Deity existed previous to the separation of the Indian from the Iranian (Persian) branch. Later, Varuna became specially associated with the rule over water, and was solicited to send flood and rain from the sky.

Indra the god of the clear blue sky.

Indra and Agni, at first less important than the foregoing, later grow in importance: they were born of parents, and have various striking qualities, and there are many features of personal description given. Indra, god of the clear sky, is handsome, ruddy or golden-haired, with long arms, but has endless forms which he can assume at will. He rides on a shining golden car drawn by two golden horses, which move more swiftly than thought; he has a thunderbolt and other weapons, and is exhilarated by the libations of *soma* offered by his worshippers. In many passages the known effects of this favourite intoxicant were supposed

AGNI (FROM MOOR'S "HINDU PANTHEON").

to be felt by the gods. One of Indra's especial functions is to encounter and vanquish the hostile demons of drought. As Muir says, the growth of these ideas is perfectly natural and intelligible to those who have witnessed the phenomena of the seasons in India. "Indra is thus at once a terrible warrior and a gracious friend, a god whose shafts deal destruction to his enemies while they bring deliverance and prosperity to his worshippers. The phenomena of thunder and lightning almost inevitably suggest the idea of a conflict between opposing forces; even we ourselves often speak of the war or strife of the elements. The worshipper would at one time transform the fantastic shapes of the clouds into the chariots and horses of his god, and at another time would seem to perceive in their piled-up masses the cities and castles which he was advancing to overthrow." Frequently Indra is saluted as the god most powerful over the external world, "the most adorable of the adorable, the caster down of the unshaken, the most distinguished of living things." His worshippers are enjoined to have faith in him, and his power is asserted against denials of scepticism. He has a love for mortals, and is the helper of all men, a wall of defence and a deliverer, hearing and answering prayers. He is supposed to be capable of bestowing all kinds of temporal benefits, and in fact arbitrarily to control the destinies of men. Yet the simplicity of the worshipper is sometimes shown by prayers that the god will prove his prowess, and statements that "little has been heard of as done upon earth by one such as thou art." Indra is especially the champion and guardian of the Aryan Hindus against the darker races whom they subjected. It appears almost as if the conception of Indra expanded with the advance of the Aryans over India, while that of Varuna declined, who is more directly related to the early common Aryan belief before India was reached, and which appears also in the Zoroastrian Ormuzd and the Greek Ouranos. Another view regards Dyaus as the god whom Indra threw into the shade; answering to the difference between the time when in the more elevated and mountainous regions of Central Asia, the brilliant radiance of heaven was the holiest and most desirable thing, and the later time, in India, when the rainy sky was most longed for, and its representation as Indra became most popular.

The Maruts, or storm-gods.

Passing by Parjanya, the thundering rain god, and Vayu, the wind, as less important deities, we find the Maruts, Rudras, or storm gods, many in number, often associated with Indra and with Agni. Some extracts from one of the hymns addressed to them will give a better idea of the conceptions attached to them than a description. "They shake with their strength all beings, even the strongest, on earth and in heaven. . . . They who confer power, the roarers, the devourers of foes, they made winds and lightnings by their powers. The shakers milk the heavenly udders (clouds), roaming around they fill the earth with milk (rain). . . . Mighty you are, powerful, of wonderful splendour, firmly rooted like mountains, (yet) lightly gliding along;—you chew up forests like elephants. . . . Give, O Maruts, to the worshippers strength glorious, invincible in battle, brilliant, wealth-conferring, praiseworthy, known to all men. Let us foster our kith and kin during a hundred winters." (M. M.)

The Sun-gods, Surya and Savitri.

The gods personifying the Sun, under different phases, are Surya and Savitri, who are praised and described in the Veda with appropriate epithets; they are drawn in cars by numerous horses, preserve all things, enable men to perform their work, and see all things, both the good and the bad deeds of mortals. Surya is sometimes said to be dependent on Indra, who causes him to shine and prepares his path. Pushan is another solar deity, a guide on roads and journeys, a protector and multiplier of cattle and of human possessions generally. A hymn addressed to him runs thus: "Conduct us, Pushan, over our road; remove distress, son of the deliverer; go on before us. Smite away from our path the destructive and injurious wolf which seeks after us. Drive away from our path the waylayer, the thief, the robber. . . . O god who bringest all blessings, and art distinguished by thy golden spear, make wealth easy of acquisition. Convey us past our opponents; make our paths easy to traverse; gain strength for us here." Another hymn more emphatically prays the god for personal favours: "Bring to us wealth suitable for men, and a manly suitable householder who shall bestow on us gifts. Impel to liberality, O glowing Pushan, even the man who would fain bestow nothing; soften the soul even of the niggard. Open up paths by which we may obtain food; slay our enemies; let our

Pushan.

designs succeed, O glorious god." With him is sometimes associated Soma, and the two are celebrated together as the generators of wealth and preservers of the world.

Soma, the Indian Bacchus or Dionysus.

Soma, the god animating the exhilarating juice of the *soma* plant, probably a species of *Asclepias*, seems to represent Dionysus or Bacchus among the early Indian gods. The whole of the hymns, 114 in number, of the ninth book of the Rig-Veda are dedicated to him. Prof. Whitney says of him: "The simple-minded Aryan people had no sooner perceived that under the influence of this liquid the individual was prompted to and capable of deeds beyond his natural powers, than they found in it something divine; the plant which afforded it became to them the king of plants; the process of preparing it was a holy sacrifice; the instruments used therefore were sacred." The worship of Soma was very ancient, as it is mentioned in the Zend-avesta. To Soma are attributed almost all divine power and honours, especially in reference to his influence on the other gods and on his human votaries; but his worship declined and almost wholly passed away with the early Vedic worship.

Ushas, the dawn goddess.

Ushas, the goddess of dawn, has many of the most beautiful hymns addressed to her. She is described as restoring consciousness, smiling like a flatterer, awakening all creatures to cheerfulness, rousing into motion every living thing, born again and again, revealing the ends of the sky. "Blessed Ushas," says the worshipper, "thou who, animated by strength, shinest forth with wonderful riches, may I obtain that renowned and solid wealth which consists in stout sons, numerous slaves, and horses." (M.) Ushas is most usually described as the daughter of the sky, and is said to have the sun for her lover. The name Ushas (Ushasa) is identical with the Greek Ἠώς (Ēōs) and the Latin Aurora (=Ausosa).

Agni, the god of fire.

Agni, the god of fire (the Roman Ignis, the Slavonian Ogni), is a most prominent deity, being only paralleled, in the number of hymns addressed to him, by Indra. His characteristics aptly portray the wonder with which our forefathers viewed fire. Agni is an immortal and messenger from and to the gods, who has taken up his abode with man. He is both sage and sacrificer, supreme director of religious ceremonies and duties. "O Agni, thou from whom, as a newborn male, undying flames proceed, the brilliant smoke goes towards the sky, for as messenger thou art sent to the gods: thou whose power spreads over the earth in a moment, when thou hast grasped food with thy jaws,—like a dashing army thy blast goes forth; with thy lambent flame thou seemest to tear up the grass. Him alone, the ever youthful Agni, men groom like a horse in the evening and at dawn; they bed him as a stranger in his couch." (M. M.) The world and the heavens are made manifest at his appearance, after having been swallowed up in darkness. He is all-devouring, has a burning head, is thousand-eyed and thousand-horned; his flames roar like the waves of the sea, he sounds like thunder, and roars like the wind. He is described as having the highest divine functions of all kinds, and his votaries prosper and live long. He protects and blesses the worshipper who sweats to bring him fuel, or wearies his head to serve him. Prayers were made to him for all kinds of blessings, and for forgiveness for any sin committed through folly. The same simple familiarity in speaking to the gods which we have noticed before is seen in such an address as this: "If, Agni, thou wert a mortal, and I were an immortal. I would not abandon thee to wrong or to penury. My worshipper should not be poor, nor distressed, nor miserable." That there was also an association of Agni with a future may be gathered from the following paraphrase. (M. W.)

"Deliver, mighty lord, thy worshippers,
Purge us from taint of sin, and when we die,
Deal mercifully with us on the pyre,
Burning our bodies with their load of guilt,
But bearing our eternal part on high
To luminous abodes and realms of bliss,
For ever there to dwell with righteous men."

Tvashtar is the artisan and skilful contriver, and in

many ways answers to Hephaistos and Vulcan. He sharpens the iron axe of Brahmanaspati and forges the thunderbolts of Indra. All kinds of created powers are attributed to him. The Asvins are the earliest bringers of light in the morning sky, before the dawn, and are often connected with Surya; they were enthusiastically worshipped and praised, being hailed as chasers away of darkness, and described as the guardians of the slow and hindmost, as physicians restoring the lame, blind, and sick, as placing the productive germ in all creatures, and as capable of renewing the youth of all. Consequently they were supplicated for varied blessings, and were begged to overwhelm and destroy the niggard who offered no oblations. It is thought by good authorities that these gods represent deified mortals who were at the same time swift in their movements and appeared to possess remarkable healing powers.

Tvashtar.

The Asvins.

A somewhat later god than these is variously known as Brihaspati and Brahmanaspati, and personifies the worshipper, represented by the priest and sacrificer interceding with the gods, thus showing a distinct advance in moral ideas. The word Brahman is one of the most difficult in all Sanskrit, having been very diversely derived and explained; but while in its highest use it came to denote the objective Self or Cause of the universe, it may have originally represented the impulse and striving towards the gods, then every sacred word, formula, ceremony, or act, and finally the priest. Brahmanaspati is represented as the god of prayer, aiding Indra in conquering the cloud demon, and in some instances appearing to be identified with Agni. He is the offspring of the two worlds (Heaven and Earth), and is the inspirer of prayer, and by prayer accomplishes his designs; he mounts the chariot of the ceremonial and proceeds to conquer the enemies of prayer and of the gods. He is the guide and protector of the pious, whom he saves from calamities and blesses with wealth.

Brahmanaspati.

Vishnu is a god comparatively little mentioned in the Rig-Veda, but attaining great importance later. He is most characterised of old by the three steps by which he strode over the world; by his threefold existence as fire on earth, as lightning in the atmosphere, and as the sun in the sky; or as the sun in his three positions of rising, culmination, and setting. Triple power and functions are variously asserted of him, and he is said to assist other gods. Only sometimes is he adored independently, as thus: "Our hymns and praises have proceeded to Vishnu, the worker of many wonders: he is the wide-stepping, the exalted, whose primeval, creative wives are indefatigable." Often he is closely associated with Indra. How different a position he afterwards assumes we shall see later on. Most of the goddesses mentioned in the Veda we must omit reference to, as they are of less importance.

Vishnu.

YAMA (FROM A NATIVE PICTURE).

Yama and a future life.

It is in the later portions, the ninth and tenth books, of the Rig-Veda, that we find a marked reference to the ideas of immortality and a future life, although they are not entirely wanting previously, as in passages where mortals are said to have attained immortality, or to have gone to the gods, who prolong their lives. Sometimes, too, the souls of ancestors, the fathers existing with the gods, are invoked. These ideas are in the later books especially connected with Yama, the divine ruler of the spirits of the dead, by some supposed to represent the first man, and having a twin sister, Yami (Max Müller dissents from this view). Sir Monier Williams thus represents Yama in verse:—

"To Yama, mighty king, be gifts and homage paid.
He was the first of men that died, the first to brave
Death's rapid rushing stream, the first to point the road
To heaven, and welcome others to that bright abode.
No power can rob us of the home thus won by thee.
O king, we come; the born must die, must tread the path
That thou hast trod—the path by which each race of men,
In long succession, and our fathers, too, have passed.
Soul of the dead! depart; fear not to take the road—
The ancient road—by which thy ancestors have gone;
Ascend to meet the god—to meet thy happy fathers,
Who dwell in bliss with him. Fear not to pass the guards—
The four-eyed brindled dogs—that watch for the departed.
Return unto thy home, O soul! Thy sin and shame
Leave thou behind on earth; assume a shining form—
Thy ancient shape—refined and from all taint set free."

The two four-eyed dogs are of interest in comparison with Cerberus, the dog of Tartarus. Yama is not represented in the Rig-Veda, though he is in the later mythology, as having anything to do with the future punishment of the wicked. His dogs are said to wander about among men as his messengers, and to guard the road to his abode; the dead are advised to hurry past them with all speed. When the remains of the dead one have been placed upon the funeral pile, Agni, the god of fire, is besought not to scorch or consume him, but to convey him to the fathers as an offering. "Let his eye go to the sun, his breath to the wind. Go to the sky and to earth, according to nature; or go to the waters, if that is suitable for thee. As for his unborn part, do thou (Agni) kindle it with thy heat; with those forms of thine which are auspicious convey it to the world of the righteous." The spirit is then imagined to enter upon a more perfect life in which all desires are fulfilled; occupation will also be found in fulfilling the pleasure of the gods. It must not be supposed that in a time when even the gods are represented as marrying and indulging in soma, the heaven of the departed would be idealised.

Virtues rewarded by Heaven.

The following passage will give an idea of the virtues for which heaven was given: "Let him depart to those who through rigorous abstraction are invincible. Let him depart to the combatants in battles, to the heroes who have there sacrificed their lives, or to those who have bestowed thousands of largesses. Let him depart, Yama, to those austere ancient fathers who have preached and promoted sacred rites." These fathers are in some hymns held up as objects of admiration to their descendants; their descendants supplicate their good will, deprecate their wrath, and pray for their protection. They are asked to give them wealth, long life, and offspring. They are supposed to rejoice in libations and sacrificial food, and to come in thousands to the sacrifices.

Future punishment.

As to future punishment, Indra is in the tenth book of the Rig-Veda prayed to consign to the lower darkness the man who injures his worshipper; but it is not always certain that this lower darkness signifies a place of punishment. In the ninth book Soma is said to hurl the hated and irreligious into the abyss; but references to future punishment are confessedly vague and indistinct in the Rig-Veda.

One of the finest of the hymns of the Rig-Veda is the 121st in the tenth book, thus translated by Max Müller :—

"In the beginning there arose the Source of golden light—He was the only born Lord of all that is. He established the earth, and the sky;—Who is the God to whom we shall offer our sacrifice? (This last clause is repeated after each verse.)

"He who gives life, He who gives strength; whose blessing all the bright gods desire; whose shadow is immortality; whose shadow is death.

"He who through His power is the only King of the breathing and awakening world; He who governs all, man and beast.

"He whose power these snowy mountains, whose power the sea proclaims, with the distant river—He whose these regions are as it were His two arms.

"He through whom the sky is bright and the earth firm, He through whom the heaven was established, nay the highest heaven, He who measured out the light in the air.

"He to whom heaven and earth, standing firm by His

will, look up, trembling inwardly; He over whom the rising sun shines forth.

"Wherever the mighty water-clouds went, where they placed the seed and lit the fire, thence arose He who is the only life of the bright gods.

"He who by His might looked even over the water-clouds, the clouds which gave strength and lit the sacrifice, He who is God above all gods.

"May He not destroy us, He the creator of the earth; or He the righteous who created the heaven; He who also created the bright and mighty waters!"

Transition to monotheism and pantheism.

Thus we have contemplated in the earliest Vedic hymns a series of conceptions of distinct deities associated with the powers of Nature, and correspondingly named. It is only later that the idea seems to arise that these were all representations of different aspects of one power, and sometimes this appears to proceed from a desire to magnify the particular god whose praises are being specially celebrated; later, new names were used to signify these more enlarged conceptions, such as Visvakarman and Prajapati, not limited to any particular department, but believed to be the divine powers governing the earth. Another kind of expression shows an early form of pantheism, identifying the godhead with Nature: Thus "Aditi is the sky, Aditi is the air, Aditi is the mother and father and son. Aditi is all the gods and the five classes of men. Aditi is whatever has been born. Aditi is whatever shall be born." (M.)

Visvakarman.

Visvakarman (at first a name of Indra), the great architect of the universe, is in the tenth book of the Rig-Veda represented as the all-seeing god, who has on every side eyes, faces, arms, and feet, the father generator, who knows all worlds, and gives the gods their names. Similar attributes are in other hymns ascribed to other divine beings, such as Brahman, Prajapati, etc.; these being probably by different authors. We see here the product of the most advanced thought among these early Aryans, including a singular variety of attempts to express the thoughts to which the great phenomena of the universe gave rise in their minds. That these conceptions should be vague and often discordant and confused, and should include much that is puerile, is to be expected, when we remember that the sum of human thought up to the present day is "man cannot by searching find out God."

Absence of later Hindu doctrines.

Sir Monier Williams thus expresses his mature conclusions on some important points: "The Vedic hymns contain no allusion to the doctrine of transmigration of souls, which is a conspicuous characteristic of the Hindu creed in the later system. Nor do they afford any sanction to the prohibition of widow marriages, the encouragement of child-marriages, the iron rules of caste, and the interdiction of foreign travel. Nor is there in them any evidence that the personifications of the forces of nature were represented by images or symbols carved out of wood or stone." Animals were killed for sacrifices as well as for food, and we find no trace of the objection to eat the flesh of cows, which became so strong at a later period.

Organisation of early Hindus.

The people of the Vedas appear to have inhabited the Punjab, and to have only gradually extended their power into the tracts watered by the Jumna and Ganges. Every father of a family at first was entitled to act as priest in his own family, every chief in his own tribe; but as the hymns or prayers or offerings began to grow elaborate, there was a tendency to restrict worship, especially on important occasions, to special priests, who knew the approved hymns or the prayers which had been believed to be successful. In time it became a part of the chief's credit to retain about him favourite or noted priests, and their offices, like those of the chiefs, tended to become hereditary. Great gifts were lavished upon the priests by the kings, and many of the Vedic hymns commend this practice. Some of the hymns themselves were composed by kings; and the Rishis gradually asserted themselves so far as to claim superior rank to the temporal rulers, and erect themselves into a distinct caste of Brahmans; this position was not, however, acquired without a struggle.

Special families were distinguished by symbols, such as the number and arrangement of their locks of hair, or their being shaven in peculiar ways.

Morals.

As to morals under this *régime*, it appears that one wife was the rule, while a plurality was tolerated; women might marry a second time, and appear to have had some freedom of choice. Immorality was by no means unknown, and Indra is said to have declared that "the mind of a woman was ungovernable, and her temper fickle." Untruth was condemned, and the gods were said to punish lying; thieves and robbers are mentioned as infesting the highways or stealing secretly. Liberality and fidelity were held in high esteem.

How forcible is the contrast between the beneficence and the brightness, the helpfulness and the kindliness of the gods, as imagined by the earlier Aryans, and the severity, the ruthlessness, the cruelty, afterwards associated with Hindu gods. Direct access to the gods, direct benefits in return for prayer and offerings; intensity of prayer and meditation, fervency of petition, inevitably securing blessing, these are cardinal features of the early Hindu religion.

The other Vedas.

The Sama-Veda, and the Yajur-Veda are smaller collections formed mainly out of the Rig-Veda, but considerably modified; the former in verse, relating to the Soma offering, the latter in prose, relating to the other sacrifices. The Yajur-Veda belongs to a period when the Aryans had progressed into Eastern India, and when the Brahmans had acquired supremacy. The fourth great Vedic collection, the Atharva-Veda, belongs to a still later period, probably that of the Brahmanas, and contains the hymns and services then in use, modified or developed from the Vedic time. They exhibit a growth of belief in evil powers, and contain a series of formulas designed to protect against these, and against diseases and noxious animals and plants, together with cursings of enemies, and magic verses about all kinds of daily events, designed to counteract unfavourable events. This Veda contains a great number of words used by the people.

Not yet within the region of dates and relation to known persons, we come to the next great division of ancient Hindu literature, the Brahmanas, which exhibit to us a fully developed sacrificial system, and are intended for the use of the priests or Brahmans. We find here a series of prose compositions describing the connection of the sacred songs and words with the sacrificial rites. They may date from the seventh or eighth centuries B.C. We see in them, as in the case of so many priesthoods, the tendency to elaborate, to develop a ritual which could only be carried out by an hereditary caste, and which furnished a means of demanding large contributions from the votaries. The length of the Brahmanas themselves is wearisome, and is matched by their dogmatic assertion and their complex symbolism. Each of the collections of Vedic hymns has its proper Brahmanas, there being no fewer than eight Brahmanas to the Sama-Veda. Besides ceremonial directions, these Brahmanas contain numerous materials for tracing the growth of Hindu religious ideas. In one story of a king who had no son, after extolling the benefits that a son brings, the king offers, if a son be born to him, to sacrifice him to Varuna. When the son was born and was told of his destiny, he refused, and left his father's home. Disappointed of his victim, Varuna afflicted the father with dropsy. The son wandering for years in the forest, at last found a Brahman hermit in distress, whose second son voluntarily offered to be sold in order that he might be sacrificed instead of the king's son. Finally the substitute, by the virtue of Vedic prayers, was released from sacrifice. Another narrative describes how the gods killed a man for their victim, and the part of him fit for sacrifice entered successively into a horse, an ox, a sheep, and a goat, which were all sacrificed in turn. The sacrificial element remained longest in the goat, which thus became specially fit for sacrifice. Here we may see how an introduced human sacrifice may have been replaced by animal sacrifice.

The Brahmanas.

Human sacrifice.

Animal sacrifice.

In the Satapatha-Brahmana, perhaps the most interesting of all these books, there is found an early tradition of a flood. Manu, a holy man, was warned by a fish that a flood would sweep away all creatures, but he would rescue him. He was directed to build a ship and enter it when the flood rose; he did so, and fastened the fish to the ship, and was drawn by it beyond the northern mountains. When the flood subsided Manu was the only man left; a daughter was mysteriously born to him by virtue of religious rites, and ultimately the world was peopled with the sons of Manu. In later times it was said that the fish was an incarnation of Brahma, who assumed that form in order to preserve Manu.

Tradition of a flood.

The doctrine of immortality is more definitely presented in the same Brahmana than in the Vedic hymns. The gods had by toilsome religious rites become immortal. Death complained to the gods that men would follow their example. The gods enacted that no being should thenceforward become immortal in his own body, but should first present his body to Death.

Immortality.

A remarkable passage shows that the ancient Brahmans had a very advanced conception about the sun: "The sun never sets nor rises. When people think to themselves the sun is setting, he only changes about after reaching the end of the day, and makes night below and day to what is on the other side. Then when people think he rises in the morning, he only shifts himself about after reaching the end of the night, and makes day below, and night to what is on the other side. In fact he never does set at all."

Idea of the sun's course.

There seems little doubt that the origin and establishment of the caste system was largely due to the successful assertion by the Brahmans of their superior rank, combined with the growth of a class of cultivators distinct from the warriors, who at first were the great majority of the people. By this time the conquering Aryans had spread themselves over the basin of the Jumna and Ganges, and the Brahmans found it necessary and advantageous to show that they had a more noble, powerful, and important religion than the

Origin of caste.

aborigines whom they conquered. Consequently we meet with such assertions as the following: "Verily the gods do not eat the food offered by the king who is without a purohita (family priest)." In the Atharva-Veda, "May perfect, unceasing and victorious power accrue to those whose purohita I am. I perfect their kingdom, their might, their vigour, their strength. With this oblation I cut off the arms of their enemies." This development was accompanied with the development of ceremonial to such an extent that several classes of priests were required.

Self-assertion of Brahmans.

It is exceedingly difficult, without entering into great detail, to give an idea of the contents of the Brahmanas. Assuming the older ceremonials to be known, they comment upon every detail supposed to require explanation, discuss the meaning of particular verses or even of the metres used, and furnish explanations of the origin of the sacrifices, frequently consisting of legends and myths, often told very diffusely. A few extracts, somewhat abbreviated, from Mr. Eggeling's translation of parts of the Satapatha-Brahmana may give some notion of their contents.

Nature of the Brahmanas.

Every Brahmanical householder, from the period of setting up a household fire of his own, was enjoined to perform two monthly sacrifices, one at new the other at full moon, each lasting two days. The first was a fast day, in which the fire-places were swept and trimmed, and the fires lighted, and the Brahman and his wife took the vow to abstain from meat and some other foods, to cut off the beard and hair, except the crest-lock; to sleep on the ground in one of the chief fire-houses; and to observe silence. "He who is about to enter on the vow touches water, while standing between the (sacrificial) fires, with his face turned towards the east. The reason why he touches water is, that man is (sacrificially) impure on account of his speaking untruth,—and because by that act an internal purification is effected, for water is indeed (sacrificially) pure. . . . Looking towards the fire, he enters on the vow, with the text, 'O Agni, Lord of Vows! I will keep

Household sacrifices.

Purification.

the vow! May I be equal to it, may I succeed in it!' For Agni is Lord of Vows to the gods, and it is to him therefore that he addresses these words." As to the fasting, it is contended that the essence of the vow consists in fasting; for the gods see through the mind of man, and when he takes the vow they know that he means to sacrifice to them next morning, and betake themselves to his house. It would then be unbecoming in him to take food before they have eaten, and he may only eat what is not offered in sacrifice, which must be only what grows in the forest.

Fasting.

Every night and morning a burnt-offering of fresh milk had to be made to Agni, and on the morning of the sacrificial day, the householder chose his Brahman or superintending priest, an official who now becomes prominent—this class having indeed been no doubt the originator of the modern Brahmans. Then follows a most complex series of directions and explanations as to the various offerings.

Equally elaborate are the directions given for the ceremony of establishing sacrificial fires by a young householder. Four officiators were required besides the sacrificer; they erected two sheds or fire-houses by strict rules, and the fire was to be produced afresh by friction, or from certain definite sources, and placed upon the carefully purified fire-place. Towards sunset the sacrificer invoked the gods and ancestors thus: "Gods, fathers, fathers, gods! I sacrifice, being whom I am; neither will I exclude him whose I am; mine own shall be the offering, mine own the toiling, mine own the sacrifice!" He and his wife then entered the respective houses, and received with various ceremonies two pieces of wood specially prepared for reproducing the sacred fire the next morning. The offerings which followed were chiefly of rice and clarified butter. Later the sacrificer, having honoured the priests by washing their feet and giving them perfumes, etc., and given to each his share, invited them to eat. The Soma ceremony, according to the Brahmanas, is still more developed; but it is quite impossible to compress an account of it into a short space.

Establishment of sacrificial fires.

The Vedas and the Brahmanas in time proved insufficient for securing the hold of the priestly class on the people. The next great group of compositions were the Upanishads or mystical doctrine. Some of these are contained in a class of writings supplementary to the Brahmanas, known as the Aranyakas, or forest-books, intended for those Brahmans who, after

The Upanishads.

BRAHMA, VISHNU, AND SIVA, FROM THE ELLORA CAVES.

having performed all the duties of a student and a householder, retired to the forest to spend their remaining days in contemplation. The word Upanishad is said by native authorities to mean "to set ignorance at rest by revealing the knowledge of the supreme spirit"; its real etymological meaning is a session, especially of pupils round a teacher. These books consequently became the most important Vedic treatises for learned Hindus. Max Müller considers that although the Upanishads are later than the Brahmanas, their germs already existed in the Rig-Veda; and the earliest of them, he says, will always maintain a place in the literature of the world among the most astounding productions of the human mind in any age and in any country.

The Khandogya Upanishad, which continues the succession of the Sama-Veda, is one of the most important Hindu philosophical books. It begins by the astonishing advice (to the Western mind), "Let a man meditate," or as some translate it, "Let a man 'worship' the syllable Om." The real meaning is, first, that by prolonged repetition of the syllable, the thoughts should be drawn away from all other subjects and concentrated on the subjects of which that syllable was the symbol. It was the beginning of the Veda, and the essence of it, the symbol of all speech and all life. Om therefore represented man's physical and mental powers, and especially the spirit or living principle, and this is identified later with the spirit in the sun or in nature; and the beginning of this Upanishad teaches that no sacrifices, however perfectly performed, can secure salvation, while meditation on Om alone, or what is meant by it, will secure salvation or immortality. Finally the discussion reaches the highest philosophical subjects. The declaration that the origin of the world is ether, "for all beings take their rise from the ether, and return into the ether; ether is older than these, ether is their rest," has a striking significance when compared with the sentiments and speculations of philosophers at the British Association in 1888. But there is a further elevation of the ether, which includes more than the physical, for after defining Brahman as the immortal with three feet in heaven, the Upanishad says: "The Brahman is the same as the ether which is around us; and the ether which is around us is the same as the ether which is within us. And the ether which is within, that is the ether within the heart. That ether in the

The syllable Om.

The origin of the world in ether.

heart is omnipresent and unchanging. He who knows this obtains omnipresent and unchangeable happiness." (M.M.)

The Atman or Self-existent.

The highest doctrine of the Upanishad, according to Max Müller, is that the human Brahman recognised his own Self or "Atman" as a mere limited reflection of the Highest Self, and aimed at knowing his own Self in the Highest Self, which may be identified with the Divine Being, the Absolute, of Western philosophers. Through that knowledge he was to return to the Highest One and to regain his identity with it. "Here to know was to be, to know the Atman was to be the Atman, and the reward of that highest knowledge after death was freedom from new births, or immortality." This Atman was also the source of all visible existence, identical with the Brahman and the Sal, the true and real, which exists in the beginning and for ever, and gives rise to every kind of existence. Although there is much associated with this philosophy that seems trivial or fanciful, it contains the essence of pantheism; modern philosophers find it hard to advance really further than the ancient Hindus. There are many references to the sacrifices and to particular gods, and it is said that he who knows or meditates on the sacrifices as enjoined, has his reward in different worlds with the gods for certain periods of time, till at last he reaches the true Brahman. In this state

FIGURE OF HINDU PRAYING.
(From Temple at Madura.)

he neither rises nor sets, he is alone, standing in the centre; to him who thus knows this doctrine "the sun does not rise and does not set. For him there is day, once and for all."

The meditation on the five senses is one of the most striking; but the one which follows must be quoted as expressing one of the essential expositions of Brahman philosophy.

"All this is Brahman. Let a man meditate on that (visible world) as beginning, ending, and breathing in it (the Brahman).

"Now man is a creature of will. According to what his will is in this world, so will he be when he has departed this life. Let him therefore have this will and belief.

"The intelligent, whose body is spirit, whose form is light, whose thoughts are true, whose nature is like ether (omnipresent and invisible), from whom all works, all desires, all sweet odours and tastes proceed; he who embraces all this, who never speaks, and is never surprised,—

"He is my self within the heart, smaller than a corn of rice, smaller than a corn of barley, smaller than a mustard seed, smaller than a canary seed, or the kernel of a canary seed. He also is my self within the heart, greater than heaven, greater than all these worlds.

"He from whom all works, all desires, all sweet odours and tastes proceed, who embraces all this, who never speaks and who is never surprised, he, my self within the heart, is that Brahman. When I shall have departed from hence, I shall obtain him (that Self)." (M.M.)

In the Talavakara Upanishad occurs the following notable passage: "That which is not expressed by speech and by which speech is expressed, that alone know as Brahman, not that which people here adore: That which does not think by mind, and by which, they say, mind is thought: That which does not see by the eye, and by which one sees the eyes: That which does not hear by the ear, and by which the ear is heard: That which does not breathe by breath, and by which breath is drawn, that alone know as Brahman, not that which people here adore." (M.M.) This Upanishad is asserted to rest on penance, restraint, and sacrifice; "the Vedas are its limbs, the True is its abode. He who knows this Upanishad, and has shaken off all evil, stands in the endless unconquerable world of heaven."

The Svetasvatara contains a more fully developed doctrine, although it at times identifies the Brahman or highest self with several of the lower divinities. It teaches the unity of souls in the one and only self; the unreality of the world as a series of figments of the mind, as phenomenal only. There is no evolution of the Brahman; he is absolute and does not directly create. He deputes that office to Isvara or Deva, the Lord, Brahman under the semblance of a personal creating and governing god.

The Svetasvatara.

It is interesting to compare the pantheism of this Upanishad with previous expressions. Thus, "I know that great Person of sunlike lustre beyond the darkness. A man who knows him truly, passes over death; there is no other path to go. This whole universe is filled by this Person, to whom there is nothing superior, from whom there is nothing different, than whom there is nothing smaller or larger, who stands alone, fixed like a tree in the sky. That which is beyond this world is without form and without suffering. They who know it, become immortal, but others suffer pain indeed. . . . Its hands and feet are everywhere, its eyes and head are everywhere, its ears are everywhere, it stands encompassing all in the world. Separate from all the senses, yet reflecting the qualities of all the senses, and it is the lord and ruler of all, it is the great refuge of all." (M.M.)

Certain of the narratives incidentally introduced into the Upanishads show a still further development of what is dimly visible in the Rig-Veda, and still more clearly expressed in the Brahmanas, namely, a struggle between the good or bright gods (devas) and the evil spirits. In one of these Indra, as chief of the devas, and Virokana, chief of the evil spirits, are represented as seeking instruction of Prajapati, as a supreme god. Prajapati said, "The self which is free from sin, free from old age, from death and grief, from hunger and thirst, which desires nothing but what it ought to desire, and imagines nothing but what it ought to imagine, that it is which we must search out, that it is which we must try to understand." (M.M.) The two seekers desire to realise that self, and are led on by successive stages of illusion, Virokana being easily satisfied with the idea that the body is the self; but Indra persists in inquiries, and finally learns that the real self is the knower or seer as distinct from the mind or the eye as instruments.

Another Upanishad introduces in full expression the doctrine of transmigration. The immortality of the Self is taught, and that after death some are born again as living beings, some enter into stocks and stones. "He, the highest Person, who wakes in us while we are asleep, shaping one lovely sight after another, he indeed is called the Bright, he is called Brahman. . . . There is one eternal thinker, thinking non-eternal thoughts; he, though one, fulfils the desires of many. The wise who perceive him within their Self, to them belongs eternal peace. . . . He, the Brahman, cannot be reached by speech, by mind, or by the eye. He cannot be apprehended, except by him who says: *He is.* When all desires that dwell in the heart cease, then the mortal becomes Immortal, and obtains Brahman."

Transmigration of souls.

Max Müller sums up the purpose of the Upanishads as being "to show the utter uselessness, nay the mischievousness of all ritual performances; to condemn every sacrificial act which has for its motive a desire or hope of reward; to deny, if not the existence, at least the exceptional and exalted character of the devas, and to teach that there is no hope of salvation and deliverance, except by the individual self recognising the true and universal Self, and finding rest there, where alone rest can be found."

Purpose of the Upanishads.

So worked the human mind in India thousands of years ago, and produced these books of wisdom, believed to be directly revealed, mixed with much that is childish; so grew that highly artificial sacerdotal system by which the Brahmans gained that supremacy in India which they have never wholly lost.

WORSHIPPING THE GANGES.

CHAPTER II.

The Brahmanism of the Codes.

The Sutras—Rationalist philosophers—The six Shastras—Common tenets—How to attain emancipation—The banefulness of activity—The Sankhya philosophy—The Yoga philosophy—Early rituals—Gautama's institutes—Rites of purification—The four orders of Brahmans—The ascetic—The hermit—The householder's duties—Kings—When the Veda is not to be recited—Various restrictions—The duty of women—Outcasts—Penances and penalties—The laws of Manu—Date—Alleged origin—Self-repression inculcated—Study of the Veda a privilege—The gods in Manu—New births and hells—Duties of the four castes—Lofty claims of the Brahmans—The four periods of life—The student—Some liberal sentiments—The householder—The chief daily rites—Sacrifices for the dead—Position of women—Gifts—Spiritual merit—The hermit in the forest—The mendicant ascetic—The duties of a king—The Brahman's superiority—Crimes—Punishments and penances—Falsehood excused—Caste—Growth of mixed castes—Transmigration of souls—Efficacy of the code—Code of Yajnavalkya.

THE very mass of the Vedic sacred literature became its bane. No one could learn it all and understand it all. There arose a need for condensed statements of the revealed truth and the laws of ceremonial, and we have these in the form of Sutras, or collections of aphorisms tersely giving the most needful information; and these were composed by different authors for different Brahmanical families, and are exceedingly numerous. They are based upon the Vedas and the subsequent Brahmanas, and exhibit many of the peculiarities of the Vedic language. They give us for the first time a full account of the castes, composed at a time contemporaneous with the rise and spread of Buddhism.

The Sutras.

During the same period, probably about 500 B.C., there arose, contemporary with Buddha, a number of rationalist philosophers, who, while accepting the authority of the Vedas and the supremacy of the Brahmans, speculated freely on questions of philosophy and the moral government of the universe. Finally these were arranged in six main systems of teaching, sometimes called the six Shastras. Which of these is the earlier cannot yet be considered settled. But a great deal is common to most of the systems, and is still held by the majority of educated Hindus. Such articles of common belief are: the eternity of the soul, both the supreme soul or Brahman and the individual soul or Atman; the eternity of matter, or that substance out of which the universe is evolved; that the soul can only exercise thought and will when invested with some bodily form and joined to mind, and has in successive ages become manifest as Brahma, Vishnu, Siva, etc., and in the form of men; that the union of the soul with the body is a bondage, and in the case of men produces misery; that consequences inevitably follow acts, whether good or bad, and these are partly suffered in heaven or hell, and partly have to be worked out through continual transmigrations of the soul in varied animal, material, or higher forms; that this transmigration is the explanation of all evil, but the soul bears the consequences of its own acts only, though these may have taken place in an inconceivable number of past existences, not recollected; and finally

Rationalist philosophers.

The six Shastras.

Common tenets.

that the great aim of philosophy is to produce indifference in thought, feeling and action, and to enable the individual to return to the condition of simple soul.

The terseness of these Sutra philosophies may be illustrated from the Nyaya of Gautama (a philosopher distinct from the great Buddha). Deliverance from the misery of repeated births is to be thus attained: "Misery, birth, activity, fault, false notions; on the removal of these in turn (beginning with the last), there is the removal also of that which precedes it; then ensues final emancipation." (M.W.) A Hindu comment on this is as follows: "From false notions proceed partiality and prejudice; thence come the faults of detraction, envy, delusion, intoxication, pride, avarice. Acting with a body, a person commits injury, theft, and unlawful sensualities—becomes false, harsh, and slanderous. This vicious activity produces demerit. But to do acts of charity, benevolence, and service with the body; to be truthful, useful, agreeable in speech, or given to repetition of the Veda; to be kind, disinterested, and reverential—these produce merit. Hence merit and demerit are fostered by activity. This activity is the cause of vile as well as honourable births. Attendant on birth is pain. That comprises the feeling of distress, trouble, disease and sorrow. Emancipation is the cessation of all these. What intelligent person will not desire emancipation from all pain?"

How to attain emancipation.

Banefulness of activity.

This system, with its supplement, the Vaiseshika, teaches the eternity of material atoms, and also of the supreme Soul and of individual souls. The Sankhya philosophy is still more positive on these points, and says: "There cannot be the production of something out of nothing; that which is not cannot be developed into that which is." It recognises that there is a being or essence which evolves or produces everything else, together with Souls which neither produce nor are produced, but become united with the world-evolver in varied degrees. The development of these ideas in later Hindu theology and philosophy will be referred to hereafter.

The Sankhya philosophy.

The Yoga philosophy is the foundation of much of the asceticism of the Hindu. It directly acknowledges the supreme Being, and aims at teaching the human soul to attain perfect union with the supreme Soul. In it we have the fuller development of the benefits of contemplating the syllable *Om*, the symbol of the deity. Mental concentration is facilitated by bodily restraint and postures, religious observances, suppression of the breath, restraint of the senses, etc., and by these in their varied forms, the devotee is supposed to attain union with the supreme Being, even in the present life.

The Yoga philosophy.

The remaining chief systems of philosophy, the Jaimini and the Vedanta, are mainly concerned with ritual. The former may be said to have made a god of ritual, and appealed to the Veda as infallible. The Vedanta professes to be based upon the Upanishads and their pantheism.

Early rituals.

Much of the ceremonial of the Hindus was also very early condensed in Sutra form, and every school had its own form. Several of these, preceding the celebrated laws of Manu, have come down to us. They are a kind of manual composed by the Vedic teachers for use in their respective schools, and only later put forward as binding on Aryans generally. The "Institutes of the Sacred Law," ascribed to Gautama, begins by acknowledging the Veda as the source of the sacred law, and proceeds to fix the period and mode of initiation of a Brahman, and the rites of purification after touching impure things. Here is a specimen of these rites.

Gautama's Institutes.

Rites of purification.

"Turning his face to the east or to the north, he shall purify himself from personal defilement. Seated in a pure place, placing his right arm between his knees, arranging his dress (or his sacrificial cord) in the manner required for a sacrifice to the gods, he shall, after washing his hands up to the wrist three or four times, silently, sip water that reaches his heart, twice wipe his lips, sprinkle his feet and his head, touch the cavity in the head with his right hand, and place it on the crown of his head and on his navel."

Students of the Vedas had to study each for twelve years, but might restrict their study to one Veda only. After the Veda had been studied, he might choose which order of Brahmans he would enter; that of the student, the householder, the ascetic, or the hermit in the woods. The ascetic was required to live by alms, to restrain every desire, and maintain an attitude of indifference towards all creatures, whether they did him an injury or kindness. The hermit was to live in the forest, and subsist on roots and fruits, practising austerities. He was to worship gods, manes (ancestor worship), men, goblins, and Rishis (great Vedic teachers). He must not enter a village, nor step on ploughed land; his dress must be made of bark and skins.

The four orders of Brahmans.

The ascetic.

The hermit.

For the householder, marriage and its rites are of the utmost importance, and full directions are given as to the choice of a wife and the ceremonies attending marriage, which vary according to the kind of marriage. The offspring of marriages with other castes give rise in each case to a distinct caste. Complex domestic ceremonies are prescribed, with offerings to the deities presiding over the eight points of the horizon, at the doors of the house to the Maruts, to the deities of the dwelling inside the house, to Brahman in the centre of the house, to the Waters near the water pot, to the Ether in the air, and in the evening to the beings walking about at night. A kindly courtesy is shown in the direction that a householder before he eats shall feed his guests, infants, sick people and women, aged men, and those of low condition. A Brahman is allowed to earn his living by varied occupations in times of distress; but he is forbidden to sell a great many specified kinds of goods.

The householder's duties.

The authority of kings is upheld in Gautama's Institutes, but at the same time high privileges are demanded for Brahmans, who, if of high rank and religious character, must not be corporally punished, imprisoned, fined, exiled, or reviled. Truth-speaking and the ascertainment of truth are strongly inculcated.

Kings.

One of the most curious chapters in these Institutes details a multitude of circumstances in which the Veda is not to be recited; as, for instance, if the wind whirls up the dust in the daytime, or if it is audible at night, if the barking of many dogs and jackals or the braying of many donkeys is heard, when the reciter is riding in a carriage or on beasts of burden, in a burial ground, in the extremity of a village, when it thunders and rains, etc., etc. Equally curious are the particulars of the gifts which may be accepted from twice-born persons (*i.e.*, pure Aryans). If the means of subsistence cannot be otherwise obtained, it may be accepted from a Sudra (one of the slave or subject races). A householder may not eat food into which a hair or an insect has fallen, nor what has been smelt at by a cow, nor what has been cooked twice, nor what has been given by various people of bad character performing low offices. The classes of animals that may not be eaten remind one of the ceremonial restrictions of Leviticus; but in fact the principle of tabooing certain things to those who belong to a higher or select order is found in many parts of the world. The milk of sheep, camels, and entire-hoofed animals was forbidden to the Brahmans. Five-toed animals were not to be eaten, except the porcupine, the hare, the boar, the iguana, the rhinoceros, and the tortoise; nor animals with a double row of teeth, those covered with an excess of hair, those with no hair, entire-hoofed animals, and indeed whole groups of creatures.

When the Veda is not to be recited.

Various restrictions.

Women were enjoined to fulfil their duty to their husbands strictly, and restrain their tongues, eyes, and actions; yet much that Christians would revolt against is declared lawful and right for her to do. Early betrothals are enjoined. The crimes for which a man becomes an outcast are very varied, including murder and many crimes against Brahmans, and association with outcasts; thus boycotting is almost as old as Brahmanism, if not older. "To be an outcast," says Gautama, "means to be deprived of the right to follow the lawful occupations of twice-born men,

The duty of women.

Outcasts.

and to be deprived after death of the rewards of meritorious deeds."

Numerous and severe penances for various offences are enjoined. He who has killed a Brahman must emaciate himself and thrice throw himself into a fire, or remaining chaste he may, during twelve years, enter the village only for the purpose of begging, carrying the foot of a bedstead and a skull in his hand, and proclaiming his deed; thus standing by day, sitting at night, and bathing thrice a day, he may be purified in twelve years, or by saving the life of a Brahman. It is most striking how vigorously the Brahman literature maintains the sanctity and inviolability of its priests, and claims to exert throughout the life of the Aryans a minute authority scarcely paralleled by the Church of Rome. Some of the severest penalties are those inflicted for touching spirituous liquor. Thus "they shall pour hot spirituous liquor into the mouth of a Brahman who has drunk such liquor; he will be purified after death." Severe secret penances are enjoined on those whose sins are not publicly known. It is not to be supposed that the worship of the gods is intentionally lowered by these regulations; but the very great importance assumed by ceremonial observances and penances naturally tended to lower the dignity of the gods and raise that of the Brahmans. It is not wonderful, therefore, that Buddhism should have arisen.

Penances and penalties.

THE LAWS OF MANU.

We have not space to compare this lawbook with later ones which bear the names of Vasishtha, Baudhayana, and Apastamba, or to give an account of the Grihya Sutras or books specially on domestic ceremonies; but must pass on to the celebrated Laws of Manu, a metrical version of the whole Brahmanical scheme, dating, according to some authorities, from the fifth century B.C.; but Prof. Bühler does not consider it certain that it existed in its present form earlier than the beginning of the second century A.D., though undoubtedly it is derived from earlier versions containing

Date.

HINDU RELIGIOUS MENDICANT.

substantially the same matter. It results, in fact, from the gradual transformation of the teaching of a school into a general lawbook. But in process of time this book became surrounded by a multitude of fictitious legends designed to support its divine authority and secure the obedience of all Aryans. The first chapter of Manu is an apt illustration of this, and we therefore quote a portion from Bühler's translation.

"The great sages approached Manu, who was seated with a collected mind, and having duly worshipped him, spoke as follows:—

"'Deign, divine one, to declare to us precisely and in due order the sacred laws of each of the four chief castes and of the intermediate ones.

Alleged origin.

"'For thou, O Lord, alone knowest the purport (*i.e.*) the rites, and the knowledge of the soul, taught in this whole ordinance of the Self-Existent, which is unknowable and unfathomable!

"'He who can be perceived by the internal organ alone, who is subtile, indiscernible, and eternal, who contains all created beings and is inconceivable, shone forth of his own will.

"'He, desiring to produce beings of many kinds from his own body, first with a thought created the waters, and placed his seed in them.

"'That seed became a golden egg, in brilliancy equal to the sun; in that (egg) he himself was born as Brahman, the progenitor of the whole world.'"

After a very fanciful account of the derivation of all creation and of the relations of the creator to the creatures, it is stated that the creator himself composed these Institutes and taught them to the author, Manu, who deputes Bhrigu his pupil to recite them.

It appears that the introduction of the Laws of Manu as a general authority was due to the great accumulation of older works, having but a local and limited authority, and to the gradual extension of the influence of a particular school of general religious and legal instruction. No doubt one factor which contributed to its wide reception was the extended description of the duties and powers of the king and of the administration of justice, and another was its general relation and suitability to all Aryans, whatever their caste. Their authority was clenched and upheld by their being given out as the work of Manu, the typical man, the offspring of the self-existent Brahman, and consequently of double nature, divine and human. Hence he was invoked as Lord of created beings, and even as identical with Brahman, the supreme Soul. In the Rig-Veda he is frequently termed Father Manu, and it is stated that "the five tribes" or "the races of men" are his offspring. We have already referred to the legend in the Satapatha-brahmana in which Manu is said to have been saved from a great flood which destroyed all other creatures. He thus naturally represents social and moral order, and is the type of the temporal ruler, the inspired teacher and the priest combined. In many passages of the Rig-Veda his sacrifices are mentioned, and the gods are begged to accept the offerings of the priests as they accepted those of Manu.

That writing was known and in considerable use when the Laws of Manu were compiled, is evident from several passages, and also from the complex translations which are mentioned, which would have been impossible without writing. The number of archaic phrases and the primitive customs described show that it is based on earlier works; and by careful study a very good idea of its development may be formed.

In giving some account of the Laws of Manu an endeavour will be made to dwell principally upon their religious aspect; but it is difficult for the Western mind to realise the extent to which every detail of a Hindu's life and conduct is connected with and supported by his religious belief. In fact the Christian ideal, that the whole life should be religious, has long been practised by a vast number of Hindus, although the form, basis, and nature of the religions differ so widely.

High religious ideal.

The assent of the heart is the inner sanction of the Hindu law, supported by the authority of Manu, the Veda, the Vedic teachers, and the customs of holy men. The desire of rewards is

Self-repression inculcated.

declared to be not laudable in itself, but it is recognised and utilised; and the man who discharges his prescribed duties is promised the attainment of the deathless state, and even in this life the realisation of all his desires. How completely the system was directed to self-repression and the production of passivity in this life may be seen by this verse: "That man may be considered to have really subdued his organs, who, on hearing and touching and seeing, or tasting and smelling anything, neither rejoices nor repines." The privilege of being instructed in the Veda is strictly fenced in, but the limitations may be relaxed by presents of money. Even in times of dire distress, however, a Vedic teacher was rather to die with his knowledge than sow it in barren soil. The Brahman unlearned in the Veda is stigmatised as useless, like a wooden elephant, having nothing but the name in common with his kind. The Veda is, indeed, extolled to a position which is only rivalled by those whom some have called Bibliolaters. Thus we read that the Veda is the eternal eye of the manes, gods and men, and beyond human comprehension. Everything not founded on it is founded on darkness, and produces no reward after death; the eternal lore of the Veda upholds all created beings. He only who knows the Veda deserves royal authority, the office of a judge, the command of armies. By knowledge of the Veda the taint arising from evil acts is burnt out of the soul. A Brahman who retains the Rig-Veda in his memory is not stained by guilt, though he may have destroyed the three worlds. Study of the Upanishads is mentioned as necessary to the attainment of union with the supreme Soul.

Study of the Veda a privilege.

As to the gods other than this universal Spirit or Soul, they scarcely go beyond the lists already given in the Vedic period, such as Indra, Surya, the Maruts, Yama, Varuna, Agni, etc., whose energetic action the king is to emulate; but they appear to occupy a very moderate place in the scheme, the Supreme Spirit and the Brahmanic rites being chief. Indeed, there is a manifest leaning towards pantheism, it being frequently declared that everything proceeds from Brahma the uni-

The gods in Manu.

versal Soul, and will ultimately be absorbed once more in the same. The whole philosophy is affected by the doctrine of transmigration of souls, new births in the same or a lower order of creation or in hells being the result of evil conduct, and absorption in the Supreme Soul being the grand result of the greatest merit. The hells described, though terrible, are consequently only temporary. Among the torments are "being devoured by ravens and owls, the heat of scorching sand, being boiled in jars," etc. Altogether, theology is largely absent from Manu. But it must be remembered that the constant study of the Veda is everywhere inculcated. There is scarcely any reference to public worship or to temples; and from its whole tone we see how the family was the keystone of the Brahmanic religion. The influence of the Brahmans over the domestic life of the people was profound and sufficient at the time when the code of Manu was composed.

New births and hells.

The original castes are stated to be four, the Brahman, the Kshatriya or warrior, the Vaisya (cultivator), and the Sudra or servant; and (as in the tenth book of the Rig-Veda) they originated respectively from the mouth, arms, thighs, and feet of Brahma, who assigned them their separate duties. To Brahmans he assigned teaching and studying the Vedu, sacrificing for their own benefit and for others, and giving and accepting of alms; to Kshatriyas the protection of the people, the bestowal of gifts, the offering of sacrifices, the study of the Veda, and abstinence from sensual pleasures; to the Vaisyas tending cattle, the bestowal of gifts, the offering of sacrifices, the study of the Veda, trading, lending money, and the cultivation of land; to the Sudras simply to serve the other three.

Duties of the four castes.

The Brahman caste is exalted far above the others, having sprung from the mouth of Brahma, being the first-born, the preserver of the Veda, and having the right of expounding it. "What created being can surpass him, through whose mouth the gods continually consume the sacrificial viands and the offerings to the dead?" The most distinguished Brahman is he who fully performs his duty and knows

Lofty claims of the Brahmans.

the Brahman; he in fact becomes one with Brahma the creator. The most extravagant claims of lordship over all creatures, of possession of everything, are made on his behalf. In fact, not only is everything bestowed upon him, his own already, but other mortals are stated to owe their subsistence to the benevolence of the Brahmans. In some passages of Manu a Brahman is even lifted to the rank of a divinity, whether he were ignorant or learned, and even if he were occupied in a mean occupation. A Brahman who studies Manu and faithfully performs his duties is said to be never tainted by sins of thought, word, or deed, and to sanctify any company he may enter, together with seven ancestors and seven descendants. Surely more arrogant self-assertion was never advanced and admitted than by these Brahmans. The king is warned not to provoke them to anger, for it is asserted that they could instantly destroy him and his army, by their power over all creation, and by the utterance of magic texts. Yet, inconsistently enough, it is allowed that just as Kshatriyas cannot prosper without Brahmans, so Brahmans cannot prosper without Kshatriyas. Their persons are declared inviolable, and the crime of threatening a Brahman with a stick will be punished in hell for a hundred years, while the actual striker of a Brahman will remain in hell a thousand years. Still more extravagant is this further threat: "As many particles of dust as the blood of a Brahman causes to coagulate, for so many thousand years shall the shedder of that blood remain in hell." This system could of course only be maintained by the receipt of heavy fees. The repetitions of the Veda and the performance of the sacrifices were made to depend upon the gifts to the officiating Brahmans. No taxes were to be paid by them; and any king who suffered a learned Brahman to die of hunger would have his kingdom afflicted by famine, while the meritorious acts of any Brahman whom he protected would increase the king's wealth, length of life, and kingdom. Yet, if, after all these injunctions, a Brahman failed to receive proper patronage and support, he might become a soldier, a cultivator, or a trader.

The four periods of life. The student.

We must give some further detail of the Brahman's life and course of study; for although it only partially applies to the other classes of Hindus, it represents that ideal which they continually looked up to and revered, and is as characteristic of Hindu religious life as that of the clergyman of the present day is of our own. We cannot fail to be astonished at the lengthy student period which the Brahman must go through. Studentship might last for nine, eighteen, or thirty-six years, or even for the whole of life. The most important of the numerous preliminary rites was the investiture with the sacred cord or sacrificial string, which must be of three threads of cotton, twisted to the right, and worn over the left shoulder and across the body to the right hip. The ceremony commenced with taking a staff as tall as the pupil, and worshipping the sun while standing and walking round the sacred fire, after which he begged alms and food in succession of each person present according to a fixed order. After having eaten, and purified himself with water, a series of formalities is required before the teacher begins to instruct his pupil in the Veda, the syllable Om being always pronounced at the beginning and end of a lesson. Once initiated, regular bathing, with libations of water to the gods, the inspired Rishis, and deceased ancestors, is required of the Brahman student, and he must reverence the deities (explained later to mean, "worship the images of the gods"), and place fuel on the sacred fire. He must live a chaste life, refrain from meat and all sensuality, from dancing, singing, and playing musical instruments, must never injure any living creature, must not wear shoes or use an umbrella, and must refrain from anger, covetousness, idle disputes, and gambling. The regulations for securing reverent behaviour towards the teacher are very elaborate; and parents and elders generally are to be highly regarded. It is declared that the trouble and pain which parents undergo on the birth of their children cannot be compensated even in a hundred years, and obedience to them and to the teacher are the best forms of austerity; the son must rejoice to do what is agreeable and beneficial to them; by honouring them the three worlds are gained;

HINDU SUTTEE (SATI), OR THE SELF-IMMOLATION OF A WIDOW.

for him who honours them not, all rites are fruitless.

Somewhat surprisingly, in the midst of these stringent regulations we come upon the following liberal sentiments: "He who possesses faith may receive pure learning even from a man of lower caste, and an excellent wife even from a base family."

Some liberal sentiments.

"Even from poison nectar may be taken, even from a child good advice, even from a foe a lesson in good conduct, and even from an impure substance gold.

"Excellent wives, learning, the knowledge of the law, the rules of purity, good advice, and various arts may be acquired from anybody."

Finally, the Brahman who has not broken his vow during his student stage is promised after death the highest abode, and that he will not be born again in this world.

The householder.

The stage of a householder being at length reached, the Brahman must marry a wife of equal caste, free from bodily defects and having various good qualities; but polygamy is allowed though not recommended, and when the first wife is one of equal caste, another wife may be taken from each of the inferior castes. Eight different forms of marriage, four laudable and four blamable, the chief differences being in the matter of dowry and attendant circumstances, the highest rank being accorded to a marriage where the parent of the bride offers her with costly garments and jewels to a learned Brahman; the son of such a wife is said to liberate from sin ten ancestors and ten descendants if he does meritorious works.

The chief daily rites.

Sacrifices for the dead.

The Brahman householder had to perform daily five chief rites: (1) muttering the Veda; (2) offering water and food to ancestors; (3) a burnt offering to the gods; (4) an offering to all creatures, including aged parents, good and evil spirits, consisting of the scattering of rice-grains on the housetop or outside the door; (5) an offering to men, consisting of hospitable reception of (Brahman) guests. This last was naturally considered of great importance, as it afforded the chief means of support to the students, ascetics, and hermits. Sacrifices for the dead were required to be performed every new moon, and at these times learned Brahmans were specially entertained. A long list of those who must not be invited or who must be shunned on these occasions is given, including physicians, temple-priests (implying that these were rising in importance and were considered to have interests opposed to those of the domestic Brahmans), sellers of meal, actors or singers, one-eyed men, incendiaries, drunkards, gamblers, those who had forsaken parents. The great importance assigned to these celebrations for deceased ancestors,—being declared much more important than the rites in honour of the gods,—seems to indicate that ancestor worship among the Aryans was later than nature worship. The funeral sacrifices further acquired importance to the Hindus as affording the basis of their law of inheritance. All who offered the funeral cake and water together were bound in one family, represented by the eldest male, although the living family had a joint interest in the family property. This part of the subject we cannot here detail, although intimately connected with and enforced by the religious sanction.

An astonishing number of daily rites and of things to be avoided is laid down for good Brahmans, and this can only be matched by the extreme of early Pharisaic restriction; but although the eating of meat is forbidden in general, it is expressly enjoined on certain occasions.

Position of women.

As regards the position of women in Manu, it is one of complete subjection; the husband was not to eat with his wife, nor look at her when she ate; women were forbidden to repeat the Veda, or to perform any religious rite separately; they must continually feel their dependence on their husbands. The wife must worship her husband as a god. Women were credited with many inbred evils. When unfaithful to her husband, she is born of a jackal in the next life, and tormented with diseases. No repudiation or divorce of a wife was (originally) recognised, and if sold or repudiated she could not be the legitimate wife of another. There is no ground for the long-current statement that Manu or the Vedas supported or enjoined the burning of widows (Sati[1]). The re-marriage of widows is mentioned, but with censure, and a widow who remains chaste is rewarded with heaven. Very early marriage of girls was permitted if a suitor was distinguished and handsome.

Gifts.

Householders are enjoined to be liberal in gifts. "If he is asked, let him always give something, be it ever so little, without grudging;" the giver receives corresponding rewards, either in worldly prosperity or in future existences. Truthfulness is highly recommended: "he who is dishonest in speech is dishonest in everything." Giving no pain to any creature, the householder is to slowly accumulate spiritual merit, the only lasting companion. "Single is each being born; single it dies; single it enjoys the reward of its virtue; single it suffers the punishment of its sin. . . . He who is persevering, gentle, and patient, shuns the company of men of cruel conduct, and does no injury to living creatures, gains, if he constantly lives in that manner, heavenly bliss."

Spiritual merit.

The hermit in the forest.

The hermit and ascetic periods of life were held up to Brahmans as the culmination of their existence. We do not know how many Brahmans went through this discipline; but it is recommended to the householder, that when his skin becomes wrinkled and his hair grey, and he has grandchildren, he should go and live in the forest, taking with him the sacred fire and implements for the domestic sacrifices which he is still to perform, and there live in control of his senses, wearing his hair in braids, and the beard and nails unclipped. He was still to recite the Veda, and to be patient of hardships, friendly towards all, of collected mind, compassionate to all living creatures. He must feed only on special kinds of vegetables. A considerable number of austerities are enjoined on him, including exposure to fires in summer, living under the open sky and clothed in wet garments in winter, with other performances con-

[1] *Sati* means, "she who is faithful," and is a feminine form of the root seen in "sooth" = truth.

ducive to short life, much study not being forgotten. Finally he may, subsisting only on water and air, walk straight on "until his body sinks to rest"; then, having got rid of his body, he is exalted in the world of Brahma, free from sorrow and fear.

The mendicant ascetic.

The forest dweller who has not found liberation may become a mendicant ascetic, absolutely silent, caring for no enjoyment, indifferent to everything, but concentrating his mind on Brahma. "Let him not desire to live, let him not desire to die; let him wait for his appointed time as a servant waits for the payment of his wages." "Let him patiently bear hard words, let him not insult anybody, and let him not become anybody's enemy. . . . Against an angry man let him not in return show anger, let him bless where he is cursed." These are only a few of the numerous precepts for promoting the high spiritual life of the ascetic. Meditation, self-repression, equability, contentment, forgiveness, honesty, truthfulness, abstention from anger, purification, etc.—these may be said to sum up the moral law for all Brahmans.

The duties of a king.

We can only lightly dwell on the duties of a king and of government as described in Manu. The king represents Agni and Indra, the Maruts, Varuna, Yama and other gods, out of all of whom he is supposed to be framed; thus he is "a great deity in human form." He has divine authority, is to protect all creatures, and be an incarnation of the law. He must have seven or eight ministers, the chief of whom must be a Brahman. Punishment is his chief instrument, indeed the only maintainer of the law. He is, however, to be obedient to the Brahmans, and be determined not to retreat in battle. The Brahmans are to be the judges, either by themselves, or as assistants to the king. The criminal code is marked by much severity, and not a little inconsistency. Offences by the low-born against the higher classes were very severely punished, often with great cruelty; while Brahmans were very leniently treated. A Brahman's life was not to be taken, however grave or numerous his crimes.

The Brahman's superiority

Crimes. Among "mortal sins" are: killing a Brahman, drinking spirituous liquor, stealing the gold of a Brahman, adultery with a Guru's (spiritual teacher's) wife, associating with those who did those things, falsely attributing to oneself high birth, falsely accusing one's teacher, forgetting or reviling the Vedas, slaying a friend, giving false evidence, stealing a deposit, incest and fornication; but the classification and punishments show a **Punishment and penances.** very crude estimate of their relative importance. Many punishments are designed as penances, to remove the guilt of the offender. Various ordeals are prescribed to ascertain if a witness speaks the truth, such as fire and water. Altogether, the rules of evidence do not inspire us with the idea that the early Brahmans had invented very excellent machinery for dis- **Falsehood excused.** covering truth; and such statements as the following are not calculated to show them in a favourable light. In some cases a man who, though knowing the facts to be different, gives false evidence from a pious motive, does not lose heaven. Whenever the death of a Sudra, a Vaisya, a Kshatriya, or of a Brahman would be caused by the declaration of the truth, a falsehood may be spoken. In cases of violence, of theft and adultery, of defamation and assault, the judge must not examine witnesses too strictly. But he is to exhort all witnesses to speak the truth, promising them bliss after death and fame here below, while false witnesses are firmly bound by Varuna and are helpless during one hundred existences.

Caste. Reverting once more to the question of castes, we may note that the Brahman was supposed to have three births; the first his natural birth, the second his investiture with the girdle of Munga grass, the third his initiation to perform the greater sacrifices; the Kshatriyas or warriors, and the Vaisyas or cultivators, were only twice born, the second birth happening on their investiture with the sacred thread. We may recall here that the term caste is not an original Hindu or even an ancient word. It is believed to be an adaptation of a Portuguese word, *casta*, race or family, from the Latin

YOGIS (HINDU RELIGIOUS FANATICS).

castus, pure. The word used in Manu is *varna*, or colour, while in later Hindu phrase caste is denoted by *jati* or *jat*, meaning birth.

Growth of mixed castes.

The code of Manu was forced to recognise that wide departures took place from the original purity of caste, although maintaining that only those born of wedded wives of equal castes were to be considered as belonging to the same caste as their fathers. Hence distinct names were given to the offspring between the different castes; some of these are declared to be ferocious in manners and delighting in cruelty. These had already been assigned to distinct occupations, which increased as the Hindu life grew more settled and diversified. Some of them are said to be inherently fit only for low and degrading offices, and unworthy to receive the sacramental rites. The modern development of the caste system must be dealt with later.

Transmigration of souls.

Finally, as to the important belief in the transmigration of souls, which in the Hindu system plays so large a part, it appears to have been wielded by the Brahmans very much as a mode of influencing actions on earth. Evil actions done with the body were to be punished by being born next in something inanimate, those done by speech were followed by birth as a bird or a beast, while sins of the mind, such as covetousness, evil thoughts, and adherence to false doctrines, led to re-birth in a low caste. Self-control in all these respects led to emancipation from all births and final blessedness. This scheme is elaborated in great detail, many gradations being fixed in descending order, each the just recompense for some fault. The specific reason for many of these cannot be imagined, although some are intelligible enough, such as these: "men who delight in doing injury become carnivorous animals; thieves, creatures consuming their own kind; for stealing grain a man becomes a rat, for stealing meat, a vulture," etc. Sensual men are said to suffer in a succession of dreadful hells and agonizing births, slavery, imprisonment in fetters. The last pages of Manu are devoted to further glorification of Brahmans who do their duty, and to the extolling of the

Self or Soul in all things; "for he who recognises the universe in the Self, does not give his heart to unrighteousness. . . . He who thus recognises the Self through

SCULPTURED FIGURES IN THE CAVE TEMPLE AT ELEPHANTA.

the Self in all created beings, becomes equal-minded towards all, and enters the highest state, Brahman. A twice-born man, who recites these Institutes, revealed by

Manu, will be always virtuous in conduct, and will reach whatever condition he desires."

It must be owned that the system thus developed in Manu does not fail for lack of penalties or of precise directions. Its efficacy is to be sought in its gradual growth, its accordance with the ideas of creation, supreme power, and morality which had long been current, and its promulgation by those who had most intellectual power and most capability of swaying the conduct of men. Thus we may imagine the extraordinary influence which the sacred class of Brahmans attained in early Indian history, an influence which has been sufficient to perpetuate itself to our own times, which remains very great, and which more than two thousand years ago was sufficient to produce by exaggeration and reaction the remarkable religion of Buddhism. But looking on it calmly, while admitting the loftiness of many of its precepts and imaginings, it cannot be said that its general moral elevation was great. The scheme was powerful enough to bind together society for centuries, but not powerful enough to diffuse itself widely among other races, or to become more than a Hindu religion.

Efficacy of the code.

There is one other code to which we must refer, besides that of Manu, namely the Darma Shastra of Yajnavalkya, possibly dating from the first century A.D. It is still the chief authority in the school of Benares. It is much shorter than that of Manu, is more systematic, and represents a later stage of development. It adds to the sources of authority the Puranas and various traditional and scholastic authorities. To some extent caste is carried farther, and a Brahman is forbidden to have a Sudra as a fourth wife. We have reached a period when writing is in regular use, and written documents are appealed to as legal evidence; coined money is in use. It is evident that Buddhism has arisen, and that the shaven heads and yellow garments of its votaries are well known; the king is also recommended to found monasteries for Brahmans, an evident imitation of Buddhists.

Code of Yajnavalkya.

Compare the following philosophy with that of Manu.

"The success of every action depends on destiny and on a man's own effort; but destiny is evidently nothing but the result of a man's act in a former state of existence. Some expect the whole result from destiny or from the inherent nature; some expect it from the lapse of time; and some from a man's own effort; other persons of wiser judgment expect it from a combination of all these." (M.W.) But there is no sufficient difference in the nature of the precepts to make it necessary to quote further.

We may here refer briefly to the celebrated rock-temples of India, excavated in solid rock many centuries ago, but by no means confined to Hinduism, having often been excavated by Buddhists and Jains. Some of them display surprising skill in construction as well as in sculpture. Many are ornamented with figures of the gods or scenes from their supposed adventures. The majority of the Brahmanic temples are dedicated to Siva. The most famous are those of Elephanta, an island in Bombay harbour; one of them contains a colossal trimurti, or three-faced bust, representing Siva in his threefold character of creator, preserver, and destroyer. Many other caves, scarcely less famous, are at Ellora in the Nizam's dominions.

THE KRISHNA AVATARA.
(From a native picture.)

CHAPTER III.

Modern Hinduism I.

Reaction from Brahmanism—Triumph of Buddhism—Downfall of Indian Buddhism—The caste system—The Mahabharata—The Bhagavad-gita—Krishna—Incarnations of the Deity—Immortality taught—The Ramayana—Partial incarnations—Conquests of Rama—Resistance of Brahmanism—Kumarila Bhatta—Sankara—Worship of the supreme Brahman—The Smartas—Vishnu worship—The Puranas—The Vishnu Purana—Description of the Supreme Being—Great Vishnuite preachers—Ramanand—Kabir—Chaitanya—Influence of Buddhism—The linga and the salagram—Brahma—Vishnu the preserver—Incarnations of Vishnu—Rama—Krishna—Buddha—Jagannath—Lakshmi—Siva the destroyer—Ascetic Sivaites—Durga—Kali--Ganesa—Gangsa—Local deities and demons—Worship of animals and trees—Deification of heroes and saints.

IN our chapters on Buddhism, it will be shown that the new religion which deposed Brahmanism from supremacy in India, and greatly depressed it for more than a thousand years, was partly a natural reaction from the haughty sway of the Brahmans and their reliance on ritual and sacrifice, and partly the development of a movement which had already risen within the older system. The educated Brahmans came to see that the Vedic gods were poetic imaginations which could not all be true, and that whereas various gods—the Sun, the Encompassing Sky, the Dawn, etc.—were represented as independent and supreme, they must be emanations of one supreme Cause. While they continued to uphold the popular ideas about the gods, and to conduct the customary sacrifices, they began to develop a theological literature, of part of which we have already given an account, the Upanishads and the Puranas, teaching the unity of God and the immortality of the soul, still mingled with many myths and superstitions. Their new system involved the brotherhood of man; but it was reserved for Gautama to break through all the old conventions, and to found the great system of Buddhism. All classes found in it something that was lacking in Brahmanism, and rejoiced in the upsetting of many things that had been irksome. From the third century B.C. to the fourth century A.D., Buddhism increasingly triumphed, until it was professed by the majority of the Indian people. But in the fifth century the Buddhists were persecuted by the adherents of the old religion. By the end of that century the Buddhist leaders had taken refuge in China, and many of its priests had carried the faith to new lands. As late as the twelfth century a few remained in India, but now they are non-existent, unless Jainism be regarded as representing the old Buddhism. But the influence of Buddhism upon Brahmanism had been profound, and modern Hinduism is a very different thing from the religion of the Vedas and Brahmanas. Indeed, Sir W. W. Hunter terms modern Hinduism the joint product of Buddhism and Brahmanism. The latter was active and slowly changing during all the time of the predominance of the former, and we have the testimony of Greeks in Alexander's time

Reaction from Brahmanism.

Triumph of Buddhism.

and later, and of Buddhist priests from China who visited India in the fifth and seventh centuries, that Brahman priests were equally honoured with Buddhist monks, and temples of the Hindu gods adjoined the Buddhist religious houses.

The Hindus date the final triumph over Buddhism from the preaching of Kumarila, a Bengal Brahman, who powerfully advanced the Vedic teaching of a personal Creator and supreme Being, against the impersonal negations of Buddhism; but he also shone as a persecutor. Sir W. W. Hunter, however, traces the change which followed to deeper-seated causes—such that the rise of Hinduism was a natural development of racial characters and systems. According to him, it rests upon the caste system and represents the coalition of the old Vedic faith with Buddhism, as well as with the rude rites of pre-Aryan and Mongolian races. We cannot here give an account of the caste system. The immense subdivision of castes is the result partly of intermarriages, partly of varied occupations, partly of locality, partly of the introduction of outside tribes to Hinduism. Religious exclusiveness and trades unionism, once grasped, made easy progress, and converted India into a vast grouping of separate classes. Caste is a powerful instrument for personal discipline and the maintenance of convention and custom, but it is a weakener of united popular action and national unity. Its great force is in its hereditary instincts and in social and religious excommunication. The offender against caste laws may be fined by his fellow-members, may be forbidden to eat or intermarry with them, and may be boycotted by the community.

Downfall of Indian Buddhism.

The caste system.

We cannot understand the growth of modern Hinduism without reference to the two great Indian epic poems, the Mahabharata and the Ramayana. The former is a vast aggregation of poems and episodes, arranged into a continuous whole, and is the longest poem in the world, being fourteen times as long as the Iliad. It includes many portions dating back to Vedic times, with others of later date up to a compara-

The Mahabharata.

tively modern time. It includes the whole cycle of Hindu mythology since the Vedas, and practically represents a deification of human heroes, side by side with views of Divine incarnation. Its central story relates a prehistoric struggle between two families descended from the Moon god for a tract of country around Delhi. It is believed to have existed in a considerably developed form five or six centuries before Christ, but it has been greatly modified by subsequent Brahmanic additions, especially didactic and religious in their nature, teaching the submission of the military to the Brahman power.

The Bhagavad-gita.

The Bhagavad-gita, or song of Bhagavat, is the most important episode of this great epic, Bhagavat being a term applied to Krishna, one of the incarnations of Vishnu, the Pervader and Preserver. Krishna makes a revelation to the hero Arjuna, just before a great battle, in order to remove his scruples about destroying human life. This revelation in effect teaches the supremacy of the soul over the body, and in fact its eternity of existence in the supreme Being, so that death cannot harm it. Duty to caste and its obligations is highly extolled; but the poem is most remarkable to us for its exposition in poetry of the Vedantist philosophy of Pantheism, which teaches that all the universe is indeed Brahma, from whom all proceeds and to whom all returns. Krishna, in giving an account of himself to Arjuna, says (we quote from Sir Monier-Williams's "Indian Wisdom"):—

> "I am the ancient sage, without beginning,
> I am the ruler and the all-sustainer,
> I am incomprehensible in form,
> More subtle and minute than subtlest atoms;
> I am the cause of the whole universe;
> Through me it is created and dissolved;
> I dwell as wisdom, in the heart of all.
> I am the goodness of the good, I am
> Beginning, middle, end, eternal time,
> The birth, the death of all. I have created all
> Out of one portion of myself. Think thou on me,
> Have faith in me, adore and worship me,
> And join thyself in meditation to me.
> Thus shalt thou come to me, O Arjuna;
> Thus shalt thou rise to my supreme abode,

Where neither sun nor moon have need to shine,
For know that all the lustre they possess is mine."

Among other revelations of Krishna, he states that he is born on earth from time to time for the establishment of righteousness. In lauding work, Krishna says:—

Krishna.

"Know that work
Proceeds from the supreme. I am the pattern
For man to follow; know that I have done
All arts already; nought remains for me
To gain by action, yet I work for ever
Unweariedly, and this whole universe
Would perish if I did not work my work."

It will be evident from these quotations that the Bhagavad-gita contains much lofty thought; indeed, it has been praised as unequalled for sublimity of conception, reasoning, and diction. Yet it is in no slight degree parallel with Buddhist ideas, in preaching deliverance through self-renunciation and devotion, ending in absorption in the deity. Although women are not raised by it, yet the declaration of Krishna is, that all who resort to him will reach the highest. He says: "I have neither friend nor foe; I am the same to all; and all who worship me dwell in me and I in them. To them that love me, I give that devotion by which they come at last to me. No soul that has faith, however imperfect the attainment, or however the soul have wandered, shall perish, either in this world or in another. He shall have new births till, purified and made perfect, he reaches the supreme abode."

The repetition of incarnations of deity is an important feature in this teaching; and from this root has developed the great "avatar" or incarnation idea of the Hindus, the idea being that the deity is continually being manifested for the guidance and protection of his people. Throughout the transition period, from Brahmanism to Hinduism, varying forms of Krishna, as the incarnation of Vishnu[1] are continually described.

Incarnations of the deity.

[1] Vishnu is a god named in the Rig-Veda as a form of the sun striding across the heavens in three paces.

He appears as the protecting hero and saint and sage, the overcomer of evil spirits, the popular wonder-worker.

From some of the characteristics of Krishna it has been imagined that he has been derived from Christ; but there

VISHNU.
(From a native picture.)

is no proof of this, and, indeed, the multiplication and varying form of the incarnations tells against this idea. In fact, the belief proceeds from a date before the Christian era. The meaning of the word Krishna, "black," also makes against the Christian relationship; it rather points to respect for common humanity of black and white alike; for Krishna is the teacher of Arjuna, "white."

This doctrine about Krishna brings into view the essential link by which the intellectual Brahmans connected their higher philosophy with the common beliefs of the people. Krishna manifests the noblest traits of Hindu genius; he also condescends to the most ordinary pursuits of men and children, and even to sportive recreation. The higher doctrine of immortality is preached in such passages as the following in the Bhagavad-gita, "There is an invisible, eternal existence, beyond this visible, which does not perish when all things else perish, even when the great days of Brahman's creative life pass round into night, and all that exists in form returns unto God whence it came; they who obtain this never return. . . . Bright as the sun beyond darkness is He to the soul that remembers Him in meditation, at the hour of death, with thought fixed between the brows,—Him the most ancient of the wise, the primal ruler, the minutest atom, the sustainer of all,—in the hour when each finds that same nature on which he meditates, and to which he is conformed. . . . They who put their trust in me, and seek deliverance from decay and death, know Brahma, and the highest spirit, and every action. They who know me in my being, my person, and my manifested life, in the hour of death, know me indeed."

Immortality taught.

The other great epic poem, the Ramayana, or the goings of Rama, is a chronicle which relates primarily to another region of Aryan conquest, Oudh, and then recounts the advance of the Aryans into Southern India. It represents perhaps a later stage than the earlier parts of the Mahabharata, but was arranged into something like its present form a century earlier—perhaps about the beginning of the third century B.C. Like the sister epic, it presents the Brahman idea of the Godhead in the form of an incarnation, Rama, of Vishnu, to destroy a demon. Briefly stated, the story is as follows. It begins by relating the sonlessness of the king of Oudh, a descendant of the sun-god. After a sacrifice to the

The Ramayana.

gods, four sons were born of his three wives, the eldest, Rama, having one-half the nature of Vishnu; the second, Bharata, one-fourth; and two others, twins, having each one-eighth. This exemplifies the Brahman doctrine of partial incarnations, Krishna being a full incarnation; and, beyond this, there might be fractional incarnations of the Divine essence, in men, animals and even inanimate objects. The wonderful youth, marriage to Sita, and exile of Rama, are next told, and the refusal of Bharata to take the kingdom on his father's death. Rama continuing an exile, Ravana, the demon king of the south, heard of his wife's beauty, and carried her off in a magical chariot to Ceylon. Rama then makes alliances with the aboriginal peoples of Southern India, invades Ceylon, slays Ravana and delivers his wife, who has to undergo the further trial of being suspected of infidelity and banished. She is the type of womanly devotion and purity, and after sixteen years' exile is reconciled to her husband, with whom she is after all translated to heaven.

Partial incarnations.

Conquests of Rama.

Such was the framework in which the change from ancient Brahmanism to modern Hinduism was developed and taught. These epics bear witness to the fact that notwithstanding the great extension of Buddhism in India, there was no time when Brahmanism was not working with great skill and intellectual force to adapt itself to the changed conditions. At a council of the Buddhist monarch Siladitya at Kanauj on the Ganges in A.D. 634, while a statue of Buddha was installed on the first day, on the second an image of the Sun-god, on the third an image of Siva, the product of later Brahmanism, was inaugurated. A great series of Brahman apostles arose simultaneously with the decay of Buddhism, beginning with Kumarila Bhatta, about A.D. 750, who revived the old Brahman doctrine of a personal God and Creator, and reconverted many of the people. He was the first of a long line of influential religious reformers, who all solemnly cut themselves off from the world like Buddha, and give forth a simple message, readily understood, including in essence,

Resistance of Brahmanism.

Kumarila Bhatta.

according to Sir W. W. Hunter, "a reassertion, in some form, of the personality of God and the equality of men in His sight."

Sankara Acharya was the disciple of Kumarila, still more famous than his master; he popularised the late Vedantist philosophy as a national religion, and "since his short life in the eighth or ninth century, every new Hindu sect has had to start with a personal God" (Hunter). He taught that the supreme God Brahma was distinct from the old Brahman triad,

Sankara.

SIVA, BRAHMA, AND VISHNU.

and must be worshipped by spiritual meditations, not by sacrifices; and he perpetuated his teaching by founding a Brahman sect, the Smartas. However, he still allowed the practice of the Vedic rites, and worship of the deity in any popular form; and it is claimed by popular tradition that he founded many of the Hindu sects of the present day. Siva worship is supposed to be specially his work, though it existed long before; and he has ever been represented by his followers as an incarnation of Siva. Siva is, as we have said before, the Rudra or

Storm-god of the Rig-Veda, recognised as the Destroyer and Reproducer. He was worshipped contemporaneously with the Buddhist ascendency and is highly spoken of in the Mahabharata; but Sankara's followers elevated his worship till it became one of the two chief forms of Hinduism.

SIVA.
(From a native picture.)

Worship of the supreme Brahman.

The doctrine of Sankara just referred to, that Brahma, or Brahman, is the supreme God, distinct from the triad Brahma, Vishnu, and Siva, who are manifestations of him. The supremeBrahman is the absolute, having no form nor shape, self-existent, illimitable, free from imperfection. There are but a few worshippers of Brahman or Brahma alone. As creator he is believed to have finished his work, and there is now only one temple to him, at Pushkara in Ajmir. Ward, in 1818, wrote: "The Brahmans in their morning and evening worship repeat an incantation containing a description of the image of Brahma; at noon they present to him a single flower; at the time of burnt-offering, ghee is presented to him. In the month of Magh, at the full moon, an earthen image of him is worshipped, with that of Siva on his right hand and Vishnu on his left."

The Smartas. The Smartas of Southern India are a considerable sect who follow the philosophic teaching of Sankara. There are numerous religious houses connected with this sect, acknowledging the headship of the monastery of Sringiri, in the western Mysore hills; and the chief priest of the sect, the head of this monastery, is specially acknowledged by all Sivaite worshippers, who regard Sankara as one of the incarnations of Siva.

Vishnu worship. "The worship of Vishnu," says Sir W. W. Hunter, "in one phase or another, is the religion of the bulk of the middle classes; with its roots deep down in beautiful forms of non-Aryan nature-worship, and its top sending forth branches among the most refined Brahmans and literary sects. It is a religion in all things graceful. Its gods are heroes or bright friendly beings, who walk and converse with men. Its legends breathe an almost Hellenic beauty." This is the lofty position assigned to Vishnuism by one of the most learned and most impartial students—a very different opinion from that which regards the car of Juggernaut as the representative of all that is vile.

The Puranas. The doctrines of modern Hinduism, in their learned aspect, are contained in the Puranas (in Sanskrit), a series of eighteen treatises, in which various Brahmans expound, in lengthy dialogues, the supremacy of Vishnu or Siva. The chief of them is the Vishnu Purana, dating from the eleventh century, but containing, as the word "purana" signifies, ancient traditions, some of which descend from Vedic times; and others are traceable to the two great epics. "It includes a complete cosmogony or account of primary creation, accounts of the destruction and renovation of worlds, genealogies of gods and patriarchs, the reigns of the Manus, the institutes of society, including caste and burial rites, and the history of the princes of the solar and lunar races, a life of Krishna, and an account of the end of the world. It is not necessary to dwell upon its contents, which would require a volume. Pantheism is woven into the general scheme, God and Nature being identified, and Vishnu, as supreme God, being incarnated in Krishna.

The Vishnu Purana.

The style of the Vishnu Purana on its philosophical side may be gathered from the following extracts, relating to the supreme deity, as translated by H. H. Wilson: "Who can describe him who is not to be apprehended by the senses, who is the best of all things, and the supreme soul, self-existent; who is devoid of all the distinguishing characteristics of complexion, caste, or the like, and is exempt from birth, vicissitude, death, or decay; who is always, and alone; who exists everywhere, and in whom all things here exist; and who is thence named Vasudeva (the resplendent one in whom all things dwell)? He is Brahma, supreme lord, eternal, unborn, imperishable, undecaying; of one essence; ever pure as free from defects. He, that Brahma, was all things, comprehending in his own nature the indiscrete (spirit) and the discrete (matter). He then existed in the forms of Purusha and Kala. Purusha (spirit) is the first form of the supreme. Next proceeded two other forms—the discrete and the indiscrete; and Kala (time) was the last. These four the wise consider to be the pure and supreme condition of Vishnu. These four forms, in their due proportions, are the causes of the production of the phenomena of creation, preservation, and destruction. Vishnu being thus discrete and indiscrete substance—spirit and time—sports like a playful boy, as you shall learn by listening to his frolics." Here it should be noted that the creation

Description of the supreme Being.

of the world is very commonly considered by the Hindu to be the sport or amusement of the supreme Being.

The life of Krishna, as given by this Purana, is so full of fabulous marvels as to read like an Arabian Night's story, without its charm. It is sufficient to say that this

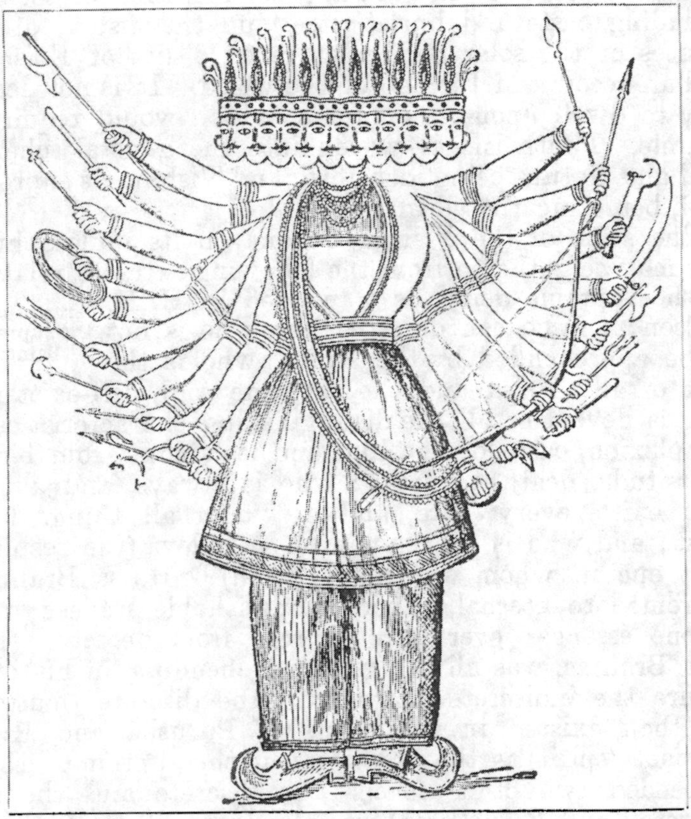

RAVANA.

(From a native picture. See account of Ramayana, p. 63.)

Purana did not work the great development of Vishnu worship, which was due to a series of Vishnuite preachers, beginning with Ramanuja in the 12th century, rising against the cruel doctrines of the Sivaites. It was not till the end of the 13th or beginning of the 14th century that the great

Great Vishnuite preachers.

development of popular religion in the name of Vishnu took place, under the apostolic leadership of Ramanand. This teacher had his headquarters in a monastery at Benares, and travelled from place to

Ramanand.

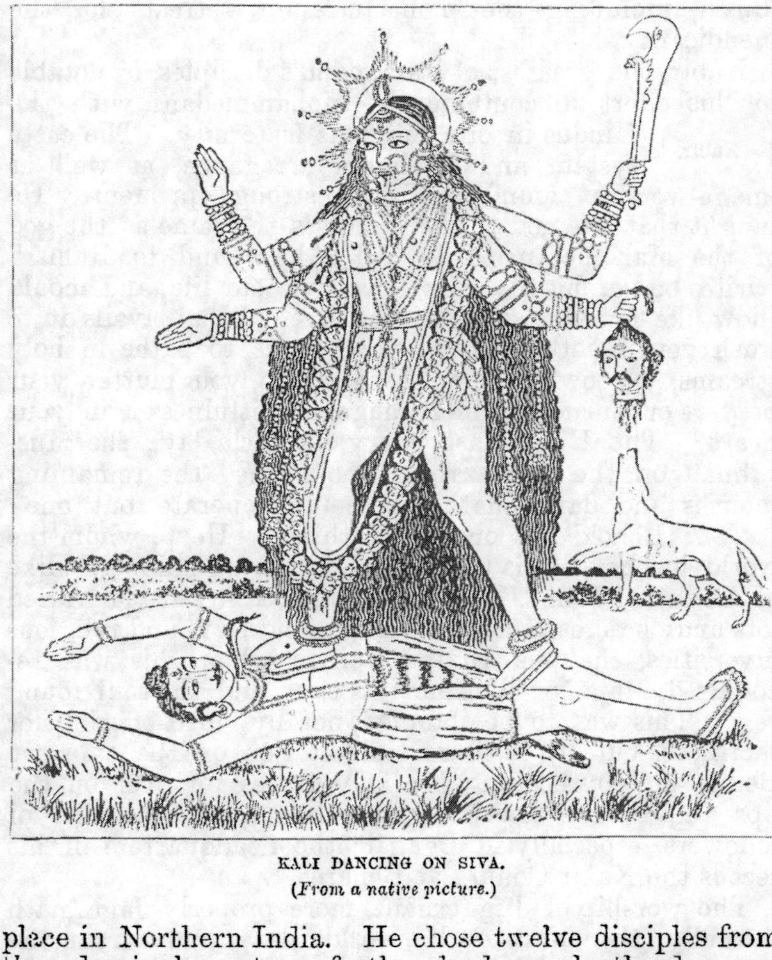

KALI DANCING ON SIVA.
(*From a native picture.*)

place in Northern India. He chose twelve disciples from the despised castes of the barbers, leatherdressers, weavers, and the like, who, like the Buddhist monks, had to forsake the world, and depend solely on alms, while they went about teaching religion. They addressed the people in the vernacular Hindi, and largely helped to make it a literary language. The inclusion of lower-caste men among Ramanand's chief disciples is a proof that his reaction was directed against Brahman exclusiveness; and it embraced many features of Buddhism, including the monasteries or retreats for the mendicants.

Kabir.

Kabir, the greatest of Ramanand's disciples, is notable for his effort to combine the Mohammedans with the Hindus in one religious fraternity. The caste system and Brahman arrogance, as well as image-worship, found in him a strong opponent. He taught that the god of the Hindu is the same as the god of the Mahometan. "To Ali (Allah) and to Rama" (writes one of his disciples) "we owe our life, and should show like tenderness to all who live. What avails it to wash your mouth, to count your beads, to bathe in holy streams, to bow in temples, if, while you mutter your prayers or journey on pilgrimage, deceitfulness is in your heart? The Hindu fasts every eleventh day; the Mussulman on the Ramazan. Who formed the remaining months and days, that you should venerate but one? . . . Behold but one in all things. He to whom the world belongs, He is the father of the worshippers alike of Ali and of Rama." Kabir recognised in all the varied lots and changes of man, his hopes and fears and religious diversities, the one Divine Spirit; when this was recognised, Maya, or illusion, was over, and the soul found rest. This was to be obtained, not by burnt-offerings or sacrifices, but by faith and meditation on the supreme Being, and by keeping his holy names for ever on the lips and in the heart. Kabir had a vast number of followers, especially in Bengal; the headquarters of his sect is the Kabir Chaura at Benares.

Chaitanya.

The worship of Juggernaut, more properly Jagannath (literally, the Lord of the world) dates only from the beginning of the 16th century, being mainly propagated by Chaitanya, who was so great a preacher of the Vishnuite doctrines that since his death he has been widely worshipped as an incarnation of

Vishnu. He preached a religion of faith to Hindus and Mohammedans alike ; but he laid great stress on obedience to religious teachers. By contemplation rather than ritual he taught that the soul would find liberty from the imperfections and sins of the body. After death the soul of the believer would dwell for ever in a heaven of perfect beauty, or in the presence of Vishnu himself, known in his supreme essence.

After the death of Chaitanya there appeared teachers who lowered the spiritual level of Vishnuism, some preaching the religion of enjoyment, others giving increased importance to the idea of physical love ; one adoring the infant Krishna as the cowherd. Vallabha-Swami (sixteenth century) was one of the chief of these ; he established a ritual of eight services in which the image of Krishna as a lovely boy is bathed, anointed, sumptuously dressed and fed, and in which beautiful women and other sensual delights figure largely. Such a religion appealed largely to the well-to-do, the luxurious, and the sensually minded, and was made the pretext for self-indulgence.

Influence of Buddhism.

Before particularising the forms of modern Hindu worship, we must briefly indicate the influence which Buddhism and other popular religions of India have had on Hinduism. The brotherhood of man is implicitly if not explicitly recognised by many of the Hindu sects ; the Buddhist communities or monasteries are reproduced in the monastic houses of many Hindu brotherhoods. Sir W. Hunter describes the rules of the Vishnuite communities as Buddhistic, with Brahmanical reasons. One of the brotherhoods of Kabir's followers has as its first rule the very Buddhistic one that the life neither of man nor of beast may be taken, the reason being that it is the gift of God. Truth is enjoined as the great principle of conduct ; for all ills and ignorance of God spring from original falsehood. Retirement from the world is commended, worldliness being hostile to tranquillity of soul and meditation on God. Similarly the Buddhist trinity of ideas, Buddha, Dharma (the Law), and Samgha (the congregation) is largely present, more or less openly, in Hinduism. Not the least strange conjunction of Hinduism with other religions is that in which Siva-worshippers visit Adam's Peak in Ceylon to worship the footprints of their deity. Buddhists revere the same impression as the impression of Buddha's foot, while Mohammedans revere it as a relic of Adam, the father of mankind. This is but a specimen of the common resorts of Hindu pilgrims, where Mussulman and Hindu alike revere some sacred object.

The linga and the salagram.

Hindus also absorbed or adopted many rites and superstitions of non-Aryan peoples, such as the serpent and dragon-worship of the Nagas, reverence for crocodiles and generative emblems, fetish and tree worship, etc. The worship of generative emblems (*linga*) found a wide field among the Sivaites, whose god was the reproducer as well as destroyer; while the fetish, or village, or local god, in the shape of an unhewn stone (known as *salagram*) or a tree, usually the tulasi plant, became the usual symbols of the Vishnuite. In not a few cases their rites are little elevated above those of primitive savagery as conducted by low-caste Hindus.

Brahma.

Coming now to a description of the chief Hindu gods as popularly worshipped, we find Brahma, the creator, represented as a red man with four heads, dressed in white, and riding upon a goose. Brahma's wife, Sarasvati, the goddess of wisdom and science, is depicted as a fair young woman with four arms; with one right hand she presents a flower to Brahma; in the other she holds a book of palm-leaves; in one of her left hands she carries a string of pearls. In the Mahabharata she is called the mother of the Vedas. She is worshipped once a year in the same month as Brahma by all who have any learning; and with this worship are connected pens, ink, paper, books, etc. Women take no part in this festival.

Vishnu.

Vishnu is adored by the Vishnuite sects as the equal or even the superior of Brahma, and is especially termed the Preserver, exempt from impatience and passion. Various legends in the Puranas describe the other gods as submitting to Vishnu, who is termed omniscient and almighty. In pictorial representations Vishnu usually appears as a black man with four arms: in one hand a club is held, in a second a shell, in the third a discus, in the fourth a lotus, and he rides upon the Garuda bird.

Sir Monier-Williams describes both Vishnuism and Sivaism as forms of monotheism, because they set aside the coequal trinity Brahma, Vishnu and Siva in favour of their special god: but it may be doubted whether many of the Vishnuites can be called intelligent monotheists, rather than superstitious worshippers of they know not what. The opinion of this great Indian scholar, that Vishnuism "is the only real religion of the Hindu peoples, and has more common ground with Christianity than any other non-Christian faith," must be taken as having but a limited application when he has to qualify it by referring to "the gross polytheistic superstitions and hideous idolatry to which it gives rise." We must acknowledge the distinguishing merit of Vishnuism to be, that it teaches intense devotion to a personal god, who exhibits his sympathy with human suffering and his interest in human affairs by frequent descents (avatars) upon earth. Of these we must give a brief account.

Incarnations of Vishnu.

As many as twenty-eight avatars of Vishnu have been enumerated in the Puranas. They represent the descent into human bodies, by birth from earthly parents, of a portion or the whole of the divine essence of the god; they do not interfere with the divine body of the god, which remains unchanged. Of these we may enumerate (1) the Fish, whose form Vishnu took to save Manu, the progenitor of mankind, from the universal deluge. Manu obtained the favour of Vishnu by his piety, was warned of the coming deluge, and commanded to build a ship, wherein he was to take the seven Rishis or patriarchs and the seeds of all living things. When the flood came, Vishnu, as the Fish, dragged the ship, by a cable fixed to a horn on his head, to a high crag where it was secured till the flood went down. The avatars of the tortoise, the boar, the man-lion, the dwarf, and Rama with the axe, we must pass over. The great Rama, Ramachandra, or the moon-like Rama, has been already referred to as the subject of the Ramayana. "Every man, woman, and child in India," says Sir Monier-Williams, probably with some exaggeration, "is familiar with Rama's exploits for the recovery of his wife, insomuch that a common phrase for an ignorant person is 'one who does not know that Sita was Rama's wife.' From Kashmir to Cape Comorin the name of Rama is on every one's lips. All sects revere it, and show their reverence by employing it on all occasions. For example, when friends meet, it is common for them to salute each other by uttering Rama's name twice. No name is more commonly given to children, and no name more commonly invoked at funerals and in the hour of death. It is a link of union for all classes, castes, and creeds."

Rama.

But Krishna is the most popular of all the incarnations of Vishnu, and is represented as manifesting his entire essence. He is especially the god of the lower orders, having been brought up among cowherds and other peasants, with whom he constantly sported. A multitude of marvellous stories are told about him; but it is evident from the history of Krishna literature and practices that he, like Rama, is a deified hero. Sir Monier-Williams identifies him as a powerful chief of the Yadava tribe of Rajputs in central India east of the Jumna, while the original of Rama was a son of a king of Oudh. So possible is it to trace gods adored by multitudes of human beings to the exaggeration and deification of heroic men.

Krishna, the preserver.

Thus we shall be little surprised to find Buddha adopted as one of the incarnations of Vishnu. The Brahmans account for this by saying that Vishnu, in compassion for animals, descended as Buddha in order to discredit the Vedic sacrifices. The Brahmanical writers, says Wilkins, "were far too shrewd to admit that one who could influence men as Buddha did could be other than an incarnation of deity; and as his influence was in favour of teaching opposed to their own,

Buddha.

they cleverly say that it was to mislead the enemies of the gods that Buddha promulgated his doctrine, that

SIVA TEMPLE, BENARES.

they, becoming weak and wicked through their errors, might fall an easy prey."

Not content with incarnations that have taken place, the Vishnuites look for a future descent which they call the Kalki avatar. He is to appear at the end of the Kali age (which began with his descent as Krishna), when the world has become utterly wicked, and will be seen in the sky, seated on a white horse, wielding a drawn sword, for the destruction of the wicked and the restoration of the world to purity.

Jagannath.

We have not included Jagannath among the incarnations of Vishnu, both because it is believed that he is an appearance of Vishnu himself, and also because it is probable that he was originally the god of a non-Aryan tribe adopted into Hinduism. It is a sight of this god that is so vehemently desired, whether as he is bathed or dressed, or being drawn on his car. Chaitanya, the reformer, is another incarnation of Vishnu, according to the popular notion, although he lived in almost modern times.

Lakshmi.

Lakshmi, the wife of Vishnu, is very considerably worshipped as the goddess of Love, Beauty, and Prosperity. She is represented as of a bright golden colour, seated on a lotus, and having only the ordinary number of arms.

Siva, the destroyer.

Siva, the destroyer, is naturally represented as of a stern and vindictive disposition; but yet this is compatible with his being regarded as a beneficent deity. Death being the transition to a new form of life, the Destroyer is truly the Re-creator, and this accounts for the meaning of his name—the Bright or Happy one. Siva is exclusively a post-Vedic god, though he has been identified by the Hindus with the Rudra of the Vedas, and numerous features of Siva's character and history are developed from those of Rudra. In the Ramayana, Rudra (Siva) is represented as marrying Uma, the daughter of Daksha; it is this same Uma who is much more widely-known under the names of Parvati, Durga, and Kali. It is stated that a great quarrel arose between Siva and Daksha, his father-in-law. In this quarrel Uma gave herself voluntarily to the flames, and became a sati (suttee), and was reborn as Parvati. Siva then became an ascetic, living with

GANESA. LAKSHMI. DURGA. SARASVATI. KARTIKEYA.

(From a native picture.)

Parvati in the Himalayas, destroying demons. He is represented sometimes with Parvati, wearing round his black neck a serpent and a necklace of skulls, and with an extensive series of emblems, such as a white bull on which he rides, a tiger's skin, etc.; he has three eyes, one being in his forehead. As Mahadeva (the great god), which is his most usual name, he may be shown as an ascetic with matted hair, living in meditation and self-discipline in a forest. It is said that Siva, in a quarrel with Brahma, cut off his fifth head, which, however, stuck to the destroyer's hand. To escape from a pursuing giant created by Brahma, Siva fled to Benares, where he became absolved from his sin and freed from the head of Brahma, thus causing Benares to become a specially sacred city.

In consequence of Siva's patronage of the bull as his steed, a strange custom has arisen in connection with the funerals of Sivaites. Whenever it is possible, a bull is set free to wander, and has a sacred character, so that

BRAHMA AND SARASVATI.

no one dares to injure it; sometimes as many as seven bullocks are thus set free. This is believed to secure the favour of Siva. Similarly, since he was an ascetic, many of his followers pay court to him by a life of austerity and painful suffering. This was much more frequent in former times than now, for the British Government has discouraged or prohibited many of the most painful ex-

Ascetic Sivaites.

hibitions. Formerly many Siva worshippers would be swung from iron hooks fixed in their backs, or would jump from a height upon the edges of sharp knives. But it is not easy to put down such practices as the maintenance of the arms and legs in one position for years, the holding of the fist clenched till the nails grow through the palm, the keeping of silence or the fixing of the eye continuously upon the sun. There are still many thousands of these devotees in India. Intoxication is also freely indulged in by Sivaites during their worship, this being believed to be pleasing to the god. After all, Siva is most worshipped under the emblem of the Linga, although he is said to have a thousand names.

SASTHI.
(From a native picture.)

Durga.

The wife of Siva occupies a comparatively subordinate position as Uma and Parvati; but as Durga she is a powerful warrior, with many stern and fierce qualities. In this character she is represented to have appeared in many incarnations, and is very widely worshipped. The name Durga was given to her as having slain a demon named Durga. The tales about this are of the most mythical and exaggerated nature. Notwithstanding her powers, Durga is portrayed with a gentle and beautiful face and a golden colour; but she has ten arms, holding various weapons, while her lion leans against one leg and her giant against the other. Of the various forms of Durga we can only refer to Kali (the black woman), probably some tribal goddess adopted into the Hindu series. She won a victory over giants by drinking their blood with the aid of Chandi, another form of Kali. The account of the image of Kali given later in describing one of the Bengal festivals will explain **Kali.** some of her qualities. Formerly human beings, as well as considerable animal sacrifices, were offered to Kali, a human sacrifice being said to please Kali for a thousand years. Cutting their flesh and burning portions of their bodies were among the actions by which worshippers sought to please the goddess. The great number of Hindus who bear the name of Kali or Durga or Tara indicates her popularity down to the present day.

Ganesa, the elder son of Siva and Parvati, the god of prudence and policy, having an elephant's head, indi- **Ganesa.** cating his sagacious nature, is the god of Bengal shopkeepers; he has a trunk, one tusk, and four hands. Kartikeya is the younger son of Siva and Parvati, and is called the god of war; in southern India his name is Subramanya. Lastly, we must notice **Ganga.** Ganga, the Ganges, whose birth and doings are the subject of elaborate legends, and whose waters are believed to have power to cleanse from all sins, past, present, and future. A specially sacred spot is that where the Ganges meets the ocean, at Sagar Island, to which vast numbers of people flock each January, to bathe with joy in the flood, and to worship the long line of deities whose images are set up by priests who take toll of the pilgrims.

But when we have exhausted the list of great gods, we have only touched as it were the more prominent of Hindu deities, which are popularly said to number three hundred and thirty millions. In fact, throughout India the old local deities and demons, so much noticed in **Local deities and demons.** China, hold extensive sway. Every village has its own special guardian mother, who has a husband associated with her as protector. But the mother is most worshipped, and is believed to be most accessible to prayer and offerings, and very liable to punish, and to inflict diseases if neglected. Many have a specialty, such as the prevention of a particular disease, or the giving of children. Many are deifications of notable women; some are in effect devils, delighting in blood. All are believed to control secret operations of nature, and to have magic powers which may be imparted to worshippers.

Some even go so far as to say that the predominant belief of the Hindus, especially in the villages, is a dread of evil spirits, who are believed to bring about all evils and diseases, and often have peculiar and special areas of destructiveness. They may have material bodies of a more ethereal structure than those of men, have differences of sex, and possess the power of assuming any shape and moving through the air in any direction. Some of these are the Asuras, or demons created at the foundation of the world or by the gods (though originally the word meant simply beings of a godlike nature). We cannot go into their classes; but it is to be noted that the majority of demons are believed to have been originally human beings, whose evil nature lives after them as demons. All crimes, diseases, and calamities are due to special devils. They mostly require food, and especially the blood of living animals. Sometimes mounds of earth, piles of bricks, etc., do duty as shrines for their "worship," the offering of food and recital of incantations being the chief rites. Every village has its own demon. A volume might be occupied in describing the devil-cults of India. In the south, where they are believed to delight in dancing, music, etc., "when pestilence is rife in any district, professional exorcisers, or certain persons selected for the purpose, paint their faces, put on hideous masks, dress up in fantastic garments, arm themselves with strange weapons, and commence dancing. Their object is to personate particular devils, or rather perhaps to induce such devils to leave the persons of their victims and to occupy the persons of the dancers, who shriek, fling themselves about, and work themselves up into a frenzy of excitement, amid beating of tom-toms, blowing of horns, and ringing of bells. When the dancers are thoroughly exhausted, they sink down in a kind of trance, and are then believed to be gifted with clairvoyance and a power of delivering prophetic utterances. The

G

spectators ask them questions about missing relatives or future events, and their deliverances are supposed to be oracular" (Monier-Williams). Many strange festivals are held in connection with this devil-worship in India, and the facts show how general must formerly have been the practices now found among the more savage races. The extensive animal worship of cows, serpents, monkeys, etc., and the worship of trees still prevailing is another considerable survival of more primitive times. It depends largely in India on the view taken of the sacredness of life, and the transmigration of the souls of men into animals. Again, the worship of great men seems even more deeply implanted in the Hindu than in the Chinese mind, and again and again great leaders, preachers, teachers or saints are deified, and regarded as incarnations of Vishnu or Siva; and even men of moderate fame are after death honoured and worshipped, and a shrine is set up to them in the place where they were best known. Surely we have said enough to show that in every way the Hindus are very remarkable for their worship of the superior powers in all conceivable forms.

Worship of animals and trees.

Deification of heroes and saints.

[See "Oriental Religions: India," by S. Johnson, English and Foreign Philosophical Library. Sir W. W. Hunter's "India," vol. vi. of the "Imperial Gazetteer of India," and also separately published. Rev. W. Ward's "View of the History, Religion and Literature of the Hindus, 1818." Rev. W. J. Wilkins's "Hindu Mythology and Modern Hinduism." Sir Monier-Williams's "Religious Thought and Life in India," and "Indian Wisdom;" "Sacred Books of the East."]

A GHAUT AT BENARES, WITH RECESSES FOR DEVOTEES.

CHAPTER IV.

Modern Hinduism II.

Inclusiveness of Hindu worship—Variations in modern times—Religiousness of the Hindus—Household worship—The guru—Initiation—Elements of worship—Brahman ritual—Ritual of the common people—Temple services—Temple priests—Frequent festivals—Images—Festival ceremonies—Miracle-plays—Festivals of Durga—Pilgrimages to holy places—Benares—Temple of Bisheshwar—Pilgrims' observances—Puri—The great temple—The images—Consecrated food—The Car festival—Reported immolation of victims—A touching incident—Vishnu temple at Trichinopoly—Vishnuite sects—Sivaite sects—The Saktas—The Sikhs—The Sikh bible—The Brahmo Somaj—Rammohun Roy—Devendra Nath Tagore—Keshub Chundra Sen—The Universal Somaj—Fatalism—Maya, or illusion—Transmigration—Rewards and punishments—Death and cremation—Ceremonies for the dead—Moral state—Condition of wives—Position of women—Widows—Suttee—Disconnection of morals and religion—Hindu virtues.

IN describing modern Hindu religious practices and worship, we are met with a most varied assemblage of rites and customs, often mutually discordant, all of which have an equal claim to inclusion under the name Hinduism. Never has there been a religion so expansive and all-inclusive. As a recent Bengal census report states, the term denotes neither a creed nor a race, neither a church nor a people, but is a general expression devoid of precision. It embraces alike the disciples of Vedantic philosophy, the high-class Brahman, the low-caste worshippers of all the gods of the Hindu pantheon, and the semi-barbarous aborigines who are entirely ignorant of Hindu mythology, and worship a stone in time of sickness and danger. There is so great a difference in the prevalent forms of worship in different districts, there are so many personal and household ceremonies, differing according to rank or locality, and also there have been so many changes in modern times, that it is quite impossible to give more than a partial view in a limited space. The common people believe their worship has lasted unchanged for long ages, and Europeans have largely adopted the same view; but while the Hindu nature remains very largely the same, variations in worship have been multitudinous. The great car festival of Jagannath is a modification of a Buddhist festival; and it would be easy to multiply proofs of the changes in modern Hinduism.

Inclusiveness of Hindu worship.

Variations in modern times.

To a greater extent than any nation under the sun, the Hindus are a religious people. As Mr. Wilkins says, "To treat of the ordinary life of the Hindu is to describe the Hindu religion. From before birth to the close of life periodical ceremonies are enjoined and, for the most part, practised." Mostly they are survivals from animism, sorcery, astrology, and the like primitive beliefs. Thus, before the birth of a child the mother must not wear clothes over which birds have flown, must always have a knot in her dress round the waist, must not walk or sit in the courtyard, in order to avoid evil spirits must wear an amulet round her neck containing flowers consecrated to the god Baba Thakur, and must drink every day a few drops of water touched

Religiousness of the Hindus.

by this amulet. The naming of a boy is a most important ceremony, including a thanksgiving service, with gifts for the benefit of ancestors. The names of gods or deified heroes are often chosen, with the addition of another chosen by the astrologer, who calculates the horoscope of the child.

Household worship.

Every household at all raised above poverty has a family priest (unless the head is himself a Brahman), who performs service, usually twice a day, in a room in which the family idol is kept. There is also a platform opposite the entrance gate of the house, to receive the images made for the periodic festivals. The priest bathes and anoints the idol, recites a ritual, and presents offerings of fruits and flowers given by the family. The family, however, are not usually present, the priest being the only person whose presence is needed. The offerings are his perquisite, and he is supported entirely by one or two families. Of course he is present at all the important family ceremonies.

The guru.

The guru, or religious teacher, is a distinct functionary; he is the initiator into the Hindu sects, and the teacher of their doctrines; but he does not live in the house of a disciple. The Hindus are taught that it is better to offend the gods than their guru, for the latter can intercede if the former are angry; but if the guru is offended, no one can intercede, and the curse of the guru brings untold miseries. He usually visits his disciples only once a year, unless he wants more money. His treatment of them is very lofty; and educated Hindus themselves describe the gurus as covetous, unprincipled, and familiar with vice. The best entertainment, new carpets and large presents are demanded by them, and few teach anything of value.

Initiation.

Every Hindu boy of eight years old (sometimes older) receives from his chosen guru, who need not be a Brahman, a sacred text or mantra, called the seed text, which is taught to him in private, with the name of the god selected by the guru for his especial worship. This text must never be repeated to others, and must be said over mentally or in whispers one hundred and eight times a day (the number is often counted by a rosary). The youth, before receiving it, fasts, bathes, and appears in

TEMPLE OF KRISHNA, NEPAUL.

spotless robes; and if he be of the twice-born (Brahman, Kshatriya, or Vaisya) castes, he for the first time puts the sacred thread round his neck. The relationship between the disciple and his guru continues throughout life. The present race of gurus are as a rule self-indulgent and ignorant men. The astrologer is an equally necessary personage to the household; no journeys can be undertaken, no new business begun without his aid; he fixes the hour for weddings and religious festivals, and numerous other matters depend absolutely on his pronouncing the time opportune.

Elements of worship.

The great elements of Hindu worship may be defined as (1) mediation, (2) works of merit, (3) purchasing the favour or arresting the disfavour of the gods by presents and sacrifices. The educated Hindu certainly has a high object, namely, to gain a realisation of his identity with the supreme Being, and to become reunited to Him. This state can only be approached by the Brahman ascetic; all others not Brahmans must by religious works seek to be reborn in some future life in a higher caste, until they reach the bliss of Brahmanism.

Brahman ritual.

We have already indicated to some extent the ritual observances laid down for Brahmans in the sacred books. These are still kept up in essence; and so numerous and laborious are they, that two hours both morning and evening, and an hour in the middle of the day, are occupied in fulfilling them all. The ascetics have plenty of time for this; but Brahmans engaged in business find them very trying, and a few perform them by deputy, through a family priest. Previous to any act of worship a complex ablution must be performed, with many details and prayers; then the sun is worshipped, with meditation on Brahma, Vishnu, and Siva; the text known as Gayatri is next repeated three times while holding the breath. It runs thus: "Om" (see p. 26), "earth, sky, heaven! We meditate on the adorable light of the resplendent generator (the sun), which governs our intellects, which is water, lustre, savour, immortal faculty of thought, Brahma, earth, sky, heaven." Thus, the light of the sun is taken as the type of all effulgent power; and, as a native commentator says, "it must be worshipped by them who dread successive births and deaths, and who eagerly desire beatitude. . . ." But this prayer must be preceded by the repetition of the names of the seven worlds: 1. This earth. 2. The world of the unconscious dead awaiting the end of the present age. 3. The heaven of the good. 4. The middle world. 5. The world of births, for animals destroyed at the end of each age. 6. The abode of the sons of Brahma. 7. The abode of Brahma the supreme. The word Om is to be repeated before and after this list. Many other ceremonies follow. The heart is supposed to be cleansed from sin by drawing up a little water by one nostril and expelling it by the other. One of the prayers is, "May whatever sin I have committed by night, in thought, word, or deed, be cancelled by day. Whatever sin is in me, may it be far removed."

Before the reading of the Vedas, which follows, offerings of grain, etc., must be made to the gods, with invitations to them to be present and cheerful during the reading of the Veda; then similar offerings must be made to Yama and the great progenitors of mankind, then for the Brahman's ancestors, and for all men, with the object of relieving the wants of sufferers in hells, or increasing the blessedness of those in heaven. After this exhausting series of ceremonies, the Brahman, before taking his meal, offers a portion to deities, ancestors, and to all other beings, and must then feed his guests before partaking himself. Finally he must wash his hands and feet, afterwards tasting the water. As his food is given him, he says, "May heaven give thee!" and when he takes it he says, "May earth receive thee!" He may not yet eat until he has passed his hand round the plate to separate it from the rest of the company, has offered five pieces to Yama, has made five oblations to breath, and has wetted hiseyes. In addition to these rites (which are here only partially given) there may be others significant of the particular sect to which the man belongs. Some will also wait for possible guests before taking food, for Brahma himself is represented as present in every guest.

But it must be owned that the mass of the Hindus

have no such elaborate daily ritual. The Sakta sect, it

IDOLS IN TEMPLE OF JAGANNATH, PURI.

is true, and the more religious members of other sects,

have a considerable daily ceremony, all including much the same ideas of purification of body, averting the anger of ghosts or ancestors, the offering of sacrifices to the great gods and goddesses, the recitation of their deeds as told in the Puranas, etc. But the majority of Hindus only bathe daily, and raise their hands and bow to the rising sun. Shopkeepers have an image or a picture of Ganesa in their shops, and burn a little incense before it in the morning; Vishnuites have one or more of the god's emblems, especially the Salgrama (a fossil Ammonite), which they guard as if it were a living being, bathing it in the hot season, etc., and before these daily prayers are offered. The names of the gods are repeated a great number of times a day. However, on days when it is not very convenient to go through a long form, the Hindu will be content with repeating the text he was taught by his guru, which is often an unmeaning jingle.

Ritual of the common people.

The public temples contain the principal religious apparatus of the mass of the Hindus. But it must not be imagined from this that their temples are as a rule large. They are not, in general, places for the assemblage of numbers of people, and in fact they are mostly not more than ten or a dozen feet square. They are simply small buildings in charge of a priest, who takes care of an idol or image, which is supposed to be a special abode of the deity, and who receives offerings from worshippers coming one by one, and prostrating themselves before the image. Many of them have been built by public contributions, others by rulers, and many by well-to-do private persons anxious to secure merits to balance their sins. If they desire to make a large offering, they do not build a larger temple, but a number of smaller ones, seven, fourteen, twenty-one, or even more, some of which may never be used. Old temples of this kind are not repaired; the new man does not wish to do what will but add to the merit of another. Usually the temple has an outer court, often with verandahs round, in which pilgrims may lodge when they come from a distance. The temple itself has two main portions—the vestibule,

Temple services.

and the shrine containing the image, only large enough to admit the priest. One of the singular forms observed is the ringing of a bell to attract the notice of the god to his worshipper, who merely walks round, hands his gift to the priest, and bows to the image.

Temple priests.

The priests of these temples are all Brahmans, who alone perform the proper worship, usually without any spectators. The sacred texts are merely muttered, and being in Sanskrit, are unintelligible to the masses; the texts, of course, differ according to the god or incarnation that is being worshipped. The essential character of this worship lies in the treatment of the image as if it were a living being, and the priest his servant; washing, dressing, feeding, decorating, putting to bed, etc., are all gone through most carefully. With all this the people have nothing to do but to bring the offerings, which become the priests' property. Of course, in the case of deities whose rites require animal sacrifices, there is a great business of slaughtering victims, and afterwards disposing of the meat not required by the priests; it finds a ready sale, being especially valuable owing to its sacred character.

Frequent festivals.

The regular daily worship of the temples forms but a small part of the religious life of the Hindu. His attention is mainly given to the festivals which occur so frequently, though somewhat irregularly, as to occupy the place of the Christian Sunday. Most of the gods have special festival days, and others are only worshipped publicly on such days. Not only are special images of the gods made for the temples, but also for many private persons, whose houses become public temples for the day or days of the festival, and are visited by crowds of people. Usually, after the proper ceremonial has been gone through, various amusements—nautch dances, plays, musical entertainments—are provided. Sometimes two or more adjoining villages will join in these celebrations, each householder paying his share.

Images are provided for these festivals by regular tradesmen. They are largely based upon bamboos tied together, and covered with hay and mud from a sacred stream. They are then dried in the sun, and afterwards painted, dressed, and otherwise decorated according to some mode presented by the sacred law-books. When they are taken to the place of worship, the priest engaged for the occasion performs a ceremony called the giving of life, in which the god is invited to reside in the image for one, two, or three days. It then becomes sacred, and must be touched by none but a Brahman,—must be approached by none but a Hindu. A full morning and evening worship is celebrated before the image, that in the evening being followed by amusements. The concluding day witnesses the farewell of the deity, who is thanked for favouring the worshippers with his or her presence, and is supplicated to return next year. When the god is supposed to have departed, the sacred image becomes once more common clay, and may be touched by any one. About sunset it is taken to a river bank, or to a tank, with a musical procession, dancing women and lighted torches. The image is rowed out to the middle of the stream and dropped into the water, there to dissolve and decay. The amount of worship performed by Hindus is increased by the necessity of averting the evil which other gods besides their own special deity may cause, and by their desire to gain any possible additional benefit. We cannot give space to a recital of the important public festivals which occur throughout the months of the year. These vary in different localities, and the total number is enormous. For instance, there are festivals all over Bengal to Jagannath, in imitation of the great ones at Puri, cars and great images being similarly provided. There are numerous special festivals to Sasthi, who watches over women in child-bearing, and protects children. At the festivals of Krishna miracle-plays form an important feature, and represent the most important events in the lives of the gods, the actors being got up to represent them, and not omitting their many indecent words and actions. By such representations, among other things, the illiterate Hindu masses come to

Images.

Festival ceremonies.

Miracle-plays.

CAR OF JAGANNATH AT PURI, ORISSA.

have a more vivid idea of the history of their gods than any people.

Festivals of Durga.

The festival of Durga in Bengal is especially elaborate, the sons of Durga, Sarasvati, the wife of Brahma, and Lakshmi, the wife of Vishnu, being attendant figures. Durga herself has ten hands, holding weapons emblematic of her victories. The forms of worship previous to the coming to life of the goddess are very long, and one or more animals may be sacrificed, sometimes a buffalo. So generally is this festival observed,—husbands and sons returning home for it, and business being suspended,—that it has been termed the Christmas of Bengal. It is celebrated in the sixth month (parts of September and October). The festival of Lakshmi, which follows, is the occasion for sitting up at night playing cards or amusing themselves, for the goddess is believed during the night to pass over all who are awake. In the seventh month there is a very repulsive celebration of Durga in her bloodthirsty aspect. "In the images which represent her at this festival," says Mr. Wilkins, "she is black, as her name Kali implies, and her husband is lying down under her feet. Her tongue protrudes from her mouth, her four arms are extended, one hand grasping a sword, another the head of a giant, and the other two signalling to her hosts. As ear-rings she has two dead bodies of her foes; her neck is adorned with a necklace of skulls, and her only garment, a zone, is made of the hands of her vanquished foes, whilst her hair falls down in long tresses to her waist. Intoxicated with the blood of her foes, her eyes flash with rage, her eyebrows are dyed with crimson, and blood flows down her breast." This worship is attended with midnight sacrifices of animals, shrieking invocations, and drunken orgies. Many of the festivals assume the aspect of carnivals. At some of the festivals of Siva hooks used to be inserted in the backs of men, which were then swung in the air at a great height; but this is now discontinued, either a dummy being used, or the hook fixed to a rope round the man's body.

The next great department of Hindu worship is that concerned with pilgrimages to particular places of great

Pilgrimages to holy places.

sanctity or to special temples. Large numbers of Hindus have given themselves up to nothing but travelling from one sacred place to another; but a great proportion of the people strain every nerve to visit a shrine at least once in their lifetime, and will exercise self-denial for many years to pay the expenses of their journey and provide offerings for the gods, believing that their pilgrimage will secure them great blessings both in this world and the next. They cheerfully endure the greatest privations or sufferings on the way, and show the most intense joy when they come in sight of their destination, or see the sacred image exhibited. "I have seen the people throw themselves on the ground," says Mr. Wilkins, "and kiss the very dust as soon as they have caught sight of the holy city of Benares; I have seen them take the dust from the wheels of Jagannath's car, and place it on their head with signs of the intensest pleasure; I have heard them shout with joy as they have come in sight of the meeting of the waters of the Ganges with the sea at Saugor Island." Many now travel by rail to the famous shrines, and thus the crowds that visit them are greater than ever; but many still go by road or boat, often being drowned, or dying by the wayside. Some take vows to perform long distances by measuring their length upon the ground. The sacrifice of life is increased by the demands of the priests, which too often do not leave the pilgrims enough money to provide for the return journey. It cannot be said that the amount or character of the worship paid is an adequate justification for the weary toil and expense of the journey. Bathing, presenting offerings, walking round the temples and seeing the place are the chief religious acts, and too often the rest of the time is occupied with immoral or degrading practices which the priests facilitate. The reputation of many shrines is kept up by the preaching or talking of travelling adherents, always engaged for the purpose of vaunting the benefits obtained by a pilgrimage. Visits are also paid in the hope of obtaining the much-valued blessing of a son, or in fulfilment of a vow in time of distress or sickness.

We can only notice in any detail the two greatest places of pilgrimage in India, Benares and Puri: the former being the special abode of Siva, the latter of Vishṇu. In no Indian city has gross idolatry a stronger hold than in Benares; ugly idols, monstrosities, and reproductive emblems are met with on all sides. More temples have been built and more money has been spent on worship under British rule than during an equal period of Mussulman domination; but this is accounted for by the greater wealth and freedom of the people. Some years ago more than a thousand temples were counted in Benares proper, exclusive of suburbs, and of images in house walls. These are devoted to a great variety of deities, sometimes Siva under different names, or relatives of other deities connected with Siva; and not content with an image of the god worshipped in a particular temple, in many cases the priests have added images of others in niches or in rows; sometimes even a hundred are to be seen in rows. The exceeding sanctity of Benares is accounted for by a legend which we have already given (p. 78), and this holy character extends to ten miles from the Ganges, the tract being bounded by a winding road fifty miles long, containing hundreds of temples. To walk along this road is itself a most meritorious act; residents are taught that they should walk along it at least once a year; and whosoever dies within this area, even a heretic or a criminal, gains heaven.

Benares.

The most important temple in the city is that of Bisheshwar (god of the world), a name given to Siva as king of all the gods in the Benares territory, the gods of the sacred road being his police force. He is supposed to reside in a stone linga emblem, and before this crowds of people pass daily with offerings of rice, flowers, grain, ghee, and money. Many of the worshippers in approaching the god show signs of great fear, dreading to call down his anger. Another of the great places of attraction is the Mankarnika well, a foul tank of water which is believed to wash out the greatest crimes.

Temple of Bisheshwar.

Pilgrims taking the fifty miles journey round Benares

have to go through a severe ritual; they must, if possible, bathe before starting, and at the end of each day, and must walk barefoot, must provide for their own wants without receiving from or giving to others, must not quarrel or use bad language on the road, and must give gifts to the priests of the Mankarnika well at the end of the journey.

Pilgrims' observances.

In a somewhat different way from Benares, Puri (the city) on the coast of Orissa is as famous and holy in the eyes of Hindus. Here Vishnu is worshipped as Jagannath (the Lord of the World); and a series of notable festivals throughout the year keep up a continual round of religious excitement, culminating in the famous Car Festival, attended by something like 100,000 pilgrims. There seems little doubt that Puri was a Buddhist sanctuary, to the reputation of which Jagannath has succeeded. The present temple dates from the end of the twelfth century, and is a pyramidal building on a site about twenty feet above the surrounding country. Vishnu worship was greatly modified by Chaitanya, who taught that faith and love were more acceptable to the deity than penance and rites. The temple already had a large double enclosure with lofty walls; and Chaitanya taught that within it men of all castes were equal, and might eat together of the sacred food. Altogether the worship of Jagannath became that of a gentle, genial deity with human feelings and sympathies, and having no trace of those bloodthirsty qualities generally associated in this country with the "car of Juggernaut." No doubt the genial has become the jovial and the voluptuous with many of the worshippers, and the worship itself is accused of licentiousness, but as warmly defended from the charge by some who have had good opportunities of knowing.

Puri.

The great temple.

The inner enclosure of the great temple, nearly four hundred by three hundred feet, includes a number of small temples and sacred places and trees as well as the large temple. The latter contains four principal halls, the Hall of Offerings, the Dancing Hall for amusements, the audience chamber, and the shrine proper, both the

BRAHMANS OF BENGAL.

latter being eighty feet square. In niches in the shrine are three large images of three of Vishnu's incarnations—the Boar, the Man-lion and the Dwarf. The principal images (p. 89), are those of Jagannath, painted black; of Balarama, his brother, white, and Subhadra, their sister, golden yellow. They are made of one block of iron-wood, and are most uncouth representations of human bodies without hands or legs, the arms being stumps to which golden hands are fixed. The male images are about six feet high, the female four and a half feet. The clothing and ornaments of these images are changed several times a day, so that they appear very different at different hours, sometimes being dressed as Buddha, sometimes as Krishna, sometimes as Ganesa. Various stories are told to account for these ugly images, one being that God is so great that no figure can properly represent Him, consequently these ugly ones are made to inspire people with fear, that they may propitiate Him by gifts. Most probably they are modified forms of Buddhist images; there is an additional shapeless stump about six feet high, which is said to have the mark of a wheel on the top, representing the Buddhist wheel of the law. A certain relic is imbedded in the image of Jagannath, and is carefully transferred when new images are made; what it is, none but the priests know, and it is probably a Buddhist relic.

The images.

Numerous other gods or forms of the principal gods have images in or near the shrine. The chief images are only moved at the great festivals; but daily services of a complete character, as if they were human beings, are performed. At the four chief meals of the day large quantities of cooked food are brought into the temple and consecrated by being set in front of the idol. It is cooked by men of low caste, and eagerly eaten by pilgrims of all castes after consecration, or even taken home as a sacred treasure. On some days this food is supplied to 100,000 people, for payment, of course, so that the profits of the priests in charge are enormous. The great festivals at Puri are the Dol Jatra festival, a sort of spring carnival; the

Consecrated food.

Snan Jatra, when the images are bathed with sacred water and beautifully dressed, after which they are supposed to have taken a fever from exposure and are put in a sick chamber for a fortnight, during which time they are repainted; and then follows the Rath Jatra, or

The Car Festival. Car Festival, when the gods are taken for a ride on their cars. These chariots have often been described; they are of immense weight and cumbrousness, that of Jagannath being forty-five feet high, and having sixteen wheels. Amid an enormous concourse the images are placed on the cars, and dressed, and have golden hands and arms attached to them. When this is complete, the chief guardian of the temple, the Kurda Raja, termed "the sweeper of the temple," sweeps the road for one hundred yards in front of the cars, worships the images, and touches the ropes of the car as if he were dragging them; then hundreds of Hindus specially set apart for the office, aided by the attendant pilgrims, drag the car slowly to a set of temples about two miles distant. This great effort, however, occupies four days, and on arrival at the destination the image of Lakshmi is taken to see Jagannath. After four or five days the return journey takes place. It is at this festival that

Reported immolation of victims. immolations of pilgrims have been supposed to take place as part of the routine, so that the car of Juggernaut has become with many almost synonymous with a system of ruthless crushing of human victims; but this is really contrary to the spirit of the worship of Vishnu. No doubt self-immolation has not unfrequently taken place, because the worshippers felt their sins were all atoned for, and they did not wish to return to the world to commit fresh sins; and in the crowds many have no doubt been accidentally crushed to death; but human sacrifice is not inculcated by the priests nor in any way encouraged by them, for a drop of blood spilt in the presence of Jagannath pollutes priests, people, and consecrated food. If a death takes place within the precincts of the temple, the worship is suddenly stopped, and the offerings are taken away from the sight of the offended deity. There is an almost continual round of festivals at Puri, which indeed lives on its religious character, having no other attraction.

Other notable localities for pilgrimages are the great temples of Tanjore, Madura, and Ramesvara (an island between India and Ceylon), these being seats of Siva worship. It is a great pilgrims' feat to visit Benares and bring from thence a pot of Ganges water to Ramesvara, to pour it on the symbol of Siva and then bathe in the sea, of course with payment of fees. Sir Monier-Williams relates a touching incident in connection with this. "Shortly before my arrival at the temple a father and son had just completed their self-imposed task, and after months of hard walking succeeded in transporting their precious burden of Ganges water to the other side of the channel. The longed-for goal was nearly reached and the temple of Ramesvara already in sight, when the father died suddenly on the road, leaving his son, a mere child, utterly destitute and unprotected. The boy, however, had one treasure left—his jar of Ganges water. This, if only it could be poured upon the sacred symbol, would prove a complete panacea for all his earthly troubles. Eagerly he grasped his burden once more and hurried on to the shrine. Imagine the child's outburst of passionate grief when the door was closed against him. He had no fee for the presiding priest."

A touching incident.

The most remarkable Vishnu temple in southern India is that of Sri-rangam, at Trichinopoly. It has a vast series of seven enclosures one within another, in which hundreds of Brahmans live. The corners of the four gateways of each square have splendid pyramidal towers. The whole is supposed to represent Vishnu's heaven. The principal image is lying down, and believed to be immovable—of course with a legend to account for the position, and there is a shrine over it in the shape of the syllable Om. A second image of Vishnu is kept for carrying in processions at the Car Festival, etc. The crown of the idol is covered with diamonds, pearls, and rubies, and the other ornaments are equally rich. Temples like this maintain large

Vishnu temple at Trichinopoly.

bands of musicians and troops of dancing girls, to take part in the festivals.

We must now give some brief account of the sects into which the Hindus are divided. To some extent these follow lines already indicated, as worshipping Vishnu or other gods under different manifestations, or following the teaching of particular reformers. Thus, to begin with the Vishnuite sects, there are the Ramanujas, or followers of Ramanuja, the Ramanandis, the Kabir Panthis, and numerous other sects founded by individuals. All these have special marks which must be painted on their foreheads, after bathing at the great festivals, with a special white earth. The Ramanujas, for instance, are distinguished by two perpendicular lines passing from the roots of the hair to the eyebrows, and a transverse line across the top of the nose connecting the other two. In the centre is a transverse streak of red. They are also marked with patches of red and white on the breast and arms, supposed to represent certain signs of Vishnu. Their chief special belief is that Vishnu is Brahman, the supreme Being. The Ramanandis specially worship Vishnu as Ramachandra, with Sita his wife. This sect has many monasteries, and many travelling members, who collect offerings and visit shrines, all these being celibates. They practically disregard caste. The Kabir Panthis, following Kabir, believe in one god, and need not join in the outward worship of the Hindu deities; but they sing hymns to Kabir, their founder. Their moral code is excellent, including truth, humanity, and hatred of violence.

Vishnuite sects.

There are very many worshippers of Vishnu under the form of the infant Gopal, child of the cowherd. This sect, founded by Vishnu Swami and extended by Vallabha, is notable for its belief in costly apparel and liberal feeding as meritorious, in opposition to asceticism. The chief temple of Gopal is in Ajmir.

The Madvas of Southern India are followers of Madhava, said to have been an incarnation of the god Vayu in the 12th century. They wear a single cloth of a dirty yellow colour, go bareheaded, and have the symbols of

THE MAHA SATI AT AHAR, RAJPUTANA (CONTAINING TOMBS OF ALL THE CHIEFS OF OUDEYPORE).

Vishnu stamped with a red-hot iron on their shoulders or breast. They worship a plurality of gods, but teach that the human spirit is distinct from the Divine Spirit, though united to it, and that absorption in the godhead is impossible, thus differing markedly from the ordinary Hindu belief.

The majority of the Vishnu worshippers of Bengal belong to the sect founded by Chaitanya, whose influence raised the festivals of Puri to such popularity. His followers believe that Vishnu is the supreme soul and the one substance in the universe, and that Chaitanya was an incarnation of him. They also lay great stress upon *bakti*, or faith, of which there are five degrees: (1) peace, calm contemplation; (2) servitude; (3) friendship; (4) filial affection; (5) sweetness. Their cult is a joyous one, qualified by the necessity of implicit obedience to the guru. Caste is laid aside at their feasts.

Sivaitic sects.

The distinguishing marks of the Sivaitic sects are horizontal lines instead of perpendicular; and differences of width and colour indicate the particular sect. The Sivaites are very largely Brahmans, and the sects are not so extensive and popular as those of the Vishnuites. Among them are the Dandis, or staff bearers, mendicants who spend most of their time in meditation. Often they become almost idiotic from their perpetual suppression of thought and speech. The Yogis are another sect of meditationists with very special regulations, which are believed to give them the power of levitation, of travelling immense distances instantly, of rendering themselves invisible, etc. Many of them are practically jugglers and fortune-tellers, travelling about and practising on popular credulity.

The Saktas.

The Saktas include those sects specially devoted to the worship of female forms of the deity, such as Sarasvati, Lakshmi, Sita, Parvati, Durga, Kali, etc. The Saktas look upon their female deity as the active energy of all things, and the source of all beings, for without the female element they could not be born. It is chiefly in modern books termed Tantras that these views are taught. They have been called the Bible of the Saktas, and are akin to the Puranas in parts, but in others deal largely with the peculiar rites of the Saktas, and charms and spells, mostly being in the form of dialogues between Siva and his wife. No doubt in this cultus the lowest grade of Hinduism was reached. It upholds and propagates the most unbridled ideas of sensuality, in the belief that to indulge the grossest appetites with the mind fixed on the supreme Being was the most pious act possible. The drinking of alcoholic liquors forms a great element in Sakti worship, as well as the eating of meat. The powers supposed to be acquired by meditating on the texts and spells of the Tantras outdo anything imaginable. By them it is possible to predict the future, work more wonders than the gods, inspire any one with love, turn plants into meal, etc. Credulity cannot go farther than in the case of the believers in Saktism. It is believed, however, that the spread of education by the English has done much to diminish the sway of these baleful notions.

The Sikhs.

Here we may call attention to an opposite phenomenon in modern Hinduism—the spread of theistic sects of an increasingly pure tendency. The Sikhs of the Punjaub owe their rise to Nanak, a follower of Kabir in the 15th century, born not far from Lahore in 1469. He became a guru or teacher, and his followers were termed Sikhs or disciples. He taught a religion free from caste and idolatry, having been largely influenced by the growing Mohammedanism around him; but he still remained more of a pantheist than a monotheist, and he taught that God should be especially worshipped under the name of Hari, one of the titles of Vishnu. After his death there succeeded him a line of chief gurus, who, at first friendly, developed great hostility to the Mohammedans, and became largely military leaders. Their political history must be read elsewhere. The fourth guru, Ram-das, set up a lake temple in the sacred tank at Umritsur, which became the head-quarters of the Sikhs. The fifth guru, Arjun, compiled the first Sikh bible largely from the precepts of his predecessors. Govind, the tenth guru, compiled a second book or supplement, devised a form of baptism, imposed a vow not to worship idols, to bow to no one but a Sikh Guru, and in many ways cemented the bonds of the party. War was made a religious duty; and while Govind refused to name a successor as guru, he created the Sikh bible (or Granth), a permanent object of worship with the title Sahib. Henceforth it was to be their infallible guide; whatever they asked it would show them. The Sikh bible is written in the old Hindi dialect, with a peculiar mode of writing. It declares the unity of God, but is based on pantheistic ideas. Many of the names of Vishnu are accepted as names of the supreme Deity. It forbids image worship, but the way in which the Granth itself is worshipped, dressed, and decorated, goes far to elevate it into an idol. Many ordinary Hindu superstitions are included in it, such as the belief in the sanctity of the cow, the vast number of transmigrations of souls, and complete submission to the guru. In recent years the Sikh faith has very considerably retrograded towards Vishnuism. Many Sikhs now adopt caste, wear the Brahmanical thread, and observe Hindu festivals and ceremonies. There is a notable temple to Govind at Patna containing many remains of him. The temple at Umritsur is one of the most striking sights in India; it is dedicated to the one god under his name Hari; but he is believed to be visibly represented by the Sacred Book.

The Sikh bible.

A very significant development of modern Hinduism is that represented by the Brahmo Somaj, which represents a revival of the theism to be found in the Vedas, influenced not a little by the teaching of Christianity. Rammohun Roy (born 1774), founder of the Brahmo Somaj, was a high-caste Brahman, son of a Vishnu worshipper, and highly educated in Persian, Arabic, and Sanskrit. At the age of sixteen he wrote a tract against idolatry, and excited such opposition that he left home for some years, studying Buddhism in Tibet. He afterwards studied English, obtained government employment, and mixed with Europeans. After his father's death he was more free in his opposition to what he considered perversions of the true

The Brahmo Somaj.

Rammohun Roy.

Vedic religion; and he particularly drew attention to the fact that suttee, the self-immolation of widows, was not sanctioned by the Vedas. In 1819, after studying Christianity, he published a book, "The Precepts of Jesus, the Guide to Peace and Happiness," in which he stated that he found the doctrines of Christ more conducive to moral principles, and better adapted for the use of rational beings, than any other that had come to his knowledge. Nevertheless he strongly objected to accept the Christian doctrine of the Trinity, for he considered it to be of the same nature as that of a plurality of gods. Thus he is properly described as a Unitarian. He preferred to choose the best from all religions, believing that inspiration was not confined to any age or nation; thus he accepted whatever was good in the sacred books of all nations.

The Brahmo Somaj was finally established in 1830, "for the worship of the eternal, unsearchable, and immutable Being, who is the Author and Preserver of the universe." No image or portrait was to be admitted, no sacrifice was to be made, and nothing worshipped by other men was to be spoken of with contempt in the building. Although he has spoken and written against the caste system, Rammohun Roy did not give it up, nor abandon the Brahmanical thread. The Vedas were still read at his meetings, while the Bible was not introduced. In 1831 he visited England with several objects, but fell a victim to the climate, and died in 1833 at Bristol. To him must be given the credit of the first striking new departure in the elevation and purification of modern Hinduism.

Devendra Nath Tagore.

His practical successor was Devendra Nath Tagore, born in 1818, who in 1839 formed a society for the knowledge of truth, and in 1841 joined the Brahmo Somaj. He prepared a scheme for organising that society as a church in 1843, including seven solemn vows to be taken by members. The members were to abstain from idolatry, to worship the great God, Creator, Preserver, and Destroyer, through the love of God and doing works dear to God,—to lead holy lives and to seek forgiveness through abandonment of sin. A minister was appointed, and by 1847, 767 persons had taken the vows, while many others adhered to them. About 1850 it was decided that the Vedas were not infallible, and that only such views as were in harmony with Theistic truth were to be accepted from them. Approved extracts were made from the Vedas, Manu, the Satapatha Brahmana, etc. The views of the church include the Fatherhood of God, who has never become incarnate, but whose providence is over his creatures, and who hears their prayers. Repentance is the one path of atonement, forgiveness, and salvation. The only necessary religious deeds are good works, charity, contemplation and devotion, and the attainment of knowledge, all penances and pilgrimages being useless. The only sacrifice is self-sacrifice, the only temple is the pure heart. Caste is not acknowledged.

Keshub Chunder Sen.

With all these advanced views, much tacit recognition of Hinduism, and even conformity with it was still maintained; and in 1865 a new reformer proclaimed his mission, the well-known Keshub Chunder Sen, imbued with more advanced views as well as a more emotional and spiritual nature. He wished to abolish all caste observances, and this led to a rupture. A new form of initiation, the admission of women, and the reform of marriage observances followed; but after vigorous work for a number of years, Keshub agreed to the marriage of his daughter while a child to the Maharajah of Kuch Behar, at which some Hindu ceremonies were observed, and this caused much scandal. Nevertheless his church, the Progressive Brahmo Somaj of India, showed much vitality under his almost autocratic rule up to his death on January 8th, 1884. The original society, now known as the Adi Somaj, continues under the guidance of Devendra Nath Tagore, but has somewhat gone back towards Hinduism. Keshub had the skill to introduce new festivals to replace the older Hindu celebrations, including religious meetings with public processions, music, and singing. He also professed himself inspired to put down sectarianism and discord between sects. His influence still lives; the apostolic

TEMPLE OF KALI, RAJGRIHA, INDIA.

Durbar of his church refused to allow the platform from which he taught to be used, and declared that Keshub was still the leader of the church. It would be curious to note if this is followed by any further step towards his deification.

The Universal Somaj.

The party who left Keshub after the marriage of his daughter have formed a stronger church than the one they left, under the title of the Universal Somaj. They have adopted a sort of presbyterian government, to prevent the autocratic rule of one man, and only those who have given up idolatry and caste in private as well as in public can be office-bearers. Altogether there are about 1,500 strict members and 8,000 adherents of these various Theistic bodies in India, distributed over 178 churches.

Fatalism.

We have said little hitherto of certain common notions of the Hindus, which however influence them very greatly and hinder improvement. For instance, fatalism is one of their strongest beliefs. All a man's life is controlled by the Deity, and it is fruitless for man to oppose the decrees of God. It is this resignation to fate which so largely paralyses the efforts of the people, especially in regard to sickness. The belief in Maya, or illusion, is another of their beliefs. It is said that all mankind are the victims of illusion, especially in imagining themselves to be something different from God. It is commonly said that the supreme Being was tired of being alone, and formed the world as a sport or amusement, and that all the miseries of life came from Maya, the creatures being ignorant that they are really one with God.

Maya, or illusion.

Transmigration.

Again, belief in the transmigration of souls pervades all India. It will be found to constitute a prominent feature in Buddhism. We may here briefly state the essential details of the creed. Existence after death is a matter of course. A predominantly good life is rewarded with heaven, an evil life with hell. After a longer or shorter time the soul returns to earth to be re-born in a higher or lower station, according to its good or evil deeds.

Rewards and Punishments.

Re-births may be indefinitely numerous, and may be alternately higher and lower, or higher only if the conduct has been sufficiently good. Many of the gods are believed to have a heaven of their own, into which they take their worshippers for a longer or shorter time, and admit them to various degrees of nearness to themselves. Many are the acts which confer these privileges, but especially pilgrimages, acts of worship, sacrifices, building temples, giving gifts to Brahmans, and honouring gurus. The higher states of blessedness are exclusively for Brahmans; but those of lower caste may by good works earn re-birth in higher castes till they at last become Brahmans.

The various hells and heavens are elaborately described in the Puranas. There are said to be a hundred thousand hells, one for each class of offence. For instance, a glutton is to be cast into boiling oil; he who injures a man of superior caste is punished by being torn by swine; one who contemptuously treats a religious mendicant is made to stick fast in the mud with his head downwards. But fortunately for both sinners and priests, these punishments may be remitted if appropriate atonements, good deeds, and offerings are made. For corporeal sins, says Manu, a man will be re-born as a plant or a mineral; for verbal sins, as a bird or a beast; for mental sins, in the lowest human state. The slayer of a Brahman will be re-born as a dog, boar, ass, bull, etc.; he who steals gold from a priest will be born a thousand times in the bodies of spiders, snakes, etc. But the earlier books are far surpassed by the later ones in their teaching on this point. Thus, in the Agni Purana it is taught that "a person who loses human birth passes through 8,000,000 births amongst inferior creatures before he can appear again on earth as a human being. Of these he remains 2,100,000 among the immovable parts of creation, as stones, trees, etc.; 900,000 amongst the watery tribes; 1,000,000 amongst insects, worms, etc.; 1,000,000 amongst birds, and 3,000,000 amongst the beasts. In the ascending scale, if his works be suitable, he lives 400,000 lives amongst the lower castes of men, and 100 amongst Brahmans. After this he may obtain absorption into Brahma."

To such an extent can the policy of frightening people into goodness, or rather into compliance with priestly demands, be developed. Happily the Hindus, as a rule, do not remember the sufferings of their imaginary previous lives or conditions; and it is a ready way of accounting for any misfortune to say that it is a punishment for sins committed in a former life.

With such views it is not surprising that death and its approach should be made the occasion for endeavouring to obtain future benefits, or relief from penalties. The Hindu is taught that after death his spirit will wander in wretchedness, unless he dies near the Ganges or some holy stream, or unless his body is burned on its banks, or at any rate near some water, and some portion of his ashes must be thrown into it. This leads to a custom of exposing the dying on the banks of rivers. Long rows of steps line the banks and rude buildings, used for the dying to lie in, called ghats. The benefits of so dying are represented as so great, that relatives often believe it to be the greatest kindness to expose them, often carrying them through terrible heat, and exposing them at imminent risk. Great numbers of lives have been sacrificed in this way when the disease was by no means mortal; the word of the native doctors is taken as sufficient, and great haste is made lest the patient should die at home. The whole scene is repulsive and injurious in the highest degree. A few minutes before death is expected the victim is brought down to the brink of the river, where he dies more or less immersed in the stream. No doubt in some cases advantage is taken of these circumstances to administer poison. A native writer says: "Persons entrusted with the care and nursing of a dying man at the burning ghat soon get tired of their charge (no women being allowed to be there); and rather than minister to his comforts, are known to resort to artificial means. The process of immersion is another name for suffocation." So tenacious are some people of life, that they will sometimes survive nine or ten immersions, and be brought home again; but their continued life is considered disgraceful.

Death.

The burning of the corpse follows quickly the higher "The corpse is removed from its resting-place it how-burning ghat, a distance of a few hundred yards, and preparations for a funeral pile are speedily made. The body is then covered with a piece of new cloth and laid upon the pyre, the upper and lower parts of which are composed of firewood, faggots, and a little sandalwood and glue to neutralise the smell. The Manipora Brahman, an outcaste, reads the formula, and the son, or nearest of kin, changing his old garments for new white clothes, at one end of which is fastened an iron key to keep off evil spirits, sets fire to the pile. The body is consumed to ashes, the portion remaining unburnt is thrown into the river. The son, after pouring a few jars of holy water on the pile, bathes in the stream and returns home with his friends." Then follow wild expressions of grief on the part of the women. Often the family cannot afford to buy enough wood to consume the corpse, and part is left for jackals and vultures. The Brahmans of course go through much more elaborate funeral ceremonies than are here indicated.

Cremation.

After the cremation come the Shradda, or ceremonies for the benefit of the dead; these may be comparatively inexpensive, or may be made the occasion of lavish expenditure. On the thirtieth day after death, offerings of food, sweetmeats, etc., are made to the spirit of the deceased and his or her ancestors, and at the same time a number of Brahmans and persons of other castes are entertained. These ceremonies are evidently much akin to the ancestor-worship of the Chinese, as already detailed, showing how powerful a factor this reverence for ancestral spirits has been in races very dissimilar. One of the prayers is "May those in my family who have been burnt with fire, or who are alive who are yet unburnt, be satisfied with the food presented on the ground, and proceed contented towards the supreme path! May those who have no father nor mother, nor kinsman, nor food, nor supply of nourishment, be contented with this food offered on the ground, and attain, like it, a happy abode!" Some of the food is cast

Ceremonies for the dead.

into the fire, by which means it is supposed to reach those for whom it is intended. Brahmans repeat these ceremonies frequently in the first year after death, and after wards annually. The title to property is most intimately bound up with the funeral rites. Only a son or near male relative is properly qualified to perform them; but if males fail, females or other heirs may undertake the duty. Large promises are made in the Puranas and other sacred books to those who properly perform the Shradda rites, including the forgiveness of all their own sins. The details, like those of all religious matters in so religious a people, are far too lengthy to be given.

Moral state. What about the influence of Hindu religious ideas upon their moral condition? Many writers agree that this is bound up with the position of women, and that until they are freed and elevated no permanent improvement can be made. Here is an extract from a Hindu lady's book on the duties of wives. "The husband is the wife's religion, the wife's sole business, the wife's all-in-all. The wife should meditate on her husband as Brahma. For her, all pilgrimages should be concentrated on her husband's foot. The command of a husband is as obligatory as a precept of the Vedas. To a chaste wife her husband is her god. When the husband is pleased, Brahma is pleased. The husband is the wife's guru, her honour, the giver of her happiness, the bestower of fortune, righteousness, and heaven, her deliverer from sorrow and from sin."

Condition of wives.

Position of women. Of course the seclusion of women is not generally possible among the lower classes, but it is often aimed at by them; and the full consequences of the belief that the birth of a girl is a misfortune follow most Indian women through life. On the contrary, Hindu women pray, make pilgrimages, fast, and make costly offerings, that they may have sons who can by performing the Shradda rites deliver their ancestors from sufferings after death. All a girl's worship is directed towards obtaining good husbands and sons, by a series of rites which we cannot particularise; nor can we enlarge upon the evils of girl marriages (at the age of from seven to ten), and of plural marriages in the higher castes, or the details of wedding ceremonies, which however are full of religious significance.

The wives of the poorer people have considerable freedom; but among the richer classes a wife is the servant

SHRINE OF THE GODDESS PARVATI, WIFE OF SIVA (EARLIER FORM OF KALI, DURGA, ETC.), IN A TEMPLE AT POONAH.

not only of her husband but of all the older women of his family. She must always be visited in the presence of her brothers-in-law, and must not speak to her husband in the daytime, nor even take her meals with him. Too frequently she is the subject of painful tyranny and abuse on the part of the older women of the zenana.

Widows.

Yet the life of a Hindu wife is heaven compared with that of a childless widow. The faithful wife was long expected to sacrifice herself on his funeral pile (suttee), and, according as she did it or not, was lauded or cursed. Many widows in the past, from lack of courage to perform what they vowed, had themselves drugged and forcibly immolated. Frequently widows would most calmly and impassionately devote themselves to the fire, never giving a cry or a sigh of pain. So powerfully can the belief that they are doing what is pleasing to the gods and their deceased husbands work upon the Hindu women. In 1830 suttee was prohibited in States under British rule; but it was still practised in some of the native States. Mr. Wilkins states that the last case he heard of was about 1880.

Suttee.

The extreme difficulty experienced in abolishing suttee is explained by the treatment to which surviving widows are subjected, especially childless widows, who are forbidden to marry again, and become the household drudges and objects of scorn of the zenana. One meal a day, with a fast for two days a month, is their hard lot; with the deprivation of ornaments and of every pleasure. In many cases the sufferings of a widow are such that she would gladly die. No doubt the older widows are able to assert themselves, and in time gain influence. But enough has been said to show that the key to much of the religious and social question in India is bound up with the condition and education of women. Some improvement has already come with the improved education of the better classes, and the partial opening of the zenanas to European ladies and to lady doctors; and herein lies great hope for the future.

Disconnection of morals and religion.

The Hindu system is such that merit and pardon can be obtained for gross offences without any reform of heart and life. Thus it is not surprising that theft, dishonesty, lying, ingratitude, forgery, perjury, revenge, cruelty, and personal immorality are very rife among them. Mr. Wilkins says: "It does not surprise me at all to find the Hindus morally what they are, as I remember that whilst their books contain some of the highest and noblest moral precepts, their deities, when incarnate, are described as ignoring these beautiful moral lessons; and still further, when I see that religion and morality are quite separate in their view. . . . When a Hindu's anger is excited, truth, honour, trust—all are forgotten, and no means are left unemployed that can injure an enemy. The term 'mild Hindu,' certainly is the purest sarcasm; they submit to oppression and cruelty because they are physically incapable of resistance. Only give them the opportunity to avenge themselves and to oppose others, and certainly they are as vindictive in their way as any race of men on earth. They do not use the knife or the dagger, it is true, but they resort to poison, and, what is sometimes even worse, the poison of their own untruthful tongues." On the other hand, we must credit the Hindus with much fraternal affection and filial regard, much charity in the form of gifts, great patience, industry, and ingenuity. Out of these elements and their great intellectual powers we may hope that there may yet arise a nation mighty in goodness and noble in character.

Hindu Virtues.

[In addition to works referred to in the previous chapter, the following are valuable: Bose's "The Hindus as They Are"; H. H. Wilson's "Hindu Sects"; "Medical Jurisprudence," by Dr. Norman Chevers; Dr. Lall Mittra on "Orissa"; Rev. T. E. Slater's "Life of Keshub Chundra Sen"; many articles in *The Calcutta Review*.]

CHAPTER V.

Life of Buddha.

The soil prepared—The founder's period—Real existence of Buddha—Buddhist sacred books—The native land of Buddha—His youth and early life—The great renunciation—His long retirement—His enlightenment—His temptation—Opening of his mission—The eightfold path—The origin of suffering—The freedom of Buddhism—Early converts—General features of Buddha's life—Alternation of itinerancy with rest—The Buddhist gardens—Buddha and the courtesan Ambapali—Anxious inquirers—The new order of monks—Buddha not a socialist—Buddha's principal adherents—Lay believers—Women and Buddhism—Reception of sisters or nuns—Opposition—Brahmans confuted—The best sacrifice—Method of teaching—Long-drawn dissertations—A noble youth's conversion—Socratic method—Parables—The book of the Great Decease—Buddha prepares for his final discourse—His last temptation—His death.

The soil prepared.

THAT Buddhism arose in a country and among people saturated with Brahmanism,[1] as we have described it, must never be forgotten in contemplating its rise and development. Without pre-existing Brahmanism it would have lacked its most essential elements, its *raison d'être.* The higher Brahman philosophy had already merged the multitude of early Vedic gods into the Universal Spirit, and had developed very considerably their Pantheistic system; but at the same time the fetters of Brahman control, the observance of expensive and frequent rites, the obligation to obey the Vedic teaching and the authorised comments upon it were made more and more strict and onerous; and a spirit of reaction naturally arose. That the reform associated with the great Buddha's name was only one

[1] [Rhys Davids' "Hibbert Lectures." Oldenberg's "Buddha" (O). Sacred Books of the East (S.E.).]

evidence of this spirit, may be seen by the account we have already given of other rationalist philosophies (p. 26, etc). But while these gave a more or less nominal assent to the Vedas, Buddhism declared the good man's independence of Brahmans and Vedas, and his power of working out his own salvation. It put forward at once a higher ideal of a religious life and claimed a release from the bonds of Pharisaism.

The founder's period.

When we come to examine into the life of the supposed founder of Buddhism, we find great uncertainty even as to the period at which he lived. Many good authorities formerly placed him in the sixth and seventh centuries B.C.; but the latest and apparently the most reasonable view assigns him to the fifth century B.C. and places his death about 420–400 B.C.

How far Brahmanism was directly connected with the origin of Buddhism can probably never be known; but the deity "Brahman" of the earlier religion is adopted, amplified, and subdivided in early Buddhism; and no doubt the encouragement of the hermit and ascetic lives had led to the formation of communities of hermits and ascetics who may be taken as the prototypes of Buddhist monastic orders. Probably there were several sects of new religionists, who did not stick closely to the Veda and professed to have found a more excellent way, of whom the Buddhists and Jains have alone remained.

Real existence of Buddha.

We need not doubt that Buddhism had a founder, though less may be attributable to him than is commonly imagined. Those who have believed that the story of Buddha was altogether a myth representing a sun-hero have had to construct more imaginary tales than those they seek to destroy. The study of the Buddhist accounts, as preserved in Ceylon, written in the Pali, or sacred language of Buddhism (an early modification from Sanskrit), shows that from a very early time (supposed to be considerably before the Christian era) their religion has been believed to have been founded by the Knowing or Enlightened One (Buddha), also designated the Exalted One (Bhagava). But it must be confessed that we have no genuine ancient biography of Buddha dating from the same age as the early Pali texts. Such information as they do contain is rather in an incidental and unconnected form; but this does not cause us to doubt his having existed and been a religious leader, for at that early period and among that people the idea of composing a biography of a man had not arisen; and all the ancient Hindu books are destitute of any specimen of an attempt at even a brief biography of a man. But the existence of numerous Buddhist sacred books, the composition of which almost certainly took place before the council of the seven hundred fathers met at Vesali in the fourth century B.C., together with the nature of their contents, suffices to assure us that they represent the teaching of a great teacher, the Buddha, who preached salvation and deliverance to the people, and was in rivalry or opposition to six other heads of sects, of whom one, Nataputta, founded the Jain system, often represented as an offshoot of Buddhism, though it is rather a representative of similar tendencies acting at the same time. "It is evident," says Prof. Oldenberg, "that Buddha was a head of a monastic order of the very same type as that to which Nataputta belonged; that he journeyed from town to town in the garb and with all the external circumstances of an ascetic, taught and gathered round himself a band of disciples, to whom he gave simple ordinances." The form in which details concerning him have been preserved is chiefly his discourses and teaching, sometimes doubtfully associated with the name of the place where they were uttered; and in addition to this the main events of his life are frequently referred to.

Buddhist sacred books.

The native land of Buddha was situated between the lower Himalayas of Nepal and the middle course of the river Rapti, in the north-east of Oudh. The little river Rohim, which joins the Rapti near Goruckpore, about 100 miles north of Benares, is its eastern boundary. Both the Rohim and the Rapti appear by the same names in early Buddhist literature. In this fertile region, liable to heavy rains and long-lying inundations, the Aryan tribe or people of the Sakyas

The native land of Buddha.

(the Powerful), grew rice and maintained a close connection with the more powerful kingdom of Kosala (Oudh) to the south-west, which ultimately absorbed them. Although it has been widely represented that the Buddha was a king's son, the oldest records only mention the father as Suddhodana, a wealthy landowner, one of whose wives, Maya, of the same tribe, died soon after the birth of her son, who was named Siddhattha, and was often called Sakya, or Sakya-muni, the Sakya sage; this event took place probably somewhere about 500 B.C. He passed his youth in Kapila, the capital of the Sakyas, and there is no early tradition of his having become a Vedic student; rather the events of his after-life tend the other way, exhibiting him as a reformer and an opponent of Brahmanic pretensions. He appears to have been married, and to have had one son, Rahula, who became one of his disciples; but there is no absolutely certain detail about the reasons and circumstances which led him at the age of twenty-nine to abandon his home, and become a wandering ascetic, thenceforward known as the ascetic Gautama (pronounced Gowtama). One of the earliest records represents him as having felt deeply and often meditated on the weakness and decay of old age, and the horror of

His youth and early life.

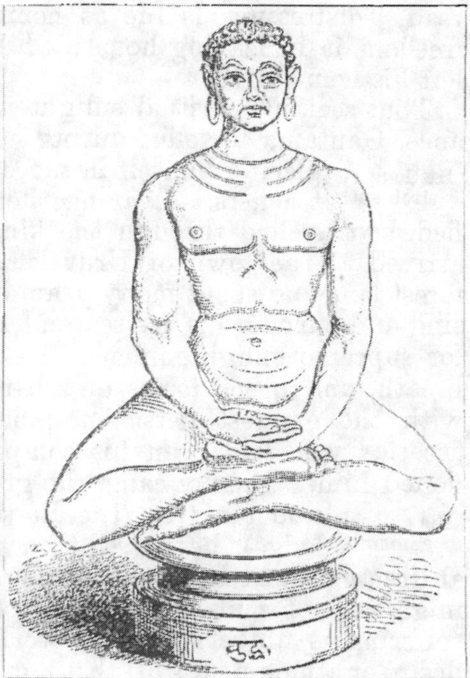

SEATED FIGURE OF BUDDHA.

The Great Renunciation.

sickness and death, and having thus lost the buoyancy of youth and the enjoyment of life. Other early records tell that "the ascetic Gautama has gone from home into homelessness, while still young, young in years, in the bloom of youthful strength, in the first freshness of life. The ascetic Gautama, although his parents did not wish it, although they shed tears and wept, has had his hair and beard shaved, has put on yellow garments, and has gone from his home into homelessness." Elsewhere we read, "distressing is life at home, a state of impurity; freedom is in leaving home; while he reflected thus, he left his home." (O.)

His long retirement.

Thus seeking spiritual enlightenment, freedom, deliverance, Gautama travelled during a period of seven years, placing himself in succession under two notable teachers. Leaving them without being satisfied, he travelled through the kingdom of Magadha, and arrived at the town of Uruvela. There, in a beautiful forest land, he spent many years in self-discipline, repressing and curbing his desires and aspirations, and waiting for supreme enlightenment. Fasting, suppression of the breath, and other forms of self-mortification were tried with the greatest persistence, but in vain. Five other ascetics, who had been his companions for a time, abandoned him. Finally came the great crisis, when, sitting under a tree (the Bo-tree, or Tree of Knowledge), he passed through successive stages of abstraction until he became enlightened about the transmigrations of souls, and the Four Sacred Truths, (1) that suffering is universal in the world; (2) that its cause is desire or attachment; (3) that it can be ended by Nirvana; (4) the way to attain Nirvana. "When I apprehended this," say the early records, "and when I beheld this, my soul was released from the evil of desire, released from the evil of earthly existence, released from the evil of error, released from the evil of ignorance. In the released awoke the knowledge of release; extinct is rebirth, finished the sacred course, duty done, no more shall I return to this world; this I knew." (O.) He had become the Buddha, the awakened, the enlightened.

His enlightenment.

For some time Buddha remained near the tree of knowledge, fasting and enjoying the happiness of deliverance; the oldest narrative states that this period lasted four times seven days. After this time, he is believed to have undergone severe temptation to enter at once into the desired condition of Nirvana instead of preaching his doctrine to the world. Meeting a Brahman, who questions his right to assume the title of Brahman, Buddha tells him that he is a true Brahman who has put away all evil from himself, who knows nothing of contempt or impurity, and has conquered himself. Finally at the request of the Supreme Being Himself, Brahma Sahampati, Buddha resolved to proclaim to the world the truth he had attained.

His temptation.

Buddha's formal mission, by general consent, opened at Benares. He is supposed to have started with preaching to the ascetics who had been his former companions, expounding to them the perfect way, a mean between mortification and self-indulgence, and leading to rest, to knowledge, to enlightenment, to Nirvana, by the eightfold path: "Right faith, right resolve, right speech, right action, right living, right effort, right thought, right self-concentration." This, his first sermon, is recorded in a form which, if it can scarcely be regarded as giving the actual words Buddha uttered, embody a very early form of what the Buddhist monks regarded as the essence of their master's teaching. As we read it, we realise more vividly how suffering was regarded by Hindus generally as the bane of existence, a feeling which might well arise in the ceaseless turmoil of strife and oppression among which they lived. "Birth is suffering, old age is suffering, sickness is suffering, death is suffering, to be united with the unloved is suffering, to be separated from the loved is suffering, not to obtain what one desires is suffering; in short, the fivefold clinging to the earthly is suffering."

Opening of his mission.

The eightfold path.

The origin of suffering.

"This, O monks, is the sacred truth of the origin of suffering: it is the thirst for being, which leads from birth to birth, together with lust and desire, which finds gratification here and there; the thirst for pleasures, the thirst for being, the thirst for power."

"This, O monks, is the sacred truth of the extinction of suffering, the extinction of this thirst by complete annihilation of desire, letting it go, expelling it, separating oneself from it, giving it no room." He then expounded to them the eightfold path, by which he had attained the supreme Buddhahood in this world and the worlds of gods. Henceforth there was for him no new birth. The new doctrine is summed up thus:—"Walk in purity, to make an end of all suffering."

The five ascetics being the first converts, others soon began to flock round them, and Buddha sent them forth to preach in the surrounding country. A conspicuous feature in their teaching, contrasting markedly with that of the Brahmans, was their freedom from constraint, from forms, from ceremonies, from Pharisaism. "I am loosed from all bands, divine and human," says Buddha. "Ye also, O disciples, are loosed from all bands, divine and human. Go ye out, O disciples, and travel from place to place for the welfare of many people, for the joy of many people, in pity for the world, for the blessing, welfare, and joy of gods and men. Go not in twos to one place."

The freedom of Buddhism.

Returning then to Uruvela, where he had entered into the knowledge of deliverance, he preaches to a band of ascetics, whose leader, Kassapa, he converts after performing numerous miracles, according to the records. The whole body then proceeded to Rajagaha, the capital of Magadha (Behar), whose king, Bimbisara, he converted; this was followed by the conversion of many of the noble youths of Magadha, so much so as to lead to much murmuring, the people fearing that the ascetic was come to bring childlessness and widowhood and the subversion of families.

Early converts.

From this time forward we can frame no proper history of Buddha's life; but from the early records about him it is easy to realise the general nature of his career, although without those touches of individuality which Hebrews and Europeans

General features of Buddha's life.

so well knew how to hand down, but which have scarcely been noted by the Hindus and Chinese. This is partly because individuality, as we understand it, was largely undeveloped among them. Their civilisation created types rather than individuals, accustomed continually to do the same thing, feel similarly, and think alike. But one thing is certain; in early Buddhism there is little trace of a contradictory spirit within the order, no trace of a disciple developing the master's teaching in new and unexpected directions, or making himself a second founder. Whether Buddha himself was all that he is described in the earliest records or not, he has no rival, and his disciples closely imitated what they believed him to have said or done. Thus the picture of Buddha's life will describe much of that of his immediate disciples.

Alternation of itinerancy with rest.

The contrast of the principal Indian seasons marks the two chief alternations in Buddha's life. The three rainy months necessitated a season of rest and retirement in or near towns and villages; and this period was devoted partly to teaching the disciples who flocked round him. The rest of the year was spent by Buddha in travelling from place to place, attended by disciples, throughout the kingdoms of Kosala and Magadha and their neighbourhood, chiefly comprised within Oudh and Behar. They do not appear to have entered Western Hindustan where Brahmanism had its stronghold. Near the chief cities of these kingdoms, Savatthi (now Sahet Mahet on the Rapti), and Rajagaha (now Rajgir), pleasant gardens were given to Buddha and his followers, well provided with places for lodging, eating, and assembling. We may gather some idea of what these places were like from a description in one of the early Buddhist books. "Not too far from, nor yet too near the town, well provided with entrances and exits, easily accessible to all people who inquire after it, with not too much of the bustle of life by day, quiet by night, far from commotion and the crowds of men, a place of retirement, a good spot for solitary meditation." Here were beautiful groves of trees, pools in which the symbolic lotus grew, and every con-

The Buddhist gardens.

venience for meetings; and such on a smaller scale were provided in many other places. Among the visitors were strangers from distant countries, and those who had accepted the teaching of his disciples and longed to see him; even kings and chiefs thronged to see him and to hear his teaching. In some cases the rulers of a town commanded every inhabitant to go forth and meet the Exalted One when arriving, under a heavy penalty.

One of the most remarkable records in the Buddhist books is that relating the conversion of a courtesan, and his preference of her invitation to that of the noblest people. This has been compared to a well-known incident in the life of Christ; but it must be confessed that the resemblance is but superficial. The following is abridged from the "Book of the Great Decease."

Buddha and the courtesan Ambapali.

"Now the courtesan Ambapali heard that the Blessed One had arrived at Vesali and was staying at her mango grove. And ordering a number of magnificent vehicles to be made ready, she mounted one of them, and proceeded with her train towards her garden. She went in the carriage as far as the ground was passable for carriages; there she alighted, and she proceeded on foot to the place where the Blessed One was, and took her seat respectfully on one side, and when she was thus seated, the Blessed One instructed, aroused, incited, and gladdened her with religious discourse.

"Then she, instructed, aroused, incited, and gladdened with his words—addressed the Blessed One and said:—

"'May the Blessed One do me the honour of taking his meal, together with the brethren, at my house tomorrow.'

"And the Blessed One gave by silence his consent. Then when Ambapali, the courtesan, saw that the Blessed One had consented, she rose from her seat and bowed down before him, and keeping him on her right hand as she passed him, she departed thence.

"Now the Likhavis of Vesali (rich noble youths) heard that the Blessed One had arrived at Vesali, and was staying at Ambapali's grove, and proceeded to invite

Buddha to dinner the next day; but he refused, saying he was already engaged to dine with Ambapali.

"And the Blessed One robed himself early in the morning and took his bowl, and went with the brethren to the place where Ambapali's dwelling-house was; and when he had come there he seated himself on the seat prepared for him, and Ambapali, the courtesan, set the sweet rice and cakes before the Order, with the Buddha at their head, and waited upon them till they refused any more.

"And when the Blessed One had quite finished his meal, the courtesan had a low stool brought, and sat down at his side, and addressed the Blessed One, and said: 'Lord, I present this mansion to the order of mendicants, of which Buddha is the chief.' And the Blessed One accepted the gift; and after instructing, and rousing, and inciting, and gladdening her with religious discourse, he rose from his seat and departed thence."

Here it will be noted that there is absolutely no teaching special to the case. The regular formulas are supposed to have been uttered, and to have proved invincible, so that the hearer yielded absolutely. The great points are the condescending to take a meal with the courtesan (a woman of considerable property, nevertheless), and preferring her invitation to that of rich young nobles, whose forms were compared with those of the Vedic gods.

Anxious inquirers.

Among those who visited Buddha are distinguished Brahmans, who seek enlightenment on their differences from him, and are brought to see the unreality of their own religious views and the truth of the Buddhist belief,—as well as logical casuists, who lay traps for him, and seek to make him contradict himself. In fact all sorts and conditions of men, except apparently the poor, resort to Buddha to obtain the knowledge he had to impart; and they usually signalise their adhesion to his order by giving him and his companions a dinner, followed again by spiritual instruction. When he had no invitation, Buddha and his companions would traverse the town carrying bowls and seeking alms. As Dr. Oldenberg says: "In the days when his reputation stood at its highest point, and his name was named throughout India among the foremost names, one might day by day see that man before whom kings bowed themselves, walking about, alms-bowl in hand, through streets and alleys, from house to house, and without uttering any request, with downcast look, stand silently waiting until a morsel of food was thrown into his bowl."

But the great achievement of Buddha, apart from his doctrine, was his formation of a new society, composed of the Bhikkhu or Bhiggu, which cannot be accurately rendered in its Buddhist sense. It has often been rendered "monks," but literally it signifies "beggar," "mendicant." Yet they did not, strictly speaking, beg at all; they had given up all worldly things, but were not secluded from society, and hence were not strictly monks; they took no vow of obedience, and could leave the order when they chose. They were not priests, as they had no rites to administer, and were not in any sense the vehicle of the worship of others. Perhaps the terms "brethren" or "members of the Order" would be least misleading; but the name of monk is most used. Their outward signs of membership were the tonsure and a yellow garment.

The new order of monks.

That Buddha should so readily have established a separated Order, shows that the idea of separation from the world to lead a religious life had already a wide influence in his time. It appears to have soon become a regular thing for convinced inquirers to profess their belief in the Blessed One, and to ask him to accept them as disciples and true believers; and he would receive them in some such form as this: "Come hither, O monk; well preached is the doctrine, walk in purity, to make an end of all suffering." Having given all his property to the Order, or at any rate having renounced it, having quitted family ties, and vowed to live a life of chastity, they in many cases set out on their travels to spread the principles taught by the Buddha. Personal ambition, personal exaltation, vanity, self-seeking, henceforth had no place among them. Caste was abolished, or rather ignored, by these men who had renounced the world.

Buddha is said to have answered a king thus: "If a slave or servant of the king puts on the yellow garment, and lives as a monk without reproach in thought, word, and deed, wouldest thou then say, Well then, let this man still be my slave and servant, to stand in my presence, bow before me, take upon himself to perform my behests, live to minister to my enjoyments, speak deferentially, hang upon my word?" And the king answers, "No, sire; I should bow before him, stand before him, invite him to sit down, give him what he needed in the way of clothing, food, shelter, and of medicine when he is ill, and I should assure him of protection, watch and ward, as is becoming." And this treatment, it is inferred, is what Buddha approved.

Buddha not a socialist.

Prof. Oldenberg strongly combats the idea that Buddha was specially a social reformer, who broke the chains of caste, and raised the poor and humble to his spiritual kingdom. There is no notion in his teaching of upsetting the established order of things and supplanting it by a new one. "Buddha's spirit was a stranger to that enthusiasm, without which no one can pose as the champion of the oppressed against the oppressor. Let the state and society remain what they are; the religious man who as a monk has renounced the world, has no part in its cares and occupations. Caste has no value for him, for everything earthly has ceased to affect his interests; but it never occurs to him to exercise his influence for its abolition or for the mitigation of the severity of its rules for those who have lagged behind in worldly surroundings." It is scarcely even true that Buddha practically presented an equal front to all classes of people. Those who were among his early chosen adherents were almost exclusively drawn from the upper classes, nobles, Brahmans, merchants, educated persons. We find in early Buddhist works such phrases as these: "Truly not undesired by the Exalted One is such an interview with such noble youths." "The goodwill of such a respected and well-known person towards this doctrine and ordinance is of the highest importance." Scarcely can an isolated story be found of the reception of a person of very low grade, such as the sweeper-away of withered flowers from temples and palaces; and in his case the moral which specially follows is directed against the exclusiveness of the Brahmans. "By holy zeal and chaste living, by restraint and self-repression, thereby a man becomes a Brahman; that is the highest Brahmanhood." The weak and children are scarcely mentioned. "To the wise belongeth this law," it was said, "not to the foolish."

Buddha's principal adherents.

We need only briefly mention Buddha's principal adherents, as all resemble one another in purity, in the attainment of perfect peace, and in devotion to Buddha: Sariputta and Moggallana, early converts from Brahmanism, following him through life, but dying shortly before Buddha; his own cousin Ananda, and his brother Devadatta; Upali, the court barber of the Sakyas. Ananda seems to have served as personal attendant to Buddha in his old age, and to have often accompanied him alone; to him many of his last discourses were specially addressed. Devadatta is the traditional traitor, who sought to supplant his brother in chief influence, and is said to have attempted to kill him, a project which was frustrated by many recorded miracles. Devadatta is related to have attempted to enforce a more ascetic discipline on the monks, and to have failed miserably.

Lay-believers.

Besides the monks, Buddha recognised lay believers, those who honoured his teaching as the truth, but who remained in the world, and were permitted to give gifts and exercise charity to the brethren of the Order. In fact this was but a recognition of the necessities of the case. If there were no adherents outside the mendicant members, and if all other persons were opponents, there would be little possibility of supporting the members; of course their maintenance in such a country as India cost very little, but still it was needed and had to be provided. No special form of reception of lay-adherents was provided, and they never had any share in the government of Buddhism. And as with regard to the brethren or monks, so with regard to the lay-adherents, much more prominence is given to the princes and nobles, Brahmans and merchants, who appear to have constituted by far the largest proportion of them, than to the poor. Thus Buddha and his monks gathered round them crowds of votaries who could receive and maintain them and convene assemblies to hear them speak, or who accompanied them in various vehicles or on foot.

Women and Buddhism.

In relation to women Buddha was in some respects more liberal and in some less so than the Brahmans. Brahmanism expected the Vedic student to become a householder, to marry, and to bring up a family to continue the sacrificial rites; yet women were kept strictly in a subordinate, practically in a servile position. Buddhist monks were to abjure marriage and intimate relations with women, as utterly inconsistent with their profession; but women were admissible as sisters of the Order, analogous to nuns, under severe restraints as to intimacy with men. Women were recognised as lay-adherents, and indeed the maintenance of the Order would have been very much more difficult without their ministrations. But the toleration and even welcome of women came rather late in the day. At an early period, when Buddha was asked by Ananda how the brethren should behave to women, he answers, "Don't look at them"; and when further pressed, "If we should see them, what are we to do?" he replies, "Don't speak to them"; and again, "If they should speak to us, what are we to do?" "Keep wide awake," is the master's advice, or as another translation has it, "Keep watch over yourselves," and that this view continued in considerable force may be gathered from the moral of one of the later Buddhist narratives,—"Unfathomably deep, like a fish's course in the water, is the character of women, robbers with many artifices, with whom truth is hard to find, to whom a lie is like the truth and the truth like a lie."

Reception of sisters or nuns.

But wider experience somewhat modified Buddha's attitude towards women, though not without much hesitation. His foster-mother and his disciple Ananda at last persuaded him, on the ground that women were capable of realising the fourfold path. He, however, imposed upon them eight rules, such as that a nun, of however long standing, was always to serve and to rise in the presence of a monk, even if only just initiated; and in several respects nuns were placed in subordination to the monks; they must be initiated by monks as well as nuns, and receive admonition from monks. But Buddha is very mournful, and is represented as saying that the good law will not now last more than five hundred years. As when mildew or blight visits a crop, it does not last long, so "under whatever discipline women are allowed to go forth from the household life into the homeless state, that religion does not last long. And just as a man would in anticipation build an embankment to a great reservoir, so have I laid down these eight chief rules for the sisters, not to be overpassed through their life." The female disciples were to adopt the same rules as the men, so far as applicable; and the general rule was applied, that whatever doctrines conduced to peace and not to passion, to veneration and not to pride, to wishing for little and not to wishing for much, to seclusion and not to love of society, to the exercise of zeal and not to sloth, to content and not to querulousness, these doctrines were the teaching of the Master. A great many disabilities and restrictions as to wearing apparel, decoration of the body and face, habits and occupations, etc., were imposed. Nevertheless, Buddha and his followers frequently received large hospitality from women, who, however, were to regard themselves as benefited by being allowed to give anything to the saints. Visakha, a rich and noble woman of Savatthi, voluntarily offered clothing, food, and medicine for both incoming and outgoing monks, asking this as a boon. Buddha's response was: "Whatsoever woman, upright in life, a disciple of the Happy One, gives, glad at heart

*** On the opposite page is represented one of the elaborate gateways of a solid stupa or tope, as old as Asoka's time; the sculptures on the gateways (about 35 feet high) represent scenes from the life of Buddha, and other Buddhist legends. They date probably from the first century A.D.

EAST GATE OF THE GREAT TOPE, SANCHI, NEAR BHILSA, BHOPAL.

and overcoming avarice, both food and drink—a gift heavenly, destructive of sorrow, productive of bliss—a heavenly life does she attain, entering upon the path that is free from corruption and impurity; aiming at good, happy does she become, and free from sickness, and long does she rejoice in a heavenly body."

Opposition.

It is striking how little we hear of active opposition to Buddha in the Buddhist literature. This of course may proceed from concealment; but seeing the undoubted great prosperity of Buddhism, serious opponents would have been mentioned, if only to show how they had been overthrown. But Buddhism arose in the eastern land where Brahmanism had not taken such strong root as in the north-west. Numerous bodies of ascetics and religious freethinkers had arisen; and we must bear in mind the predominant religiousness of the Hindus, which would lead them naturally to revere a seeker after religious truth, especially one who renounced worldly possessions, and who did not in any way disturb the general peace and order. In fact the asceticism sanctioned or encouraged by the Brahman literature and practice had numerous points of resemblance to that of Buddha. Yet it could only be in a country where high Brahman pretensions were already questioned, or denied, that Buddha could have so severely criticised their system. Sacrifices, Vedic teaching, caste, were to him as nothing. In a kind of Socratic method, when questioned by Brahmans as to the right path, Buddha makes them acknowledge that the paths announced in the Vedas have not enabled any of the Brahmans to see Brahma face to face, or to know him, or where and whence he is; and he declares that the boasted knowledge of the Brahmans is foolishness: "As when a string of blind men are clinging one to the other, neither can the foremost see, nor can the middle one see, nor can the hindmost see." This is followed by an elaborate series of images demonstrating the same thing. The Brahmans, he says, are hindered from knowing the truth by five obstacles,—lustful desire, malice, sloth and idleness, pride and self-righteousness, and doubt. All these things are

Brahmans confuted.

absent from Brahma, and consequently the Brahmans could never become united with him. In answer to the appeal that he would show the Brahmans the way to a state of union with Brahma, Buddha says that from time to time an unsurpassed teacher is born into the world as a guide to erring mortals, a fully enlightened one, a blessed Buddha. He thoroughly understands the universe, gods and men, and makes his knowledge known to others. "The truth doth he proclaim both in its letter and in its spirit, lovely in its origin, lovely in its progress, lovely in its consummation; the higher life doth he make known, in all its purity and in all its perfectness." A householder hears the truth and believes in the Buddha and then considers, "Full of hindrances is household life, a path defiled by passion; free as the air is the life of him who has renounced all worldly things. How difficult is it for the man who dwells at home to live the higher life in all its fulness, in all its purity, in all its bright perfection! Let me then cut off my hair and beard, let me clothe myself in the orange-coloured robes, and let me go forth from a household life into the homeless state!"

"Then, before long, forsaking his portion of wealth, be it great or be it small; forsaking his circle of relatives, be they many or be they few, he cuts off his hair and beard, he clothes himself in the orange-coloured robes, and he goes forth from the household life into the homeless state.

"When he has thus become a recluse, he passes a life self-restrained according to the rules of the Pattimokka; uprightness is his delight, and he sees danger in the least of these things he should avoid; he adopts and trains himself in the precepts; he encompasses himself with holiness in word and deed; he sustains his life by means that are quite pure; good is his conduct, guarded the door of his senses; mindful and self-possessed, he is altogether happy." (S.E.)

Buddha is equally prepared to expound to Brahmans the essentials of a proper sacrifice. A great king of former days, he says, after great exploits, and establishing peace and prosperity in his land, and remedying evils, made a great sacrifice at which no animals were slain and no trees were cut down; simply libations of milk, oil, and honey were offered. But Buddha proclaims that a better and easier sacrifice than that, is to make gifts to pious monks, and build dwelling-places for him and his Order. A higher offering was to accept Buddha's doctrine; higher still to become a monk; while the highest offering was to obtain deliverance, and the knowledge, "I shall not again return to this world."

The best sacrifice.

How far the rival ascetic bodies and their leaders openly disputed the progress of Buddha we cannot tell. Later we find some traces of interchange of civilities between them, and also some attempts to deprive each other of the aid of influential people. Buddha's greatest distinction from the various brotherhoods was his disparagement of self-mortification. He had discovered that this last was gloomy, unworthy, unreal. The life of pleasure and sensual enjoyment was base and ignoble. The perfect life was the middle way, the eight-fold path. Thus he exemplified with remarkable force the strength which lies in a middle course; it certainly powerfully helped to make his the religious community with the largest following in the world.

The general method of Buddha's teaching was oral and conversational. Such a thing as *writing* a book was not then dreamt of, although book-learning was highly developed. But learning by heart seemed then the only possible or stable form of it; and no doubt it was once thought a great innovation, and probably an unreasonable thing, for any one to attempt to write out a book in full, when it was so easy and so common to commit the contents to memory. We, with our comparatively feeble recollections of the contents of any given book, do not realise a state of society when people who were learned knew their few books by heart more perfectly than most of us know anything. But personal teaching was then as influential as it ever has been, perhaps more so. The accounts given of Buddha's interviews with disciples, even if not precisely accurate, must represent a kind of interview which was the com-

Method of teaching.

mon type of such teaching, and which at that very early age was accepted as the type of his teaching. Unlike the Vedic books, which are in the pure high Sanskrit, the books of Buddhism are in the popular dialect; and in the sayings attributed to Buddha there is no trace of Sanskrit being used. Indeed, he is reported to have given directions that every believer should learn the words of Buddha in his own tongue.

Everything in the Buddhist narratives bears the stamp of an age which had become accustomed to solemn, long-drawn dissertations, and in which people of leisure, or who had abandoned the world, gave themselves up to continual speculation on the causes of various phenomena, or of troubles and difficulties. There is no trace of a life like our hurried modern one, in which only the smallest possible time is given to any one thing. With these old Hindus there was always plenty of time if a discussion was on foot, and it must be conducted in an orderly, sober fashion, with due ceremony and full elaboration. The great heat caused a tendency to indolent gravity and long-drawn-out expression. Compression and selection were scarcely attempted. The Upanishads, even if not composed before the Buddhist books, were in existence about the same time, and testify to the widespread spirit of abstraction and philosophising. So that the form of Buddhist teaching was due to the spirit of the more educated among the Hindus, as it had been developed by the Vedic and post-Vedic literature. Although there is considerable variety in the matter and often much beauty in the illustrations used in the discourses attributed to Buddha, the following gives an idea of a method frequently followed by him.

Long-drawn dissertations.

He is expressing the thought that all the senses and the outer things which they perceive are eaten away by the sorrows and the fleeting nature of mortal affairs. He thus addresses the thousand disciples or monks who were with him. "Then said the Blessed One to the disciples: 'Everything, O disciples, is in flames. And what Everything, O disciples, is in flames? The eye, O disciples, is in flames; the visible is in flames; the knowledge of the visible is in flames; the contact with the visible is in flames, the feeling which arises from contact with the visible, be it pleasure, be it pain, be it neither pleasure nor pain, this also is in flames. By what fire is it kindled? By the fire of desire, by the fire of hate, by the fire of fascination, it is kindled; by birth, old age, death, pain, lamentation, sorrow, grief, despair, it is kindled: thus I say. The ear is in flames,'" and so on through a similar repetition of every detail; and the same with the senses of smell, taste, touch, and with the mind, forming a long discourse, very monotonous to us, but probably delighting the hearers. It then goes on, "Considering this, O disciples, a wise hearer, walking in the noble path, becomes weary of the eye, weary of visible things," and so on through the whole detail once more. Then, "becoming weary of all that, he becomes free from desire; free from desire he becomes delivered; in the delivered arises the knowledge, I am delivered; re-birth is at an end, perfected is holiness, duty done; there is no more returning to this world; he knows this." When this discourse had been delivered, the minds of these thousand disciples became free from attachment to the world. (O.)

The mode of converting a noble youth who was already mentally prepared is thus represented (Mahavagga I. 7, S.E.). "At that time there was in Benares a noble youth, Yasa by name, the son of a treasurer, and delicately nurtured. He had three palaces, one for winter, one for summer, and one for the rainy season. In the palace for the rainy season he lived during the four months of that season, surrounded with female musicians among whom no man was, and he did not descend from that palace all that time. Now one day Yasa, the noble youth, who was endowed with and possessed of the five pleasures of sense, while he was attended by those female musicians, fell asleep sooner than usual: and after him his attendants also fell asleep. Now an oil lamp was burning through the whole night.

A noble youth's conversion.

"And Yasa, the noble youth, awoke sooner than usual; and he saw his attendants sleeping; one had her lute leaning against her armpit, one had her tabor leaning against her neck, one had her drum leaning against her armpit, and one had dishevelled hair, one had saliva flowing from her mouth, and they were muttering in their sleep. One would think it was a cemetery one had fallen into. When he saw that, the evils of the life he led manifested themselves to him; his mind became weary of worldly pleasures. And Yasa, the noble youth, gave utterance to this solemn exclamation: 'Alas! what distress; alas! what danger!' So he went on into the night and sought Buddha, who was walking up and down at dawn. To him he expressed his distress. Buddha replied to him, 'Here is no distress, Yasa; here is no danger. Come here, Yasa, sit down; I will teach you the truth' (Dhamma). And Yasa, the noble youth, when he heard that there was no distress, and that there was no danger, became glad and joyful; and he put off his gilt slippers, and went to the place where the Blessed One was; having approached him and having respectfully saluted the Blessed One, he sat down near him. Then the Blessed One preached to him in due course: that is to say, he talked about the merits obtained by almsgiving, about the duties of morality, about heaven, about the evils, the vanity, and the sinfulness of desires, and about the blessings of the abandonment of desire.

"When the Blessed One saw that the mind of Yasa, the noble youth, was prepared, impressible, free from obstacles, elated, and believing, then he preached what is the principal doctrine of the Buddhas, namely, Suffering, the cause of suffering, the cessation of suffering, the Path." So Yasa became a convert and subsequently a monk; and his father also received the truth, which fact is thus elaborately expressed: "The treasurer, the householder, having seen the truth, having mastered the truth, having penetrated the truth, having overcome uncertainty, having dispelled all doubts, having gained full knowledge, dependent on nobody else for the knowledge of the doctrine of the Teacher, said to the Blessed One: 'Glorious Lord! Glorious Lord! just as if one should set up, Lord, what had been overturned, or should reveal what had been hidden, or should point out the way to one who had lost his way, or should bring a lamp into the darkness, thus has the Blessed One preached the doctrine in many ways. I take my refuge in the Blessed One, and in the Truth, and in the Order of the monks; may the Blessed One receive me from this day forth while my life lasts, as a disciple who has taken his refuge in him." These are typical stories; whether it is that there was not much necessity for adaptation to the individual cases, or that such individual touches have been lost by the narration, we find little but general teaching. There is one simple consistent teaching, one refuge for all who would attain full knowledge,—to join the Order of monks.

Something like the Socratic method is not infrequently made use of when an argument is held with a learned person. Thus, in arguing with Brahmans, Buddha says: "Is Brahma in possession of wives and wealth, or is he not?"—"He is not." "Is his mind full of anger, or free from anger?"—"Free from anger." "Is his mind full of malice, or free from malice?" —"Free from malice." "Is his mind depraved, or pure?" —"It is pure." "Has he self-mastery, or has he not?" —"He has." "Now, what think you, are Brahmans versed in the Vedas in the possession of wives and wealth, or are they not?"—"They are." And so on through all the questions; leading to the triumphant reply: "Can there then be agreement and likeness between the Brahmans with their wives and property, and Brahma who has none of these things?"

Socratic method.

It is noteworthy how frequently parables and similes are made use of in the higher Buddhist teaching. Here is an instance.

"Just as when a hen has eight or ten or twelve eggs, and the hen has properly brooded over them, properly sat upon them, properly sat herself round them, however much such a wish may arise in her heart as this, "Oh, would that my little chickens should break open the egg-shell with the points of their claws, or with their beaks, and come forth into the light in safety!" yet all the while those little chickens are sure

Parables.

to break the egg-shell with the points of their claws, or with their beaks, and to come forth into the light in safety. Just even so, a brother thus endowed with fifteenfold determination is sure to come forth into the light, sure to reach up to the higher wisdom, sure to attain to the supreme security." The lesson is, that the result is quite certain, however much doubt the hen or the believer may have about it. (S.E. xi.)

In one place Buddha says: "I shall show you a parable; by a parable many a wise man perceives the meaning of what is being said." His own preaching is compared to the physician's work, drawing poisoned arrows from wounds, and overcoming the venom by remedies. Like the lotus flower, raising its head in the lake, unaffected by the water, so the Buddhas are unaffected by the world's impurity. One of the most elaborate parables is the following, part of which we quote. "As when, O disciples, in the forest, on a mountain slope, there lies a great tract of lowland and water, where a great herd of deer lives, and there comes a man who desires hurt, distress, and danger for the deer; who covers over and shuts up the path which is safe, good, and pleasant to take, and opens up a fresh path, a swampy path, a marshy track: thenceforward the great herd of deer incurs hurt and danger, and diminishes. But now, O disciples, if a man comes, who desires prosperity, welfare, and safety for this great herd of deer: who clears and opens up the path which is safe, good, and pleasant to take, and does away with the false path, and abolishes the swampy path, the marshy track, thenceforth will the great herd of deer thrive, grow, and increase. I have spoken to you, O disciples, in a parable, to make known my meaning. But the meaning is this. The great lowland and the water, O disciples, are pleasures. The great herds of deer are living men. The man who devises hurt, distress, and ruin, is Mara, the evil one. The false path is the eightfold false path, false faith, false resolve, false speech, false action, false living, false effort, false thought, false self-concentration. The swampy way is pleasure and desire. The swampy track is ignorance. The man who devises prosperity, welfare, salvation, is the Perfect One, the holy

COLOSSAL FIGURE OF BUDDHA, CEYLON.

supreme Buddha. The safe good way in which it is well

to walk, is the eightfold path," etc. "Everything th. a master who seeks the salvation of his disciples, whoa pities them, must do out of pity for them, that have I done for you." (O.) Fables, too, were not infrequently introduced into Buddha's discourses.

THE BOOK OF THE GREAT DECEASE.

We now come to the record of Buddha's death and the events immediately preceding it, contained in the "Book of the Great Decease," which has been compared to a gospel. This book comes to us apparently from the latter end of the fourth or beginning of the third century B.C., about a hundred years after Buddha's death. The author is unknown. The date of Buddha's death cannot be determined from it, but he appears to have been about eighty years of age, and to have exercised his public mission for about forty-four years. He is represented as journeying from Rajagaha, the capital of Magadha, to Pataliputta (Patna), the new capital, whose future greatness he prophesies. The narrative throughout contains summaries of discourses and directions which Buddha had probably given on previous dates. Journeying on, he was attacked by a severe illness, which he subdued temporarily by great resolution, having a strong desire to give a farewell address to the Order. He asserts to Ananda that he has kept back nothing, and he no longer wished to lead the brotherhood or thought that the Order was dependent upon him. "I too, O Ananda, am now grown old and full of years, my journey is drawing to its close, I have reached my sum of days, I am turning eighty years of age; and just as a worn-out cart, Ananda, can only with much additional care be made to move along, so, methinks, the body of the Enlightened One can only be kept going with much additional care." He advised his people to be a refuge to themselves, and not look for any other, and above all, be anxious to learn. The tempter Mara came to him, suggesting that he should voluntarily die at once, as all his objects were accom-

Buddha prepares for his final discourse.

His last temptation.

prished; he however still elected to live three months. And the narrative goes on: "Thus the Blessed One deliberately and consciously rejected the rest of his allotted sum of life, and on his rejecting it there arose a mighty earthquake, awful and terrible, and the thunders of heaven burst forth, and when the Blessed One beheld this, he broke out into this hymn of exultation:—

> 'His sum of life the sage renounced,
> The course of life immeasurable or small;
> With inward joy and calm, he broke,
> Like coat of mail, his life's own cause.'"

He then gave a summary of his most essential teachings to the assembled disciples, and concluded thus:—

> "My age is now full ripe, my life draws to its close:
> I leave you, I depart, relying on myself alone!
> Be earnest then, O brethren! holy, full of thought!
> Be steadfast in resolve! Keep watch o'er your own hearts!
> Who wearies not, but holds fast to this truth and law,
> Shall cross this sea of life, shall make an end of grief."

His death.

After still a few days' journeying, Buddha was seized with dysentery attended with sharp pain, which he bore without complaint. At last he arrived at Kusinara where he died, even in his last hours converting new disciples. His last words were, "Behold now, brethren, I exhort you, saying, Decay is inherent in all component things. Work out your salvation with diligence." His death was followed by earthquakes and thunders, and Brahma, the Supreme Deity or First Cause, is represented as uttering some of the most characteristic Buddhist doctrines, while his venerable disciple Anuruddha spoke thus:—

> "When he who from all craving want was free,
> Who to Nirvana's tranquil state had reached,
> When the great sage finished his span of life,
> No gasping struggle vexed that steadfast heart.
>
> All resolute, and with unshaken mind,
> He calmly triumphed o'er the pain of death.
> E'en as a bright flame dies away, so was
> His last deliverance from the bonds of life!"

His funeral was celebrated by the nobles of Kusinara with the honours due to a king of kings, wrapping his body in five hundred alternate layers of cotton wool and new cloth, enclosing it in two iron vessels, and finally cremating it on a funeral pile made of perfumes. Finally, the legend says that neither soot nor ash was left, but only the bones. Then the relics were divided into eight portions, over each of which a mound was erected by the respective groups who had claimed and obtained them.

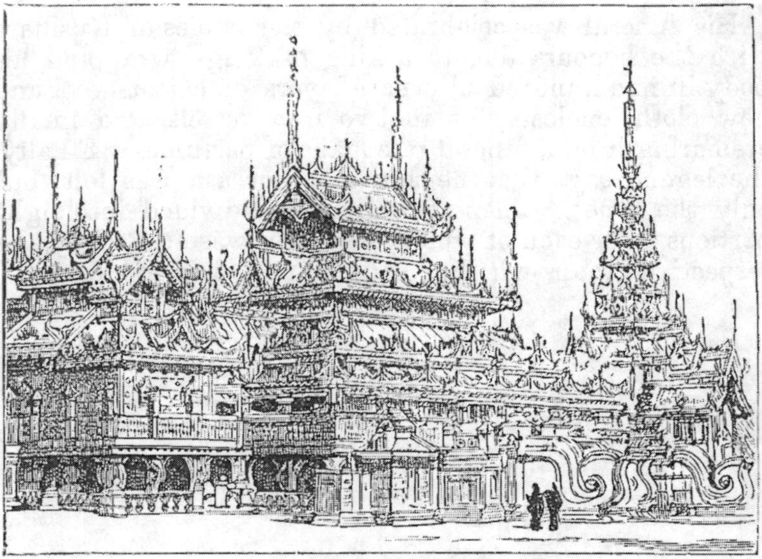

THE ROYAL MONASTERY AT MANDALAY.

CHAPTER VI.

The Buddhist Doctrines and Sacred Books.

Reaction from Brahmanism—Suffering and ignorance—The Eternal Immutable—Vanity of earthly things—The causal nexus—Human responsibility—Punishment of evil—Being and causality—The soul—Nirvana—Moral precepts—Negative morality—Benevolence—Beneficence—Self-discipline—Temptation—Mara—The struggle and victory of the soul—States of abstraction—The four grades of attainment—The person of Buddha—The Buddhist Scriptures—The Dhammapada.

Reaction from Brahmanism.

IT is one of the strangest phenomena, that the system holding itself forth so prominently as the bringer of happiness and extinguisher of suffering should be fitly called a philosophy of pessimism, of negation, of agnosticism. Yet it was a natural reaction from the Brahman assumption of knowing everything, and that everything would be right if its management were committed to Brahmans. In only one direction did the Buddhists claim to attain knowledge, that was the path by which to attain deliverance from suffering, and ultimate Nirvana. The kernel of this doctrine we have already given (p. 122). The suffering which Buddha bewails is not merely active pain and misery, but also the want of control which our self has over the body and consciousness. Everything, too, is non-permanent, and that is a sorrow; consequently a man is not sure of himself, and cannot say, "That is mine, that is I, that is myself." The root cause of this is ignorance; but while we might agree with the Buddhists that ignorance lies at the root of much if not of all evil, the Buddhists have their own interpretation of what ignorance constitutes this great evil; it is the ignorance of their four sacred truths, and these truths contain no allusion to any notion of nihilism, to the Nothing and nothingness as the supreme attainment, which is sometimes represented as the essential of Buddhist pessimism. Far from being of this nature, Buddhism has a positive if limited philosophy, and elevates its gaze to the highest and most permanent existence, regarding the Eternal Immutable, supremely free and happy. There is the only refuge of man from suffering, where birth and death, change and decay have no dominion. Man must seek deliverance from the mutable, and return to the Immutable: whether that may lead to eternal existence or not, is left undetermined. Buddha never pretended to know; rather he left it to be inferred that he did not know. His object was gained, as well as the happiness of his followers in this world, when they had attained "deliverance," release from desire, union with the Immutable.

Suffering and ignorance.

The Eternal Immutable.

Never has the vanity of earthly things, so succinctly expressed by the Old Testament Preacher, been so elaborately set forth as in the Buddhist books. Listen to its sad strain. "The pilgrimage of beings, O disciples, has its beginning in eternity. No opening can be discovered, from which proceeding, creatures, mazed in ignorance, fettered by a thirst for being, stray and wander. What think ye, O disciples, whether is more, the water which is in the four great oceans, or the tears which have flowed from

Vanity of earthly things.

you and been shed by you, while ye strayed and wandered on this long pilgrimage, and sorrowed and wept, because that was your portion that ye abhorred, and that which ye loved was not your portion? A mother's death, a father's death, a brother's death, a sister's death, a son's death, a daughter's death, the loss of relations, the loss of property, all this have ye experienced through long ages; and while ye experienced this through long ages more tears have flowed from you and have been shed by you, while ye strayed and wandered on this long pilgrimage, and sorrowed and wept, because that was your portion which ye abhorred and that which ye loved was not your portion, than all the water which is in the four great oceans." (O.) And so on through the whole range of mortal affairs.

The Dhammapada, that notable collection of Buddhist apophthegms, proverbs, and similes, which existed before the second council (377 B.C.), contains some of the most pithy sayings of melancholy. "Man gathers flowers; his heart is set on pleasure. Death comes upon him, like the floods of water on a village, and sweeps him away." "How can ye be gay? How can ye indulge desire? Evermore the flames burn. Darkness surrounds you: will ye not seek the light?" "Look upon the world as a bubble; look upon it as a mirage." "There is no satisfying lusts, even by a shower of gold pieces." "Let no man love anything; loss of the beloved is evil. Those who love nothing, and hate nothing, have no fetters." "From love comes grief; from love comes fear." Yet in association with these sad views throughout we have the joyful standard raised aloft. He who has learnt the sacred truths of Buddhism has overcome these evils and entered into joy. "The virtuous man is happy in this world, and he is happy in the next; he is happy in both. He is happy when he thinks of the good he has done; he is still more happy when going on the good path." "Earnest among the thoughtless, awake among the sleepers, the wise man advances like a racer, leaving behind the track." "Let no man think lightly of good, saying in his heart, it will not come nigh unto me. Even by the falling of water-drops a waterpot is filled; the wise man becomes full of good, even if he gather it little by little." "Let us live happily, free from greed among the greedy." "His good works receive him who has done good, and has gone from this world to the other; as kinsmen receive a friend on his return."

The causal nexus.

We cannot fully expound what is known as the causal nexus in Buddhism, but this in itself has never been taught to the masses, and was only for the more intellectual; while to western minds it is confused and inconclusive and more or less self-contradictory. We find that Buddhism, like most other human systems, has failed to express, though it has verged near to the core of, philosophical questions. What is certain is, that the early Buddhists regarded the consciousness as the sole continuing thing, while at death the body, sensations and perceptions vanish; and this consciousness was connected with a sort of spirit-stuff or element, undemonstrable, everlasting, all-illuminating; it passes over at death to become associated with the germ of a new material being to be born again. The succession of rebirths must continue until the being attains "deliverance," as made known by Buddhism.

Human responsibility.

Although expressed in a widely different form from our own, we see throughout Buddhism an assertion of human responsibility which tends in the highest degree to morality. However much we may be conditioned by our previous state as by our environment, we are always affected by our own actions. As explicitly as in the Christian Bible, we find stated that "not in the heavens, not in the midst of the sea, not if thou hidest thyself away in the clefts of the mountains, wilt thou find a place on earth where thou canst escape the fruit of thy evil actions" (Dhammapada v. 127). Even when the way of deliverance has been attained, a man will still suffer punishment for evil-doing not yet expiated. Thus, a robber and murderer who became a Buddhist was violently attacked when he went to collect alms; and Buddha tells him he was now receiving the penalty for evil deeds for which otherwise he would have had to suffer thousands of years in hell. A judgment scene is depicted, in which the wicked man is brought up from hell before King Yama, who inquires of him whether he did not see on earth the five visions of human weakness and suffering,—the child, the old man, the sick man, the criminal under punishment, and the dead man. He is further asked whether he did not consider that he was not exempt from old age and death, and ought to do good in thought, word, and deed. Confessing that he had neglected it, he is told that he alone is responsible, and must gather the fruit. The warders of hell take him away and subject him to the severest physical torments, ending in death only when his guilt is fully expiated.

Being and causality. One aspect of the Buddhist doctrine of causality is well illustrated by the following. "Whoever perceives in truth and wisdom how things originate in the world, in his eyes there is no 'it is not' in this world. Whoever perceives in truth and wisdom now things pass away in this world, in his eyes there is no 'it is' in this world. . . . Sorrow alone arises where anything arises; sorrow passes away where anything passes away. 'Everything is'; this is the one extreme: 'everything is not,' this is the other extreme. The Perfect One, remaining far from both these extremes, proclaims the truth in the middle. 'From ignorance come conformations (sankharas),'" forms of being determining their own successions and successive forms. There is no thought of an independent matter apart from an existence or being. Every perception, every condition, bodily or spiritual, is one of these sankharas, and all are transitory, all under the control of causality. Beyond this Buddhism does not attempt to go; it does not know the Eternal, or how the world was created, or whether it is everlasting or finite.

The soul. Buddhism even does not allow that there is a soul distinct from the body. Practically it only recognises the combined being that is seen or is conscious of itself, and that suffers; and it has no explanation beyond. Reduced to its lowest term, Buddhism recognises simply that suffering is going on, or keeps coming and going; without defining any permanent soul that suffers. All on this earth is under the dominion of causality.

The state of Nirvana, Buddha held, may be entered upon before the death of the body, and therefore it is not identical with annihilation, as has often been represented. Although its meaning is extinction, it is the extinction of desire, of suffering, of error, of ignorance; and it is termed the eternal state. What that eternal state is, early Buddhism in no way determines. Hence the Nirvana may perhaps best be regarded as the perfection which the Buddhist attains in this life. "What is to be extinguished has been extinguished, the fire of lust, hatred, bewilderment." In this state the devout disciple says, "I long not for death, I long not for life; I wait till mine hour come, like a servant who awaiteth his reward." Yet the Buddhist may truly be said to anticipate extinction of the consciousness on dying. Yet even that is consistent in his eyes with an imagined completion of his being, which no terms applicable to earthly things can possibly describe. And those who wished to cherish a hope of continual existence and perfect happiness were permitted to do so.

Nirvana.

The moral system taught by Buddha as obligatory upon his followers can be separated from the system and rules of his monastic order. It is not a little curious to find moral precepts at that early time not based upon obedience to a Supreme Ruler of the world, or a Creator, and consequently not based upon any duty of human beings to obey a Supreme Ruler. In fact, this moral law is entirely utilitarian, taking its stand solely upon benefits obtainable by the doer, or punishments to be incurred by him. Further than this, that we hear of no one being repelled by Buddha who sought to learn the truth, it does not appear that Buddhism concerned itself with the mass of mankind even so far as to give precepts available for them all, or to preach deliverance to them all. It is evident that this has not hindered the very wide spread of the society; and the

Moral precepts.

declaration that they had a message only for those who recognised their evil state and desired deliverance no doubt acted as a stimulus to the outer masses so far as they were in an intellectual state capable of aspiring after something better. But Buddhism did not lay itself out to tell all people that they ought to do or to be so-and-so every day, always, everywhere. Only when they sought discipleship, lay or mendicant, did Buddhism furnish them with a code of observance, which included moral duties, undertaken for the purpose of elevating their own state Thus "He who speaks or acts with impure thoughts, him sorrow follows, as the wheel follows the foot of the draught horse. He who speaks or acts with pure thought, him joy follows, like his shadow, which does not leave him."

The third to the sixth portions of the noble eightfold path more specially concern morals. The first and second, correct views, free from superstition or delusion, and right aims or correct thoughts, worthy of an intelligent man, are specially intellectual. The third, right speech, perfectly truthful, as well as kindly; the fourth, right conduct, pure, honest, peaceable; the fifth, a right mode of gaining a livelihood, doing harm to no living thing; and the sixth, right effort, self-control, self-training, embrace the sum of Buddhist morals. The seventh and eighth, mindfulness and contemplation, are again purely inward. The whole moral code may thus be expressed as uprightness in word, deed, and thought; but the great importance of wisdom as the crown of uprightness is fully expressed.

Negative morality.

A great portion of the Buddhist morality, however, was negative, made up of prohibitions. Five special hindrances, veils, or entanglements are specified, which must be mastered, namely, lustful desire, malice, sloth, self-righteousness or pride, and doubt. Five main commands are often repeated. The Buddhist must (1) kill no living thing, (2) not steal, (3) live chastely, (4) speak no untruth, (5) not drink intoxicating drinks. But in the rules for the monks, we find such positive additions as the following:—" The cudgel and the sword he lays aside; and full of modesty and pity, he is compassionate and kind to all creatures that have life. What he hears here, he repeats not elsewhere to raise a quarrel. . . . He lives as a binder-together of those who are divided, an encourager of those who are friends, a peacemaker, a lover of peace. . . . Whatever word is humane, pleasant to the ear, lovely, reaching to the heart, urbane, pleasing to the people, such are the words he speaks. . . . Putting away foolish talk, he abstains from vain conversation. In season he speaks; he speaks that which is; he speaks fact . . . that which redounds to profit, is well defined, and is full of wisdom. He refrains from injuring any herb or any creature. He takes but one meal a day. He abstains from dancing, singing, music and theatrical shows" (S. E. xi.).

Benevolence.

It cannot be said that the Christian virtue of love is taught by Buddhism. There is sometimes some approach to it, but it is not clear. The virtue enjoined by Buddhism is rather the extinction of hating than positive love. Thus, "He who holds back rising anger like a rolling chariot, him I call a real driver. . . . Let a man overcome anger by not becoming angry; let a man overcome evil by good; let him overcome the greedy by liberality, the liar by truth." "Enmity never comes to an end through enmity here below; it comes to an end by non-enmity; this has been the rule from all eternity." A notable story is found in the Mahavagga, which illustrates this last doctrine. But the benevolence which an early Buddhist felt was far removed from Christian benevolence. His body, which might be hurt by others, was not really himself; so he felt no bitter resentment at anything done to it. "Those who cause me pain and those who cause me joy, to all I am alike, and affection and hatred I know not. In joy or sorrow I remain unmoved; in honour and dishonour throughout I am alike." This benevolence was not a spontaneous sympathy rising in the good man's heart, but a result of meditation and intentional mental exercise; and this benevolence, radiating from him, is said to exert a kind of magical influence, bringing about harmonious relations between Buddhists and all people and even animals.

Beneficence.

But what of beneficence, so highly esteemed in Christianity? To outward appearance, it was just as highly esteemed in early Buddhism; but the forms of its exercise were different. From all that we can gather, poor people, in the sense of those wanting daily food or means to get it, were by no means abundant at that time in India; and the higher modes of Christian beneficence were not yet dreamt of. Joining the Buddhist order itself gave rise to the very practical step of renunciation; but in the case of those who were already married and had families it released the adherents from their family responsibilities and cares. This renunciation can scarcely be called beneficence, for it was not done in order that other persons might be benefited. Practically the chief beneficence exercised by Buddhists was by the lay adherents, who were expected to show liberality to all individual monks and to the Order generally. This beneficence was for the sake of their religious profession, however, and can hardly be called pure beneficence. And all through early Buddhism the special virtue of beneficence is overshadowed by the broader and deeper necessity for renouncing every worldly possession; even lay adherents were not to count things their own, by which they might confer on the Order needed benefits. In some of the narratives a little later than the earliest, the giving away of wife and children is represented as of no moment compared with winning the Buddhahood. We see clearly that it was not by means of beneficence that the character advocated by Buddhism was to be acquired.

Self-discipline.

That discipline was essentially internal. "Rouse thyself by thyself, examine thyself by thyself, . . . curb thyself as the merchant curbs a good horse. . . . Cut off the five senses, leave the five, rise above the five. . . . In the body restraint is good, good is restraint in speech, in thought restraint is good, good is restraint in all things" (S.E. x., Dhammapada). Everything is to be done with a self-conscious effort and watchfulness. Self-examination is to be practised after every contact with the world, after every begging excursion; and all emotions or desires, which are stigmatised as evil and treacherous, are to be suppressed. In no religion is it more sternly insisted on that the character is the inner self. "All that we are is the result of what we have thought; it is founded on our thoughts, it is made up of our thoughts," says the first verse of the Dhammapada.

Temptation, Mara.

Temptation to evil is associated with a personal spirit or essence called Mara, not believed to be the originator of evil and sorrow—for on that point Buddhism had no belief—but the chief tempter to evil in thought, word, and deed. He, like Yama in the Brahman system, is Death or the King of Death, and so is king of all the pleasures of this world. The foundation of the Buddhist Order is a deadly blow at this kingdom, and consequently the Buddhists are objects of his continual attack. He offers Buddha himself the rule over the whole earth, if he will renounce his spiritual mission. He is tempted by Mara's daughters, Desire, Unrest, and Pleasure, and resists their temptations. In all the narratives addressed to the people generally, Mara appears as a real personage, not everlasting, but capable of attacking every one. The higher Buddhist philosophy sees Mara in everything which is subject to change. "Wherever there is an eye and form, wherever there is an ear and sound, wherever there is thinking and thought, there is Mara, there is sorrow." (O.) But in the details relating to the tempter, as given by the Buddhist books, we find nothing grand, nothing great even in evil. The attacks made upon Buddha and his followers are comparatively simple, and are easily foiled. Buddha was, it is related, tempted with a kingdom in order that he might do what he asserted to be possible, "rule as a king in righteousness, without killing or causing to be killed, without practising oppression or permitting oppression to be practised, without suffering pain or inflicting pain on another," and he is told that he could turn the Himalayas into gold if he chose. Buddha answers: "What would it profit a wise man if he possessed even a mountain of silver or of gold?

He who has comprehended sorrow, whence it springs, how can he bend himself to desire? He who knows that earthly existence is a fetter in this world, let him practise that which sets him free therefrom." Then Mara, the Evil one, said, "The Exalted One knows me, the Perfect One knows me," and disconcerted and disheartened he rose and went away. Other narratives represent Mara as constantly watching the avenues of the senses that he may gain access to the mind; and this continual siege is only to be met by continual watchfulness, which will at last make Mara give up the hopeless task.

The struggle and victory of the soul.

Dr. Oldenberg graphically describes the struggle between the individual soul and the sorrow-producing chain of suffering, and the tempter Mara, as pictured by the early Buddhists. "The struggle is neither slight nor brief. From that moment forward, when first the conviction dawns upon a soul, that this battle must be fought, that there is a deliverance which can be gained—from that first beginning of the struggle up to the final victory, countless ages of the world pass away. Earth worlds and heavenly worlds, and worlds of hells also, pass away as they have arisen and passed away from all eternity. Gods and men, all animated beings, come and go, die and are born again, and amid this endless tide of all things, the beings who are seeking deliverance, now advancing and victorious, and anon driven back, press on to their goal. The path reaches beyond the range of the eye, but it has an end. After countless wanderings through worlds and ages the goal at last appears before the wanderer's gaze. And in his sense of victory there is mingled a feeling of pride for the victory won by his own power. The Buddhist has no god to thank, as he had previously no god to invoke during his struggle. The gods bow before him, not he before the gods."

States of abstraction.

The place of prayer in other religions is in Buddhism taken by abstraction, meditation, withdrawal as far as possible from the world of sense. How far this may proceed by an artificial system we may see later. Some portions of the Buddhist scriptures describe methods of producing self-concentration; and frequently they approach pathological or morbid conditions. It is no wonder that hallucinations of the senses should arise in men who have torn themselves from every home tie, and devoted themselves to homelessness and abstraction. But heavenly visions, heavenly sounds, forms of supernatural beings are only rarely seen; rather the condition commonly attained was that known as clairvoyant, in which the spirit was believed to be peculiarly refined, pure, pliant, and firm. Then the monks imagined they saw the past clearly, even their own past existences, saw into the thoughts of others, acquired miraculous powers, became invisible and again appeared on earth. Many of these may be paralleled by various accounts in the Bible; but there are no parallel results flowing from them.

The four grades of attainment.

Among the monks no gradation was at first recognised except the higher order of those who had attained deliverance; but later four grades were acknowledged: (1) the lowest, those who had attained the path, and were not liable to re-birth in the lower worlds (hells, world of animals, spirit worlds); (2) those who return once only to this world—these have destroyed desire, hatred, and frivolity; (3) the non-returning, who only enter the higher worlds of the gods, and these attain Nirvana; (4) the Saints (Arhats). But these grades did not give those who had attained them any special place in the Order.

A special grade was occupied by those who gained participation in the Buddhahood by their own inherent force, having won the knowledge bringing deliverance by their own exertions. They were believed to have lived chiefly in the ages previous to Buddha himself; but they were not equal to the "universal Buddhas" of whom Gautama was one.

The person of Buddha.

The position claimed by and assigned to Buddha is peculiar in that he had no special commission from a supreme Being, and did not put himself forward as the representative of the invisible powers. He was simply, in the present order of things, the first who had obtained universal Buddhahood. He taught to others the truths that he had himself discovered. He was their helper, but it was by their own effort and meditation that it could really be received by them. And yet the claims attributed to Buddha are nothing less than omniscience and perfection. He says: "I have overcome all foes; I am all-wise; I am free from stains in every way; I have left everything; and have obtained emancipation by the destruction of desire. Having myself gained knowledge, whom should I call my master? I have no teacher; no one is equal to me; in the world of men and of gods no being is like me. I am the Holy One in this world, I am the highest teacher, I alone am the perfect Buddha; I have gained coolness by the extinction of all passion, and have obtained Nirvana." (Mahavagga, S.E. xiii.) "He appears in the world for salvation to many people, for joy to many people, out of compassion for the world, for the blessing, the salvation, the joy of gods and men." But Buddha is by no means represented as the sole person who has attained Buddahood. Many Buddhas had been before him and would come after him; but they were supposed all to be born in Eastern India, and to be all of the Brahman or soldier (Kshatriya) castes; and their teaching prevailed for longer or shorter periods, after which faith vanished for a time in the earth. Thus we see that Buddha was the starter of the new religious life, and essential to it; but by no means a god, or a heaven-sent messenger.

THE BUDDHIST SCRIPTURES.

Those which are pre-eminently worthy of this designation, as being the oldest and purest, are the Pali books preserved by the Ceylonese Buddhists. They are arranged in three collections or "Baskets" (pitakas). The first, or Vinaya-pitaka, includes books containing regulations for the external life of the order of monks. The second, or Sutta-pitaka, contains a number of miscellaneous works, each composed of suttas or short pithy sentences, some relating sayings of Buddha, others legends and stories of the preceding Buddhas. The third contains various disquisitions, an enumeration of the conditions of life, etc.

The most interesting of all these, and the most deserving of attention for its literary excellence, is the Dhammapada, or Path of Virtue (or Footstep of the Law), from which we have already quoted. The word subsequently came to mean generally "a religious sentence." Its date, like that of the rest of the scriptures, is stated by the Buddhists to be fixed by the first Council of the Church immediately after the death of Buddha; what appears to be certain is that this book existed before Asoka's council, about B.C. 242, after which date it was introduced into Ceylon by Mahinda, Asoka's son. And we may take the Dhammapada as having been believed to have been personally uttered by Buddha. Even if he did not compose it (which there is nothing to prove positively), it was composed soon after his death, by some one or more persons whose genius rose as high as his. A point of great importance in judging of this whole canon is that it contains no mention of Asoka's council, but does mention the first and second councils (of Rajagaha and Vesali), and describes them at the end of the Kullavagga.

The Dhammapada.

We will now give some further extracts from the Dhammapada, to illustrate its literary character, apart from the special points we have already drawn attention to. Sometimes we find in it dogmatic teaching quite straightforwardly put, thus: "He who wishes to put on the yellow dress without having cleansed himself from sin, who disregards also temperance and truth, is unworthy of the yellow dress." "By oneself the evil is done, by oneself one suffers; by oneself evil is left undone, by oneself one is purified. Purity and impurity belong to oneself, no one can purify another." "That deed is not well done of which a man must repent, and the reward of which he receives gladly and cheerfully." "Do not speak harshly to anybody; those who are spoken to will answer thee in the same way." Here we have the Eastern representative of the Proverbs of Solomon.

How much wisdom is to be found in the following·

"Let the wise man guard his thoughts, for they are very difficult to perceive, very artful, and they rush wherever they list." "The fool who knows his foolishness is wise, at least so far. But a fool who thinks himself wise, he is called a fool indeed." "One's own self conquered is better than all other people." Here is a condensed censure of asceticism: "Not nakedness, not platted hair, not dirt, not fasting, or lying on the earth, not rubbing with dust, not sitting motionless, can purify a mortal who has not overcome desires."

The following is a varied selection of these gems. "Bad deeds, and deeds hurtful to ourselves, are easy to do; what is beneficial and good, that is very difficult to do." "This world is dark, few only can see here; a few only go to heaven, like birds escaped from the net." "Health is the greatest of gifts, contentedness the best riches; trust is the best of relationships, Nirvana the highest happiness." "If any thing is to be done, let a man do it, let him attack it vigorously. A careless pilgrim only scatters the dust of his passions more widely." Similes of great aptness or beauty abound. "As the bee collects nectar and departs without injuring the flower, or its colour or scent, so let a sage dwell in his village." "Like a beautiful flower, full of colour, but without scent, are the fine but fruitless words of him who does not act accordingly." "There is no fire like passion, there is no shark like hatred, there is no snare like folly, there is no torrent like greed." "The fault of others is easily perceived, but that of oneself is difficult to perceive; a man winnows his neighbour's faults like chaff, but his own fault he hides, as a cheat hides the bad die from the gambler." "If a fool be associated with a wise man even all his life, he will perceive the truth as little as a spoon perceives the taste of soup."

It is natural to find in these pithy sayings the pervading truth of the universality of suffering and the vanity of life. "Before long, alas! this body will lie on the earth, despised, without understanding, like a useless log." "As a cowherd with his staff drives his cows into the stable, so do Age and Death drive the life of men." Old age is thus depicted: "Look at this dressed-up lump, covered with wounds, joined together, sickly, full of many thoughts, which has no strength, no hold. This body is wasted, full of sickness and frail; this heap of corruption breaks to pieces, life indeed ends in death." We are told to "look upon this world as a bubble, as a mirage." But watchfulness and the true knowledge preserves a man in safety. One of the later sentences gives a fine picture of a stoic. "Him I call indeed a Brahman who, though he has committed no offence, endures reproach, bonds, and stripes, who has endurance for his force, and strength for his army." Indeed, the whole section on the true Brahman is fine: he is tolerant with the intolerant, mild with faultfinders, free from passion among the passionate, is thoughtful, guileless, free from doubts, free from attachment, and content.

CASKET CONTAINING BUDDHA'S TOOTH, IN THE TEMPLE OF DALADA MALIGAWA, KANDY, CEYLON.

CHAPTER VII.

The Buddhist Order.

The Buddhist order—The Mahavagga—Fortnightly meetings—Confession and penance—Strict regulations—Profession of faith—Not a body corporate—No head after Buddha—Assemblies or Councils—Limitations on admission—Form of reception—The four resources—The four prohibitions—Quitting the order—Its advantages—No silver or gold—Seemly outward appearance—Companionship—Tutelage—Recitations and discussions—Retirement and love of nature—Few ceremonies—Reverence and Buddha—Regard for holy places—The confessional—The Kullavagga—Offences and penances—The Pavarana or invitation—The nuns or sisters—The laity—Esoteric Buddhism—Karma.

SOME attention must now be given to the great Order of mendicants or monks which perpetuated Buddha's influence and extended his teaching. Very early in Buddha's career they became an organised Brotherhood; and a formal system of admission and rules of conduct were framed as need arose. At first candidates who professed belief in this doctrine were simply admitted by the great teacher, but it is a natural development that this should be delegated to others as the Order grew.

The Mahavagga.

The Mahavagga, one of the oldest Pali books, contains the records of these events, and of the regulations imposed on the Order, preceded by a narrative embodying many of the early events in Buddha's preaching, including not a few marvels and miracles. Soon it became customary to hold meetings of the Order twice a month, at

Fortnightly meetings.

the periods of full and new moon, already sacred periods in India, observed by Brahmans with ceremonies of long standing. The special purpose of these Buddhist meetings was the confession

Confession and penance.

of faults one to another and the acceptance of the due penance. A list of common or possible offences was drawn up, and read out at each meeting, every member present being called upon to answer three times as to his innocence of each offence. Among these offences are some which show how strictly from the

Strict regulations.

first Buddhist monks were regulated. Even in building a hut it must be of prescribed measurement; no extra robes must be kept; no rug or mat with silk in it must be used by a monk, and a rug must last six years; spare bowls must not be possessed; no monk must encroach on the hospitality already given to another; no monk might take more than one meal at a public rest-house.

The members of the Order had to go into the neighbourhood of houses completely clad, clean, with downcast eye, making but little noise, not swaying the limbs about with excited gestures. Their heads must be uncovered. Various observances are connected with taking the food given to them. They were not to preach the Buddhist doctrine to persons in unseemly attitudes, nor to any one sitting.

After Buddha's death a different system of receiving

monks of course arose. The following is the profession of faith which early became prevalent:

Profession of faith.

"To Buddha will I look in faith; he, the Exalted, is the holy, supreme Buddha, the knowing, the instructed, the blessed, who knows the worlds, the Supreme One, who yoketh men like an ox, the Teacher of gods and men, the exalted Buddha.

"To the doctrine will I look in faith; well preached is the doctrine by the Exalted One. It has become apparent; it needs no time; it says 'Come and see'; it leads to welfare; it is realised by the wise in their own hearts.

"To the Order will I look in faith; in right behaviour lives the Order of disciples of the Exalted One; in proper, honest, just behaviour lives the Order of the disciples of the Exalted One, the four couples, the eight classes of believers; that is the Order of the disciples of the Exalted One, worthy to have men lift their hands before them in reverence, the highest place in the world, in which man may do good.

"In the precepts of rectitude will I walk, which the holy love, which are uninfringed, unviolated, unmixed, uncoloured, free, praised by the wise and not counterfeit, which lead on to concentration."

Not a body corporate.

Although we have spoken of the Buddhist Order, somewhat as if it were a body corporate, it never became strictly so. No central authority or representative council was ever constituted; no person was deputed by the founder of the religion to represent him after his death. And indeed mankind had not then arrived at the conception of a Pope, or a general authority exercising sway through widely different and separate regions. The only device that then occurred to the monks was to attribute every new regulation which they wished to enforce, to Buddha himself. He was the one person to whom authority was conceded; and in so far as his authority was acknowledged, his supposed behests were likely to be obeyed. The only other way of imposing new regulations was by means of assemblies or councils of monks, but though sometimes spoken of as general councils as

No head after Buddha.

Assemblies or councils.

of a Church, they were only assemblies of monks at a particular centre at one time, not called from all Buddhist centres, and not representative. Probably the first of these, said to have been held at Rajagaha immediately after Buddha's death, included the most prominent and revered of his followers; but there was no way of imposing its decisions on those who were not present, except by a purely intangible influence. The same was the case with the later councils. No doubt they were assembled because evils had arisen, or questions required decision. But the more Buddhism spread, the more independent spirits entered its ranks, the more difficult was it to heal divisions or to prevent divergences of doctrine and practice from arising. And this went on, antagonised only by the cohesion produced by the sacred books, the devotion and reverence for Buddha, the greater or less consciousness of a common interest to advance and a common battle to fight. Hence it was that, as its founder predicted, Buddhism was destined to die in India, and to maintain itself in other countries in widely different forms from those in which it had originated.

Limitations to admission.

At first no limitations were imposed as to admission to the Order; any applicant was received. But it was soon necessary to lay down certain rules of exclusion. Criminals, those afflicted with serious deformities, soldiers and servants of kings, debtors and slaves, and sons whose parents refused their consent, were thus excluded. No youth might enter the first stage till twelve years old, or might be fully received as a monk till twenty. Two stages were marked, the preliminary reception or outgoing from lay life or from another sect of ascetics, and the complete entry (Upasampada) into the Order. The latter was conferred at a general meeting (Samgha) of monks in any place, a resolution asking for it being proposed, and any one who objected being required to declare his objection. The petitioner was asked if he had certain diseases, if he was a freeman, if he had no debts, if he had a proper alms-bowl and robes, if his parents consented, if he was in the royal service, etc. He had

Form of reception.

further to offer some experienced monk as his sponsor or teacher. He was then proposed for formal reception; and if no monk objected, he was declared to be received. He was next formally told what were the four resources of the Order, (1) morsels of food given in alms, (2) a robe made of rags taken from a dust heap, (3) dwelling at the foot of a tree, (4) the filthiest liquid for medicine. All other food, drink, shelter, and clothing were to be regarded as extra allowances. After this, four great prohibitions were communicated: (1) the command to live a chaste life, (2) not to take even a blade of grass that had not been given to him, (3) not to take the life of even the minutest creature, (4) not to boast that he possessed any superhuman perfection. Thus the whole reception was confined to declarations on the part of both the candidate and the assembly. Nothing like prayer, special initiation, or conferment of power was included.

The four resources.

The four prohibitions.

It followed that it was equally easy to leave the Order. This was a direct consequence of Buddha's teaching, which was only open to those who voluntarily received it. Perhaps no Order ever held its members so lightly; and in this lay one of the secrets of its strength. The monks were bound to lead a very temperate life, but their subsistence was sure so long as the Order had any repute; the thoughts to which they were exhorted chimed in with their own natural prepossessions, and an undoubted position of respect and influence was occupied by every monk. Then again, while not coercing any one to stay (a monk might leave on simply declaring that he wished to return to relatives, or home, or a worldly life), the Order had a considerable hold on him by reason of the censure and the exclusion which it might pronounce. The breaking of any of the great prohibitions caused exclusion, provided any monk took notice of it and brought the case before an assembly. So the double mode—forcible exclusion, and voluntary retirement—were in easy operation, and thus the Order, retaining only voluntary and well-behaved members, was strong.

Quitting the Order.

Its advantages.

In one thing Buddhist monks differed from many other Orders: they were strictly forbidden to accept or possess silver or gold, or even to treasure them for the Order. Thus they were kept far from "the root of all evil." If a monk nevertheless accepted such a gift, he was compelled to hand it over to some lay adherent in the neighbourhood, who was to purchase with it butter, oil, or honey, for the use of the monks, the guilty receiver excepted. Or, again, the gold or silver might be cast away. Such a severe restriction was steadfastly maintained for centuries.

No silver or gold.

Another distinction of the Buddhist monks from other Orders, in India and elsewhere, was in the seemliness of their outward appearance. Far from cultivating dirt or unseemliness in any form, they were scrupulously careful about bathing, the care of the body, ventilation, and other things conducive to health. Their garments, though they might be very poor, were to be seemly and decent, and it was not forbidden to accept a sufficiency of food and clothing from any lay adherent. The whole picture of the Buddhist monks of early times is a remarkable one in its preservation of the medium between asceticism and excess, a resolute choice which has no doubt preserved it from the extremes of Hindu asceticism, though it has not always kept it equally free from excesses of other kinds. Shelter was always obtainable and allowable, and even comfortable quarters were not disdained. Everything was, as far as known, conducted on sanitary principles, in many points reminding us of the domestic legislation of the Jews. The seniors and teachers were especially revered and well attended to, their pupils and the novices who were their *protégés* being expected to travel ahead of them and prepare quarters for them when on their journeys, and to do every kindly office for them. Solitude, in fact, was discouraged. We everywhere hear of groups of monks residing together, helping one another in difficulties, sickness, or temptation, and looking after one another's spiritual welfare. For five years after his admission to

Seemly outward appearance.

Companionship.

the Order each monk had to be under the tutelage of two monks of ten years' standing whom he was to accompany and attend upon, and from whom he was to receive instruction. Where many monks resided together, offices became somewhat subdivided, but only in relation to domestic matters; thus different individuals were charged with the distribution of fruit, of rice, the care of the sleeping and assembly rooms, etc.

Tutelage.

It is noteworthy how little importance the Buddhist monks attached to labour apart from absolute necessities. Like the strict Brahmans, to whom the recitation of the Vedas was all-important, the monks regarded the repetition of Buddha's sayings and discourses and the rules of the Order as essential. But this was varied with discussions on points of difficulty or the fuller exposition of the leading doctrines: "He who abides in the Order talks not of many topics and talks not of vulgar things. He expounds the word himself, or stirs up another to its exposition, or he esteems even sacred silence not lightly." (O.) On the whole we have a picture of an Order living in the world, yet not of the world, almost daily contemplating the turmoil and distractions of a suffering, changeful life, yet never taking part in its affairs; a standing witness to self-seeking, quarrelling people that something existed far better than their life, that passions could be quelled, that there was a life which gave relief from sorrows and produced a philosophic calm. Perhaps in this life too there was more pure love of nature than was always acknowledged; and the rule as to sparing life was certainly in accord with this. Some of their poets have beautifully expressed this love of nature. "The broad heart-cheering expanses, crowned by *kareri* forests, those lovely regions, where elephants raise their voices, the rocks make me glad. Where the rain rushes, those lovely abodes, the mountains where sages walk, where the peacock's cry resounds, the rocks, make me glad. There is it good for me to be, the friend of abstraction, who is struggling for salvation. There is it

Recitations and discussions.

Retirement and love of nature.

good for me to be, the monk, who pursues the true good, who is struggling for salvation." (O.)

The fortnightly meetings already referred to (p. 163) were almost the only regular assemblies of Buddhists, and confession and questioning of one another was almost the only religious form. We must constantly keep in mind the burdensome and expensive nature of the Brahman observances, and likewise the authority which the Brahmans claimed over all kinds of concerns of other people. Thus the contrast to the latter was very evident in Buddhism: little ceremony, retired life, modest demeanour, pure living, no profession of supernatural power, no assumption of authority. Herein was a great part of its strength. It is surely one of the most remarkable phenomena in the world that a religion —if it can be truly called a religion,—which professes no knowledge and inculcates no worship of a god, and which is not bound in reverence to a supernatural Person, should have obtained sway over one-third of the population of the globe. Buddha, it is true, is ever held in reverence, but he is not believed in as existing; he is in Nirvana, but whether Nirvana is a state of present existence or not is doubtful, and thus there is no prayer to Buddha, no answer to prayer by Buddha; yet his memory is fresh, his name is sanctified, his teaching is influential as ever.

Few ceremonies.

Reverence to Buddha.

The only thing in early Buddhism approaching the pilgrimages and acts of worship in other religions, is the holding in reverence of the four notable places in Buddha's life: his birthplace, the spot where he attained knowledge and perfect insight, the place where he started the kingdom of righteousness, and the place of his death. Those who died while journeying to these places were promised that their re-birth should be in heaven. The care of Buddha's relics, the building of monuments to contain them, and the holding of festivals in their honour were entirely left to lay members.

Regard for holy places.

Perhaps the institution most nearly parallel with the Buddhist assemblies is the class-meeting among the Methodists as instituted by John Wesley. The "leader" of the meeting was the monk of longest standing in the district, and every member of the Order was to be present, even if ill, unless he were able to send by another monk his assurance of freedom from the faults which the sacred form (Pattimokkha, the words

The confessional.

WORSHIPPERS BEFORE THE ENTRANCE TO THE SHRINE OF THE TOOTH, CEYLON.

of disburdenment) inquired into. No woman, no lay member, no novice, might take part in or be present at this solemnity. Three times every question must be put, and silence was an assertion of purity. In later times it was held necessary that every monk should have previously confessed his fault and done the appropriate penance (unless it were one for which exclusion was the punishment); and it was the duty of any brother who knew of an offence committed by another to demand his confession and performance of penance.

The Kullavagga.

A full procedure (contained in the Kullavagga) gradually grew up to meet all cases of transgression. Buddhist monks, like other human beings, proved themselves liable to err, and we find recitals such as this at the beginning of various sections of the Kullavagga: "Now at that time the venerable Seyyasaka was stupid, and indiscreet, and full of faults, and devoid of merit, and was living in lay society in unlawful association with the world, so much so that the monks were worn out with placing him on probation and with throwing him back to the beginning of his probationary term," etc. (S. E. xvii.). The various narrations show that some monks at times were guilty of almost every kind of offence or frivolity, and so regulations for warning, punishing, or excluding them were devised. If an individual, even a lay person, had been offended or put down, his pardon had to be asked. Suspension was the punishment for not acknowledging and not atoning for an offence. How severe this "cutting" could be, is shown by the following recital: "And the monks did no reverence to him, rose not from their seats to welcome him, rendered him not service, offered him not salutation, paid not respect to him, offered him not hospitality, nor esteemed him, nor honoured him, nor supported him." The various penances and forms connected with them are too numerous for us to attempt a further account of them.

Offences and penances.

The Pavarana or invitation.

One other simple annual ceremony there was, known as the Pavarana or invitation. At the end of the rainy season, before commencing the season of itinerancy, the monks met in assembly, each sitting down on the ground, raising his clasped hands, and inviting his brethren to charge him with any offence he might be suspected of, promising, if he had been guilty, to make atonement. If any monk happened to be isolated, he could hold this service by himself.

Thus utterly devoid of show, of stately formality, of imposing accompaniments, was Buddhism; priestless, templeless, agnostic as to the Supreme Being, its undeniable power and influence drew to it multitudes of adherents; and they were not all sound or docile fish that came to the net. Hence we early hear of dissensions in the Order, and whole chapters in the sacred books are devoted to their consideration. There are procedures for settling disputes, for dealing with charges against the innocent, the insane, etc.; and when peaceable reconciliation proved impossible, matters were to be decided by a vote of the majority, unless the subject was too trivial, or a vote would lead to an open schism.

The nuns, or sisters.

The "nuns," or "sisters," of Buddhism were regarded as constituting a separate Order, with their own fortnightly assemblies, yet in complete subordination to the monks, so that none of the higher ceremonies were complete without the co-operation of monks. Every sister had to bow reverently, rise, and raise her clasped hands before every monk, however newly admitted. Both the confession meetings and the preaching of the true Buddhist doctrine had to be conducted for them by the monks; and the nuns, after having held their own annual meeting, had to send to the corresponding meeting of monks asking them if they had any fault to reprehend in them. They were forbidden to revile or scold monks, or to accuse them. Ordination of the sisters, penances for transgressions, settlement of disputes, all had to be performed or arranged by the monks. Every fortnight the sisterhood had to obtain audience of a monk who had been appointed by his assembly to instruct and admonish them; but he was strictly forbidden to enter their abode, or to journey or have any intimate companionship with them. No sister might live alone, or in a forest; they lived within the walls of towns and villages, and never seem to have been at all comparable in numbers or influence to the monks. Indeed, it would have been against the spirit of the Buddhist system that they should be so; for it could only exist by the keeping up of family life, the provision of food and dwelling-places, which could not be continued if women made a practice of living in nun-like separation.

The laity.

The relations between the Order and the laity were unlike those of almost every other church. Lay believers must have been very numerous, to admit of the support of such large numbers of monks, and the extensive dedication of parks and buildings to their use; but the monks never thought it necessary to institute a formal method of admitting lay adherents, nor to keep a roll of them. Practically in each district the followers of Buddha were well known, and it was not desirable to exclude any one from the class of givers without some potent reason. It was usual, however, for a declaration to be made to a monk by believers, that they took refuge in Buddha, in the Doctrine, and in the Order; but a monk might recognise a beneficent person as a lay believer before such profession. Instruction in the doctrines of Buddha would be readily given to any person who offered hospitality to the monks, and as readily withdrawn from any one who maligned or insulted them. A serious offence was visited by withdrawal of the alms-bowl, and refusal of hospitality; but such mild excommunication would probably be quite in accordance with the desire of any one who could speak ill of the Order. The monks showed considerable readiness to re-admit any one who apologised for his fault and became reconciled to them. Beyond this they did not greatly concern themselves with the private life of the laity. Their true church consisted of the Order; the rest of mankind was scarcely within measurable distance of bliss. And their moral state was but faintly cared for. It is true that an eightfold abstinence was enjoined on them, including abstinence from killing animals, stealing, lying, drinking intoxicating liquors, unchastity, eating after mid-day, and from perfumes and garlands; and they must sleep on hard beds on the ground. General meetings of believers do not seem to have been held, nor were they admitted to meetings of the monks. But praises and promises of bliss were freely bestowed after this fashion: "To give houses to the Order, wherein in safety and in peace to meditate and think at ease, the Buddha calls the best of gifts. Therefore let a wise man, who understands what is best for himself, build beautiful houses, and receive into them knowers of the doctrine. Let him with cheerful mind give food to them, and drink, raiment and dwelling-places, to the upright in heart. Then shall they preach to him the doctrine which drives away all suffering; if he apprehends that doctrine here below, he goes sinless into Nirvana." Naturally there was sometimes a tendency for monks to exact too much, and the sacred books exhibit a stern repression of such practices, together with considerable sensitiveness as to the opinion of the lay-believers.

Esoteric Buddhism.

We may here briefly refer to the modern doctrine termed "Esoteric Buddhism," which finds favour with some persons in our own land. In the Book of the Great Decease, Buddha expressly disclaims any secret doctrine of this kind. Modern Esoteric Buddhism should rather be called a form of Theosophy, which takes hold of some points in Buddhism, especially that of transmigration or reincarnation, and expresses the belief that souls become reincarnated in successive bodies, without remembering what took place in a previous state of existence; the successive lives being separated from one another by "intervals of spiritual consciousness on a plane of nature wholly imperceptible to ordinary senses." During this stage, the lower passions of earth are forgotten and the higher alone enjoyed; and the vividness of this joy will depend on the impulse and intensity of previous upward aspirations. Reincarnation, when this impulse is exhausted, provides an appropriate punishment for ordinary evil doing.

Karma.

The word "karma," or "doing," is very important in Esoteric Buddhism: it is explained as the law of cause and effect in the moral world. It determines, according to fixed consequences, the state and condition in which reincarnations take place; on earth good karma may be laid up, and bad karma worked out by suffering. (See A. P. Sinnett, "Esoteric Buddhism.")

BURMESE BUDDHIST PRIEST AND PUPILS

CHAPTER VIII.

Modern Buddhism. I.

Missionary religions—Buddhism many-sided—The first Buddhist councils—King Asoka—The third council—Asoka's edicts—Divergence of branches—The fourth (Kanishka's) council—Fa-hien—Siladitya's council—His good deeds—Huen-Siang—Decline of Indian Buddhism—Its causes—The Greater and the Lesser Vehicles—Wide range of Buddhism—Number of Buddhists—Singhalese Buddhism—Gradual modification—Images of Buddha—Viharas in Ceylon—Cave temples—Worship of the laity—Worship of the Bo-tree—Dagobas—Relics of Buddha—Impressions of Buddha's foot—Vassa and public readings—The Pirit ceremony—Buddhist monks in Ceylon—Schools—Services of monks in illness—Burmese Buddhism—Burmese monastery schools—Novices—A Burmese monastery—The Phongyees—Life of a monk—Monastery buildings—Burmese pagodas—The great Rangoon temple—Pagahn—Burmese worship—Images of Buddha—Pagoda feasts—Nat worship—Animism—Funerals of laity—Funerals of monks—Siamese Buddhism—Siamese temples—Newborn children—Reformed sects in Siam.

AS a missionary religion, Buddhism[1] is only comparable with Mahometanism and Christianity. No other

[1] See Spence Hardy's "Eastern Monachism" and "Manual of Buddhism"; Sir Monier-Williams's "Buddhism"; "The Burman," by Shway Yoe (Mr. Scott), (B.); Alabaster's "Wheel of the Law."

religions have set themselves to conquer many races outside their original home; no others have achieved so much peacefully. Hinduism professedly restricts itself to the Hindus, though it has displayed great powers of absorbing aboriginal races into itself. Buddhism, Mahometanism, and Christianity are for all people who will receive them; and their followers have proved their faith by their missionary efforts.

Missionary religions.

Sir Monier-Williams, in his recent work on Buddhism, well expresses the great variety of aspects under which it is necessary to study Buddhism. In various countries and periods, "its teaching has become both negative and positive, agnostic and gnostic. It passes from apparent atheism and materialism to theism, polytheism, and spiritualism. It is, under one aspect, mere pessimism; under another, pure philanthropy; under another, monastic communism; under another, high morality; under another, a variety of materialistic philosophy; under another, simple demonology; under another, a mere farrago of superstitions, including necromancy, witchcraft, idolatry, and fetishism. In some form or other it may be held with almost any religion, and embraces something from almost every creed."

Buddhism many-sided.

At the first Buddhist Council, held at Rajagriha, after the death of Gautama, the teachings of the Enlightened One were sung in three divisions, namely, the Sutras, or Suttas, or words of Buddha to his disciples; the Vinaya, or discipline of the Order; and the Dharma, or doctrine; forming together the Tripitakas, or three baskets or collections. A hundred years later, a second council, held at Vesali, condemned the system of indulgences which had arisen, and led to the splitting of Buddhism into two parties, who afterwards gave rise to as many as eighteen sects. But these controversies did not hinder the spread of Buddhism in Northern India. About the middle of the third century B.C., Asoka, the king of Magadha, or Behar, grandson of Chandragupta (Greek Sandrokottos), founder of the kingdom, and noted for his connexion with Alexander the Great and Seleucus, became a sort

The first Buddhist councils.

King Asoka.

of second founder of Buddhism. He founded so many monasteries that his kingdom received the name of Land of the Monasteries (Vihara or Behar). He made it the religion of the State, and held at Patna the third Buddhist council in 244 B.C., which rectified the doctrines and canon of Buddhism. Asoka subsequently did much to spread the Order by sending out missionaries; and he inculcated its principles by having them cut upon rocks and pillars, and in caves, through a wide extent of India. A number of these still exist. The form which the Buddhist scriptures took under his influence, in the dialect of his time and country, has been the basis of the manuscripts preserved in Ceylon, in what is now known as the Pali language. In every way Asoka showed himself to be one of the most enlightened of religious monarchs; and he in no way sought to make his views triumph by force. His missionaries were directed to mingle equally with all ranks of unbelievers, and to "teach better things." His edicts include the prohibition of the slaughter of animals for food or sacrifice, the statement of the happiness to be found in virtue and the contrast of the transitory glory of this world with the reward beyond it, the inculcation of the doctrine that the teaching of Buddhist doctrine and virtue to others constitutes the greatest of charitable gifts, an order for the provision of medical aid for men and animals, the appointment of guardians of morality, etc.

The third council.

Asoka's edicts.

From the time of Asoka we may date the divergence of Buddhism into its varied national forms; henceforth it is only possible to treat the subject either by the comparative method or by referring in turn to the development of each main branch. Space will only permit us to treat each very briefly. The fourth great Buddhist council, held under Kanishka, who reigned from Kashmir widely over north-western India, in the first century A.D., drew up three commentaries on Buddhism, which were the basis for the Tibetan scriptures. This council indicates that Buddhism was firmly and widely established in India, and up to at least A.D. 800 it continued widely

Divergence of branches.

The fourth (Kanishka's) council.

prevalent there, though Brahmanism was never suppressed, and in fact it was gradually absorbing many Buddhist ideas, and preparing, when that operation was completed, to take its place entirely. In the beginning of the fifth century A.D., Fa-hien, a Chinese Buddhist, visiting India, found Buddhist monks and Brahman priests equally honoured, and Buddhist religious houses side by side with Hindu temples. In the seventh century the Buddhists were being outnumbered by the Hindus, although there were still powerful Buddhist monarchs and states in India. At this period Siladitya appears as a great patron-king, who in 634 held another great council at Kanauj on the Ganges; but the progress of Brahmanism was manifest in the discussions which took place at this council between Buddhists and Brahmans, and by the worship of the sun god and of Siva on days succeeding the inauguration of a statue of Buddha. The divergences among followers of Buddha were seen in the disputes which took place between the advocates of the Northern and the Southern Canons, or the greater and lesser "Vehicles" of the law. Siladitya was further notable for his public distribution of his treasures and jewels every five years, after which he put on a beggar's rags; thus he celebrated Buddha's Great Renunciation. Near Gaya he supported the vast monastery of Nalunda, where it is said that ten thousand Buddhist monks and novices pursued their studies and devotions; but Gaya was already a great centre of Hinduism. Huen-Siang, who travelled from China through India in the seventh century, found Brahmanism gaining ground, though Buddhism still flourished in Southern India. Some of the Hindu reformers persecuted it, as already related. It was still comparatively strong in Orissa and Kashmir in the eleventh century, and Magadha continued Buddhist until the Mohammedan conquest at the end of the twelfth century. After that, Buddhism was practically extinct in India.

Fa-hien.

Siladitya's council.

His good deeds.

Huen Siang.

Decline of Indian Buddhism.

Why was this? Partly because, as we have already

pointed out, Hinduism seized upon the more valuable doctrines of Buddhism, and combined them with the stronger and more popular elements of its own faith and ritual. Buddhism, too, did not set itself to extinguish Brahmanism; that would have been contrary to its principles; and its composure and extinction of desires was not calculated to put down any active opposition. Moreover, the Buddhists' celibacy contradicted one of the great instincts of humanity; and we must allow for the full effect of their ignoring the existence of God, of their denial of revelation, and of the efficacy of prayer and priesthood. Again, and perhaps chiefly, Buddhism left too little for the lay adherent to do. Those only were true Buddhists who became monks; the Church outside was not defined; almost its only privilege was to wait on and feed the monks; consequently, Vishnuism and Sivaism, in which the people had a most important part to play, most special ends to gain, and a most vital interest, conquered the affections and devotion of the masses of India.

Its causes.

It is in Ceylon, Burmah, and Siam that the nearest resemblance to primitive Buddhism is to be found at the present day. These countries adhere to the canon of scriptures, as given in preceding chapters, called by the Northern Buddhists the "Lesser Vehicle," in depreciation. Mahinda, the son of king Asoka, was the great apostle of Buddhism in Ceylon; and now it has a history of over two thousand years. The canon was first translated into Singhalese and then translated back into Pali by Buddaghosa in the fifth century, since which the texts have remained practically unchanged in Pali, not very different from the language of Asoka's day and kingdom. They have been translated into modern Singhalese, and commented upon at great length.

The Greater and the Lesser Vehicles.

The council held by Kanishka was the starting-point of the Northern Canon, often called the "Greater Vehicle" (Mahayana), written in Sanskrit. There are nine principal books of these scriptures, of which the best known are the "Lotus of the true Law," and the "Legendary Life of Buddha." All of them were translated into Tibetan;

and a large number of commentaries upon them were written. It is upon this "Greater Vehicle" that the Buddhism of Nepaul, Tibet, China, Manchuria, Mongolia, and Japan is founded; but these all differ considerably from one another. Extending over so wide and so populous an area of the earth's surface, Buddhism has been described as being the religion professed by more persons than any other, and has sometimes been credited with five hundred millions of adherents. The mistake that is made in such a calculation is evident when we remember that in China, where the greatest number of nominal Buddhists exists, a vast proportion of the population profess Confucianism, Taoism, and Buddhism equally or indifferently; and the study of our chapters on the former will have shown how deep a hold Confucianism, ancestor worship, and the varied forms of Taoism, have upon the Chinese. If they were called upon to exclude one of their religions, it is almost certain that Buddhism would be excluded. It is very doubtful if it is proper to reckon so many as a hundred millions of Chinese as Buddhists. Again, we have seen that Shintoism prevails in Japan, where, nevertheless, many people generally show some adhesion to Buddhism. Buddhism, essentially, has no lay standard of adherence, since the true Buddhists are the monks only. Sir Monier-Williams reckons the number of Buddhists at one hundred millions; Dr. Happer, an experienced American missionary in China, estimates that there are only twenty millions of real Buddhist believers in China, and a total of seventy-two and a half millions in Asia. But it is a very doubtful thing to attempt to reckon the numbers of adherents of a religion, and especially such a religion as Buddhism. It is certainly one of the four most prevalent religions in the world.

Wide range of Buddhism.

Number of Buddhists.

SINGHALESE BUDDHISM.

Great indeed is the contrast between modern Buddhism, with its elaborate organisation, its wealthy monasteries, its considerable ritual, its image worship and deifications, and the simplicity of its early

Gradual modification.

state as we have sketched it. No doubt this has come to pass by a gradual process of adaptation to those instincts and desires of the masses of the people which have compelled recognition in all quarters of the globe and in almost all religions, together with the regard which grew around Gautama as a perfect man; and from the first, great importance seems to have been attached to his relics. Yet it was long before images of him came into general use. In Ceylon these are called "Pilamas," meaning counterpart or likeness

Images of Buddha.

A BURMESE FUNERAL PROCESSION.

They had become numerous in the third, fourth, and fifth centuries A.D., some being over twenty feet high and resplendent with jewels. "The viharas in which the images are deposited," says Spence Hardy, "are generally, in Ceylon, permanent erections, the walls being plastered and the roof covered with tiles, even when the dwellings of the priests are mean and temporary. Near the entrance are frequently seen four figures in relief, representing the guardians and champions of the temple. Surrounding the sanctum there is usually

Viharas in Ceylon.

a narrow room, in which are images and paintings; but in many instances it is dark. Opposite the door of entrance there is another door, protected by a screen, and when this is withdrawn, an image of Buddha is seen, occupying nearly the whole of the apartment, with a table or altar before it, upon which flowers are placed. Like the temples of the Greeks, the walls are covered with paintings; the style at present adopted in Ceylon greatly resembling, in its general appearance, that which is presented in the tombs and temples of Egypt. The story most commonly illustrates some passages in the life of Buddha, or in the births he received as Bodhi-sat. The viharas are not unfrequently built upon rocks or in other romantic situations. The court around is planted with the trees that bear the flowers most usually offered. Some of the most celebrated viharas are caves, in part natural, with excavations carried further into the rock. The images of Buddha are sometimes recumbent, at other times upright, or in a sitting posture, either in the act of contemplation, or with the hand uplifted in the act of giving instruction. At Cotta, near Colombo, there is a recumbent image forty-two feet in length. Upon the altar, in addition to the flowers, there are frequently smaller images either of marble or metal. In the shape of the images, each nation appears to have adopted its own style of beauty, those of Ceylon resembling a well-proportioned native of the island, whilst those of China present an appearance of obesity that would be regarded as anything but divine by a Hindu. The images made in Siam are of a more attenuated figure, and comport better with our idea of the ascetic."

Cave Temples.

The cave temple at Damballa is one of the most perfect. One of its halls contains a gigantic recumbent figure of Buddha in the solid rock forty-seven feet long; at its feet stands an attendant, and opposite to the face is a statue of Vishnu, who is supposed to have assisted at the building; another has more than fifty figures of Buddha, and statues of several Brahmanic devas, Vishnu, Natha, etc. There is a handsome dagoba in this vihara, the spire nearly touching the roof. The whole interior—rock, wall, and statues—is painted in brilliant colours, yellow predominating. These, and other cave temples in Ceylon show that they were constructed through the same impulse and in the same art epoch with those at Ajunta and Ellora. No recent vihara of importance has been erected in Ceylon.

Worship of the laity.

The laity, on entering a vihara, bend the body or prostrate themselves before the image of Buddha with palms touching each other and thumbs touching the forehead. They next repeat the threefold formula of taking refuge, or they take upon themselves a certain number of the ten obligations. Some flowers and a little rice are then placed upon the altar, and a few coppers are cast into a vessel. No form of prayer is used, and to all appearance there is no feeling concerned in the worship, which is a matter of course and convention, with a desire of gaining some boon. Buddha, the Doctrine, and the Order, appear in Ceylon to be almost co-equally invoked for protection. The protection of Buddha is to be obtained by listening to the scriptures or keeping the precepts, and thus the evil consequences of demerit are overcome. The protection of the Order is gained by a small gift. The protection of the three takes away the fear of successive existences, mental fear, bodily pain, and the misery of the four hells. Buddha will not protect one who refrains from worship when near a dagoba or other sacred place, or covers himself with his garment, an umbrella, etc., when in sight of an image of Buddha. The Doctrine will not protect one who refuses to listen to the reading of the scriptures when called upon, or who listens irreverently or does not keep the precepts. The Order will not protect one who sits near a priest without permission, who reads the precepts without being appointed, or argues against a priest, or has his shoulders covered or holds an umbrella up when near a priest, or who remains seated when riding in any vehicle near a priest. Many notable legends attest the importance of these statements.

The worship of the Bo-tree (Pipul, or sacred fig) under which Gautama was accustomed to sit is no doubt very ancient, and in the court-yard of most viharas in Ceylon there is one, said to be derived from the original one brought to the island in the fourth century B.C. Usually one was planted on the mound under which the ashes of Kandyan chiefs and priests were placed.

Worship of the Bo-tree.

The dagoba next claims attention, but this word appears in another guise, as "pagoda"; it is derived from "da," an osseous relic, and "geba," the womb, meaning the shrine of an osseous relic. The word "tope," otherwise "stupa," a relic, is used for the same buildings. It is a circular building of stone, built on a natural or artificial elevation, and its summit is crowned with a hemispherical cupola, formerly terminated by spires. One of the great dagobas in Ceylon, at Anuradhapura, was originally 405 feet high, but is now not more than 230 feet; another, formerly 315 feet, is now not more than 269 feet. All are built of brick and covered with a preparation of lime, of a pure white, and capable of high polish, so that when perfect the building resembled a crystal dome. At various periods in modern times these dagobas have been opened. One, opened in 1820 in Ceylon, contained in the interior a small square compartment of brickwork, set exactly towards the cardinal points. In the centre, directly under the apex, was a hollow stone vase with a cover, containing a small piece of bone, with some thin pieces of plate-gold, a few rings, pearls, and beads, a few clay images of the sacred naga, or snake-god, and two lamps. Such relics are either supposed to have been those of Buddha himself or of some Buddhist saint, and many miracles are ascribed to their virtues. The most celebrated relic of Buddha now existing is in Ceylon, namely, the dalada, or left canine tooth, a piece of discoloured ivory two inches long (much too long for a human tooth). This is preserved in a small chamber in the vihara attached to the old palace of the Kandyan kings, enclosed in nine successive bell-shaped golden and jewelled cases, each locked, and the key kept by a separate official. On the walls of the corridor of entrance are coloured frescoes of

Dagobas.

Relics of Buddha.

the eight principal hells of Buddhism, in which evildoers are represented being torn asunder by red-hot tongs, or sawn in two, or crushed between rocks, or fixed on red-hot spikes. Thus does the spirit of gentle Buddhism find place for practical threats of horrible torture.

Impressions of Buddha's foot.

Next to the relics in regard are impressions of Buddha's foot. The most celebrated is on Adam's Peak in Ceylon, annually visited by 100,000 pilgrims. It is a depression or excavation over five feet long, and three-quarters of a yard wide. Representations of it are divided into 108 compartments, each containing a design or figure, with a wheel in the centre.

Vassa and public readings.

The Vassa, or residence in a fixed abode during the rainy season, celebrated by reading the Buddhist scriptures to the people, is well kept up in Ceylon. The reading takes place in a temporary building of pyramidal form, with successive platforms, built near a vihara. In the centre is an elevated platform for the monks, and the people sit around on mats. Lamps and lanterns of great variety and gay colour are held by the people in their hands or on their heads during the reading. Sometimes the scene is a very attractive one. "The females are arrayed in their gayest attire, their hair being combed back from the forehead and neatly done up in a knot, fastened with silver pins and small ornamental combs. The usual dress of the men is of white cotton. Flags and streamers, figured handkerchiefs and shawls, float from every convenient receptacle. At intervals, tom-toms are beaten; the rude trumpet sends forth its screams; and the din of the music, the murmur of the people's voices, the firing of musketry and jinjalls, and the glare of the lamps, produce an effect not much in consonance with an act of worship" (Hardy). Usually only the Pali text is read, so that the people do not understand a word, and many fall asleep or chew betel. Whenever the name of Buddha is repeated by the reader, the people call out simultaneously "Sadhu," an exclamation of joy. In many ways these readings are observed as festival occasions; they take place at each change of the moon, or four times in the lunar month. Great merit is said to accrue to all hearers who keep the eight precepts upon these service days. It is not proper to trade or to make trade calculations on them, still less to injure any one.

Another of the ceremonies in which the laity have a share is the "Pirit," or reading certain portions of the scriptures as an exorcism against demons, *i.e.*, really malignant spirits who were formerly men. Certain portions of the scriptures are supposed to avail specially in this work, and these are collectively termed the Pirit. One of these contains the following: "All spirits here assembled, those of earth and those of air, let all such be joyful; let them listen attentively to my words. Therefore hear me, O ye spirits; be friendly to the race of men; for day and night they bring you their offerings; therefore keep diligent watch over them. Ye spirits here assembled, those of earth and those of air, let us bow before Buddha, let us bow before the Law, let us bow before the Order." The recitation of the Pirit on a great occasion continues without interruption through seven days and nights, relays of priests being engaged, with many attendant circumstances of festivity.

The Pirit ceremony.

We now pass to the Buddhist order of monks in Ceylon, "priests" as they call themselves now-a-days. "In nearly all the villages and towns of Ceylon," says Hardy, "that are inhabited by the Singhalese or Kandyans, the priests of Buddha are frequently seen, as they have to receive their food by taking the alms-bowl from house to house. They usually walk along the road at a measured pace, without taking much notice of what passes around. They have no covering for the head, and are generally barefooted. In the right hand they carry a fan, in shape not much unlike a hand-screen, which they hold up before the face when in the presence of women, that the entrance of evil thoughts into the mind may be prevented. The bowl is slung from the neck, and is covered by the robe, except at the time when alms are received." There are several thousands of these living as celibates in simple leaf-huts or in

Buddhist monks in Ceylon.

viharas; they follow substantially the rules given in the last chapter. Their countenances are usually less intelligent-looking than those of the common people, with an appearance of great vacancy approaching imbecility; a few rise above this state, but it is only the natural physical result of the kind of meditation and rote-worship in which they engage. Yet the populace regard them as a kind of inferior Buddhas, and pay them great deference. In their dress they repeat that attributed to Buddha; it is assimilated to a yellow garment of rags, by the pieces being torn and sewn together again. The left shoulder is usually covered, the right bare. There is generally a school attached to the vihara, in which boys are taught to read, recite, and write, this last being first effected on sand with the finger. A large proportion of the books read relate to Buddhism. Latterly the Ceylon Buddhists have established a college at Colombo for the study of Sanskrit, Pali, and Singhalese. Each vihara has a head, and frequently possesses considerable landed property, but there is no organised hierarchy. One of the most important services rendered by the Buddhists has been in their maintenance of schools; the pupils in general become qualified to enter upon the Buddhistic novitiate at once, and the ceremony of initiation is a very simple one.

Schools.

Notwithstanding the limited sacerdotal functions assigned to the monks, they are to a certain extent recognised in birth and marriage ceremonies, especially in fixing auspicious days for weddings. In case of illness, a monk is sent for, an offering of flowers, oil, and food being at the same time forwarded. A temporary audience-place is fitted up close to the house, and here the monk reads from the scripture for six hours to the relatives and friends, and, if possible, the sick man also. Offerings are again given to the priest, who finally says, "By reverence do the wise secure health, by almsgiving do they lay up treasures for themselves." If he appears about to die, the monk recites the formula of profession of Buddhism, the five prohibitions (p. 152), and the four earnest reflections. As

Services of monks in illness.

ON THE SACRED PLATFORM OF THE RANGOON PAGODA.

a rule, in Ceylon, the dead are buried; but the bodies of monks are burnt under decorated canopies, which are left to moulder away.

BURMESE BUDDHISM.

A very vivid picture of Buddhism in Burmah has been given by Mr. Scott in his fascinating book, "The Burman," published under the pseudonym of "Shway Yoe." Every boy goes to the monastery school from the age of eight, and is taught to read and write, the chief part of the teaching consisting of Buddhistic formulas and precepts; and, until the English took possession of the country, every boy took the yellow robe at the close of his schooling, although he might retain it but for a short time; and as yet comparatively few have thrown off the conventional mode of education in favour of the Government schools. On entering the Order as a novice, at the age of twelve or more, there is an elaborate ceremony, corresponding to baptism, at which the youth receives a new name, showing that it is now possible for him to escape from suffering; but this is again lost when or if he returns to the world, though having borne it enables him to add to his merits by good works. The ceremony includes the putting off of fine clothes, the shaving of the head, reciting a Pali prayer to be admitted to the Order as a novice, that he may walk steadily in the path to perfection, and finally attain to the blessed state of "Neh'ban," as Nirvana comes to be rendered in Burmese, and the reception of the yellow robes and the begging-pot from the chief or abbot of the monastery. Finally, there is a feast at the parent's house. The stay of the novice in the monastery is not usually long, sometimes even only one day, but usually at least through one rainy season, or Wah (Vassa, sometimes called Lent by Europeans). Those who resolve to adopt the religious life enter upon advanced studies of Buddhist writings; but many things hinder the novice, especially the duty of attending on the monks, begging, carrying umbrellas or books for his seniors. In Lower Burmah the parents

Burmese monastery schools.

Novices.

sometimes send food regularly for their son, but this would not be allowed in Upper Burmah.

A Burmese monastery.

In a Burmese monastery the whole community is roused a little before daylight, awakened by a big bell, and after washing, each brother recites a few formulas, one of which is, "How great a favour has the Lord Buddha bestowed upon me in manifesting to me his law, through the observance of which I may escape hell and secure my salvation." The entire brotherhood assemble round the image of Buddha, recite the morning service, and then perform various domestic duties, the elder only meditating. A slight meal and an hour's study are followed by the procession of all the monks through the town, to receive food in the alms-bowl. On their return a portion is offered to Buddha's image, and then breakfast is taken. Strictly it ought to consist of the morning's gift, not specially dressed; but usually this is now given to the scholars or any chance wanderers, while a tasty meal is prepared for the monks. Visits of courtesy or honour fill up part of the day, at which great ceremony is observed, the conversation, according to Shway Yoe, coming round to the merit of almsgiving. After a light meal at noon, all return to work, some teaching, others studying the Buddhist books, overseeing the writers who copy manuscripts; but the work of many is merely meditation, repeating the formulas of the Order, "while, throughout all, sounds the din of the schoolroom, where the pupils are shouting out their tasks at the top of their voices. The novices and monks may take a stroll in the evening, but at sunset all are summoned back, and the scholars recite the whole or part of their day's work to the abbot. So the evening passes till 8.30 or 9, when all assemble for devotion, before the image of Buddha. Then a novice loudly proclaims the hour, day, and year; all bow before Buddha thrice, and similarly before the abbot, and then retire. The testimony of Shway Yoe is, that "the effect of such a school, presided over by an abbot of intelligence and earnestness, must infallibly work for the good of all connected with it, and especially so in the case of an impulsive, impressionable people like the

Burmese. As long as all the men of the country pass through the monasteries, the teachings of western missionaries can have but little power to shake the hold of Buddhism on the people."

The Phon-gyees.

Among those who are fully recognised as monks, the Phon-gyee of "great glory" is distinguished, having been at least ten years a monk, and having proved himself steadfast and self-denying. From this class the Sayah (head or abbot) is chosen. Beyond these is recognised the Provincial, overseeing a number of monasteries in a district, and the Sadaw, or royal teacher, of whom there are eight, forming a sort of supreme Burmese religious board. It is always possible to leave the monastery, in which point Buddhist monasteries differ from most others.

BURMESE IMAGE OF GAUTAMA.

Life of a monk.

The life of a monk is an ideal one in many respects; food is supplied to him; he has no sermons to prepare; he has few outside religious rites to attend; and if he observes the cardinal precepts of Buddhism, he is continually accumulating merit. There is nothing in the admission or routine of the full monkhood which is not in essence contained in our chapters. Discipline is strictly maintained, the breaking of the prime commands being severely punished; unfrocking, expulsion, possibly stoning, are penalties sufficiently heavy. The condition of an expelled monk is pitiable: "no one may speak to him; no monk will take alms from him; he can neither buy nor sell; he is not allowed even to draw water from a well." If there is evil living or neglect of religious duty in a neighbourhood, the brethren invert their alms-bowls and cease to go out begging. This is felt to be so grave a censure that it does not fail to influence the most hardened in a very short time, yet laxities are not unknown. Some monks will receive money or gold, or will adopt circuitous methods of getting what they desire. So far has this proceeded that an active sect has arisen in lower Burmah to restore and maintain the true austerities and ordinances of Buddhism, and it has gained many adherents among laity as well as monks. On the whole, the monks are greatly reverenced by the people, who make obeisance when they pass, the women kneeling down by the roadside in Upper Burmah. The oldest layman terms himself the disciple of the youngest monk, whose commonest actions are spoken of in magniloquent language.

The monastery is an essential accompaniment of the Burmese village, away from bustle, surrounded by fine

Monastery buildings.

trees. Usually it is built of teak, sometimes of brick. All are oblong, and one storey high, the living rooms being raised eight or ten feet on pillars. The woodwork is ornamented with varied carving of figures and scroll-work; the roofs appear as if constituting successive storeys—three, five, or seven. The main hall is divided into two portions—one for the scholars and a higher one for the reception of visitors. At the back of this, against the wall, are images of Buddha on a sort of altar, with candles, flowers, praying flags, etc. Near this are various treasures, books, manuscripts, chests, models of monasteries and pagodas, etc. This hall is also used as the sleeping place of the monks. Sometimes a number of these buildings are contained within one enclosure.

The most gorgeous group of monastic buildings in the world probably is the Royal Monastery outside Mandalay. "Every building in it is magnificent; every inch carved with the ingenuity of a Chinese toy, the whole ablaze with gold leaf and a mosaic of fragments of looking-glass. . . . The interior is no less elaborate. The wood-carving is particularly fine." But this is only one among many. The whole space between Mandalay Hill and the

FUNERAL PYRE OF A BURMESE PHON-GYEE.

city is full of monasteries, some with excellent libraries of palm-leaf books; while in Lower Burmah many do not possess even a complete copy of the three chief books of the "Lesser Vehicle." It being the special privilege of the lay believers to build and support monasteries, plenty of scope for such philanthropy is always allowed; but many monasteries have a good deal of cash laid away. The Burmese are taxed most seriously by Buddhism, for abundant almsgiving must be supplemented by regular worship at the pagodas.

Burmese pagodas.

The pagodas of Burmah are still more numerous than the monasteries, old crumbling ones beside new glittering buildings, as in India, with very many imaginary relics of Buddha or other saints. All these buildings the Burmese call Zaydee, the offering place, or place of prayer; while the more notable pagodas are termed Payahs. A relic or sacred object is buried or enclosed in each; without it no "htee," or umbrella, could crown its spire. Often these include golden images of Buddha with the hooded snake. They are based on the primitive mound plan, combined with the lotus, extended in many cases into an inverted bell with a spire. They are all made of sun-dried brick, very liable to decay, and only a few are renewed or made substantial enough for permanence. Some of the pagodas are surrounded at the base by a circle of smaller pagodas, each enshrining an image of Buddha.

The great Rangoon temple.

The most magnificent Buddhist temple is that at Rangoon, the Shway Dagohn Payah, containing, it is said, eight hairs of Gautama Buddha, beside relics of the three Buddhas who preceded him. It stands upon a huge mound of two terraces, the upper 166 feet above the ground outside, and in extent 900 feet by 685. The long flights of steps by which the ascent is made are covered by long ranges of handsome teak roofs, with frescoes showing scenes in Buddha's disciples' lives, and horrible scenes of the torments of the wicked in hell. From the centre of the upper terrace rises the solid octagonal brick payah, 370 feet high, abundantly gilt. At the top is the htee, or gilt umbrella of iron work of many rings, each with many jewelled bells of gold and silver, tinkling with every movement of the air. Four chapels at the foot of the pagoda have colossal sitting figures of Buddha, with hundreds of smaller ones in every style and posture, surrounding or even fixed upon them. The decorations and carvings upon and around these are elaborate beyond description; the multitudes of bells of all sizes, from the great one of 42 tons downwards, deserve special mention. The great bell was carried off by the English after the second Burmese war, but by accident it capsized and lay at the bottom of the Rangoon river, and the English failed to raise it. The Burmese begged to be allowed to try, and with primitive appliances and great perseverance succeeded in raising it, and so got it back again, to the great triumph of Buddhists; and indeed the carrying off of religious emblems or property of any kind from a conquered people is a feat no Englishman has reason to be proud of. The original temple, 27 feet high, has been again and again encased with bricks rendering it larger and taller, and has thus attained its present height, and it is periodically regilt; also the faithful are never tired of climbing as high as they can, and fixing squares of gold leaf upon it. "Lepers and cripples and nuns in their white robes line the steps and cry out in piteous tones for alms. Round the platform itself are sellers of candles and coloured tapers, Chinese incense sticks, and prayer flags, along with abundance of gold leaf. Numbers of young girls sit about with flowers, especially of the lotus, and meats of different kinds for offerings. The platform is never deserted. Even long after midnight the voice of the worshipper may be heard in the night air, chanting in solemn monotone his pious aspirations, while on a duty day, and especially on a feast day, the laughing, joyous crowd of men and maidens, in their gay national dress, makes the platform of the Shway Dagohn one of the finest sights in the world." (B.)

The Shway Maw-Daw, the lotus-shrine of Pegu; the depository of the sacred hair at Prome, and the great temple at Mandalay, are among the more remarkable temples in Burmah. But we must not omit to mention the great collection of pagodas at Pagahn, the deserted capital on the Irrawaddy, extending for eight miles along the bank and for two miles inland. Colonel Yule, in his "Mission to Ava," has described them in detail. Some are cruciform vaulted temples, with great galleries and transepts, and remind visitors of old-world cathedrals; others have minarets, pyramids of fretwork; some are like huge bulbous mushrooms. It is said that there are nearly ten thousand more or less complete, but

Pagahn.

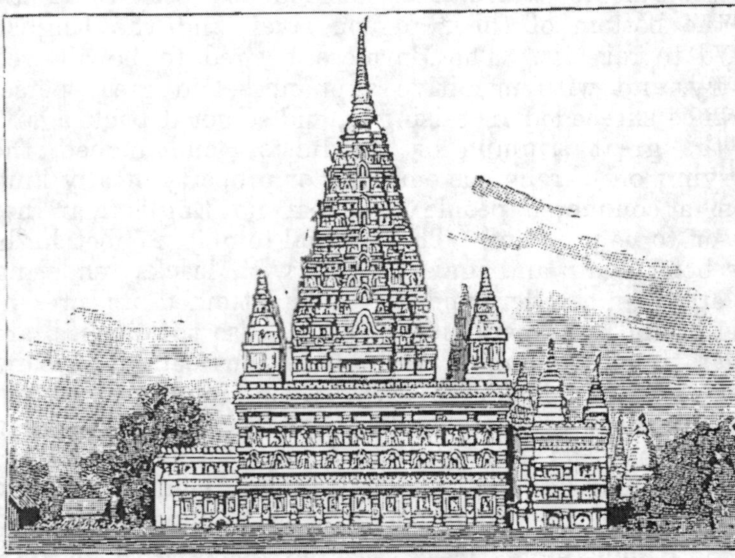

PAGODA AT PAGAHN.

ruin is on many, and jungle-bushes have overgrown them. Very many contain colossal figures of Buddha and sculptured groups. Again, Shway Goo, an island between Mandalay and Bhamo, is a great centre of temples, having nine hundred and ninety-nine.

Thus we may gather some faint idea how deeply the belief in securing merit by building a pagoda has entered into the nature of the Burmese; but, says Shway Yoe, they are not idolaters; they worship neither relics nor images. The pagoda and the figure

Burmese worship.

only furnish a fitting place to praise the great Buddha and to resolve to imitate his charity and sinless life. No actual prayers are offered to them; simple praises learnt at the monastery school, or special forms made by the worshipper are repeated, and their character is similar to those we have already given samples of. They are not merely addressed to the image, but also to the entire building, and may be repeated anywhere, at a distance from it. Pilgrims to the Rangoon temple prostrate themselves now and again, from the time they catch sight of the spire, repeating simple formulæ or Pali sentences of which they may or may not know the meaning. Many of them have little paper prayer flags in various fanciful shapes, having written in the centre some pious sentence in Pali or Burmese. These are laid on the shrine, and add to the merit of the worshipper, as do the candles, lamps, flowers, incense-sticks, etc., which are offered. The worshippers, if they are men, squat down, resting the body on their heels. The body is bent a little forward, and the hands are joined together and raised to the forehead. The women kneel down altogether, and take especial care to cover up their feet. All are of course barefooted. Before commencing the repetition of the formulæ, three prostrations are made with the forehead to the ground. It is usual to hold some offering between the hands during worship, and this is afterwards reverently deposited on the altar.

Images of Buddha.

Strange to say, the Burmese have but little idea of perpetuating their images of Buddha; few are of marble or brass; most are of short-lived brick, mortar, and wood. The utmost period for which they could endure would be as nothing in comparison with the countless future ages. Their variety, too, is not great; they are either standing in the preaching attitude, sitting cross-legged, or recumbent and representing the approach of death. The erect figures are usually very large; these are common in Upper Burmah, some forty feet high; many have been and are frequently gilt. In Lower Burmah the whole of the receptacles near the shrines are crammed full of little images of all kinds. Only a few great images are carved or placed in the open.

The ignorant in some cases ascribe miracles to particular images or relics, but all enlightened Buddhists strongly repudiate those beliefs, and only unprincipled monks can now and then be got to propagate them. There is one noteworthy marble Buddha at the foot of Mandalay Hill, twenty-five feet high, carved out of one block, scores of tons in weight. Another on the top of the hill has gold leaf only on the eyeballs, and its constant renewal by the faithful causes the pupils to protrude frightfully. Other notable images are formed of bricks laid against rock surfaces. Many are deserted, marks of past populations, still reverenced by the chance visitor, but regarded more with curiosity than adoration.

Pagoda feasts.

The pagoda feasts are the great holidays of the Burmese, each shrine having its own day, and they considerably resemble the great fairs of medieval Europe, a few minutes spent at the shrine, reciting sentences in praise of Buddha, sufficing for the devotions of most of the visitors, while a few listen to the reading and expounding of the sacred books by the head of the monastery. The four feast days every month are also well observed, and have in general been made to coincide with Sunday in Lower Burmah since the British occupation; but there is much variation in the strictness with which the day is kept. The three months of Wah (corresponding to Vassa) are kept as a sort of Lent, without fasting, but with special observance of religious duties, and absence of feasts and marriages. Often the richer people get monks to expound the law in their houses, and invite their friends to hear them. The end of this season is celebrated by a carnival, including in Rangoon much feasting and even plays in the monasteries and grand illuminations.

Nat worship.

Notwithstanding the firm hold which Buddhism has upon the Burmese, they still propitiate the nature-spirits or nats, as if Buddhism were unknown. The word "nat" in Burmese has two distinct meanings, one kind of nats being the inhabitants of the six inferior heavens, the devas, transferred from the Vedic mythology, and the other the spirits of the air, water, and forest. The last are most diligently propitiated, for

ENTRANCE TO THE SHWAY DAGOHN, RANGOON.

fear of the harm they may do, at a little shrine at the end of each village. Sometimes, it is a mere bamboo cage with a gaudy image or images of a fetish-like ugliness, to which offerings are made by the villagers.

In fact, the whole category of local spirits, disease spirits, demons, omens, and magic-workers is to be found in considerable force in Burmah, though greatly frowned upon by the Buddhist priests. Lucky and unlucky days, days proper for special things or improper for others, have also very great influence in Burmese life, and in them the astrologers find great profit. So that concurrently with the more advanced notions of Buddhism, there may be found in Burmah practically the whole round of primitive notions about the spirit world. The butterfly spirit is the Burmese idea of the essential spirit of human life, which may wander in dreams, be charmed or afflicted by demons and wizards, be preserved by witch-doctors, and which finally departs at death.

Animism.

Marriage in Burmah is not a religious ceremony, being contrary to the celibate ideas of the monks; but in burials the latter are largely concerned. They are summoned to stay in the house of death as a protection from evil spirits; they deliver addresses on the vanity of human desires and the uncertainty and wretchedness of life; they receive large alms, determining the extent of their services, and at the grave they recite the five commandments and the ten good works, and various sentences in Pali. When they are leaving with their alms, the chief mourner pours water on to the ground and says, "May the deceased and all present share the merit of the offerings made and the ceremonies now proceeding," that the earth may remember it when men forget. For a week after, feasting and mourning go on in most cases, the monks receiving offerings, reciting Pali sentences, driving off evil spirits, and purifying the house. Many people in Burmah are still cremated.

Funerals of laity.

The funeral of a monk is very different. When he dies, he simply returns to one of the various heavens, and his funeral is called "Phongyee byan," the return of the great glory. A notable monk has a funeral that is attended by people from all around. After elaborate preparations, the body is enclosed in a gorgeous sarcophagus, painted with religious subjects and variously decked. It lies in state for months under an

Funerals of monks.

open teak building called a "monastery for the dead," hung with gift-paintings of all kinds of subjects and various other gifts, and is visited by streams of pilgrims, who say their religious sentences, make offerings of flowers and fruit, and give contributions towards the final ceremony. This is the erection and burning of the funeral pyre: an elaborately decorated seven-roofed building, with a spire rising to seventy feet, is erected in a space cleared of jungle; the funeral car, previous to the coffin being placed upon it, is the subject of a prolonged "tug of war," the victory of those who are privileged to drag the car bringing abundant merit to them and being highly prized. The coffin is at last dragged to the pyre and lifted to its platform, beneath which an abundant supply of combustibles is heaped. Finally the whole is lighted by rockets fired from a distance. The bones of the deceased are gathered up and buried near the pagoda. Unlike other Buddhist countries, a shrine or pagoda is not erected over the dead in Burmah.

SIAMESE BUDDHISM.

After this account of Burmese Buddhism it will not be necessary to say much of its Siamese form, which is very similar. The Siamese monks, though their monasteries are sometimes elaborate buildings, only remain in them during the rainy season. The sacred footprint of Buddha, five feet long by two broad, known as the Phra Bat, is greatly venerated, and has a shrine erected over it, at which valuable gifts are offered. There is no real likeness to a foot, and the cavity has scarcely any markings on it; but it is venerated as a genuine relic. There are plenty of markings on the supposed genuine copies of it, divided into 108 compartments, with figures having an elaborate symbolic relationship to Buddhism. On the whole, it may be said that Buddhism is more strictly observed in Siam than in Burmah.

Siamese temples.

The great temple, "Wat Poh," in Bangkok, contains an enormous gilt figure of the dying Buddha, about 160 feet long, constructed of bricks, lacquered and heavily gilt. The huge foot-soles are inlaid with mother-of-pearl figures illustrating stories of Buddha's life. The floor is of tesselated marble. Another great temple,—the "Wat Chang," or Elephant Temple,—has a lofty spire with external decoration in remarkable patterns which at a distance look like mosaics of precious stones, but are in truth nothing but a mixture of broken glass, crockery, and shells. A representation of the three-headed elephant is prominently placed on each of the four façades of this temple.

Cremation.

Cremation is the usual mode of disposing of the dead. Priests pray day and night in the house until the body is removed to the temple-grounds. The interval between death and burial varies according to the rank and wealth of the family; it may even be protracted for months, during which the prayers go on continuously, the coffin being covered with flowers. But the devouring of bodies by vultures and dogs is not at all uncommon.

Newborn children.

The Laos believe that children are the offspring of the spirits; and when newly born, they are placed on the top of the ladder leading to the house, and the spirits are called to take away the child at once or not to molest it afterwards. Various offerings to the spirits are made; and on the second day the child is considered out of their power, and is nominally sold to some relative for a trifle, it being supposed that the spirits would not take what has been thus sold.

The Siamese as a rule have but one wife. The Buddhist priests are called in to the marriage ceremony, read an extract from their scriptures, and pray for a blessing on the pair, who are then sprinkled with holy water. After further prayers and feasting the marriage is complete.

Reformed sects in Siam.

It is significant of possibilities of Buddhist revival, that in Siam in recent years free Buddhist churches have arisen, rejecting the miraculous and mythical elements, and recurring to the pure moral teachings of the founder. The late king gave a powerful support to these churches and their efforts. His foreign minister, Chao Phya Phraklang, wrote "a book explaining many things," showing that much of the popular mythology was not essential to Buddhism, although he retained the belief in Buddha having visited the heavens and taught the angels. He may be called a Buddhist rationalist, teaching a universal morality. Having studied Christianity very carefully, he rejected it, terming it "a foolish religion." His book, as translated by Mr. Alabaster, is worth reading as a specimen of the keen criticism Christian missionaries encounter from educated Buddhists. A brief quotation from a passage relating to the future state will be found of interest. "We observe that some die young, others live to old age; some are born great, others not; some rich, others poor; some beautiful, others ugly; some never suffer illness, others are continually ill, or blind, or deaf, or deformed, or mad. If we say that God made these, we must regard Him as unjust, partial, and ever changing; making those suffer who have never done anything to deserve suffering, and not giving to men in general that average of good and bad fortune which attends even the speculations of the gambler. But if we believe in the interchange and succession of life throughout all beings (*i.e.*, the transmigration of souls), and that good and evil arise from ourselves, and are the effects of merit and demerit, we have some grounds for belief.

"Those who believe that after death the soul passes to hell or heaven for ever, have no proof that there is no return thence. Certainly it would be a most excellent thing to go direct to heaven after death, without further change, but I am afraid that it is not the case. For the believers in it, who have not perfectly purified their hearts, and prepared themselves for that most excellent place, where there is no being born, growing old, and dying, will still have their souls contaminated with uneradicated evil. . . . How is it possible that those who have not cleared away the evil disposition from their soul should attain the most excellent heaven, and live eternally with God the Creator? And of those who are to remain in hell for ever, many have made merit and done much good. Shall that be altogether lost?"

THE THREE PRECIOUS ONES (CHINESE BUDDHISM).

CHAPTER IX.

Modern Buddhism. II.

Tibetan Buddhism—Tibetan Scriptures—Worship of the Triad—The Bodhisatvas—Maitreya—The Dhyani-Buddhas—Buddhist heavens—The Lamas—The Grand Lama—History of Tibetan Buddhism—The Mongol emperors—The Dalai and Panchen Lamas—Succession of Grand Lamas—Great monasteries—The Vatican of Buddhism—Interview with Grand Lama—Tashi Lunpo—Praying by machinery—Prayer cylinders—Prayer walls and flags—Daily worship of monks—Festivals—Fasts—The Papal domain of Buddhism—Chinese Buddhism—Introduction of Buddhism to China—Chinese life of Buddha—Mythical details—Buddhist patriarchs—The Buddhist books translated—Opposition of Confucianists—Bodhidharma—The Mongol emperors—Modern discouragement—Present state—Temples—Images in the halls—Realism of images—Kwan-yin—Anntabha—Halls of 500 saints—Tien-tai—Schools of Chinese Buddhism—The Lin-tsi—Monasteries and monks—Ascetics—Nunneries—Popular aspect—Buddhist calendar—Influence of Buddhism on China—The Do-Nothing Sect—Japanese Buddhism—The Shin-Shin.

TIBETAN BUDDHISM.

THE Buddhism of Tibet may be said to pervade and dominate the national life. The Buddhist leaders practically rule and possess the entire land, paying little more than nominal allegiance to China.[1] Their hierarchy,

[1] See Sir Monier-Williams's "Buddhism"—Edkins's "Chinese Buddhism" and "Religion in China"—Beal's "Chinese Buddhism."

monasteries, ceremonies, and images are repeatedly instanced as the most elaborate parallel which can be found to the Roman Catholic system; and it is certain that Buddhism in Tibet presents an almost complete contrast to the simplicity of Gautama's Order. It did not reach Tibet till the seventh century A.D., when it had already a history of more than a thousand years behind it, and had gained predominance in Kashmir and Nepal. The Tibetans, like other Mongoloid peoples, had a Shamanistic nature worship, with much magic and sorcery and dread of spirits; and it is little doubtful that their previous beliefs largely influenced the modification which Buddhism underwent.

Tibetan Scriptures.

We will first give some notion of the developments which the central doctrines of Buddhism underwent in the Tibetan Scriptures. The Triad, Buddha, the Law or Doctrine, and the Order had already become venerated, and we find that Fa-hien on his travels committed himself to the Order as a sort of personality, invoking it by its "dread and supernatural power." Images of Buddha became common, and at a later period the Law and the Order began to be symbolised among the northern peoples. The Law is now often represented as a man (a woman in Sikkim) with four arms, two hands folded in worship, or raised, a third holding a book or a lotus, the fourth a rosary or a garland; but the Law is in some cases only represented by a book. The Order is depicted as a man with one hand holding a lotus, and the other lying on his knees. Strangely enough, the order of arrangement of these three representative figures is not uniform.

Worship of the Triad.

The Bodhi-satvas.

The next further development of Buddhism was connected with Gautama's Bodhi-satva state. Before he was born on earth, he was believed to have last existed in a state of self-enlightened knowledge as a Bodhi-satva, and to have voluntarily chosen to become a saviour of the world before attaining the Nirvana to which he was entitled. He led his followers to look for the advent of another Buddha, now a Bodhi-satva, known as Maitreya, "the compassionate one," after 5,000 years, when Gautama should have been forgotten and the Law no longer obeyed. At present he is believed to preside in the heaven of contented beings and to watch over all Buddhists and their interests. Inasmuch as he lives and is the future Buddha, not merely one who has passed away, he has become an object of worship and prayer. Huen-Siang reported that it was said, "No words can describe the personal beauty of Maitreya. He declares a law not different from ours. His exquisite voice is soft and pure." And his worshippers look forward to attaining his heaven and listening to his voice.

Maitreya.

Beyond this, the memory of the leading disciples of Buddha and those who became prominent later for their holy life, ability, or zeal in propagating the faith, was in process of time exalted into what could only be properly compared with canonisation or almost deification. Also an idea grew up that there were self-dependent solitary Buddhas and many Bodhi-satvas. The Great Vehicle or Maha-yana teaches that there will be numberless supreme Buddhas, Bodhi-satvas and solitary Buddhas, who will attain their position by their virtues and wisdom; and these Bodhi-satvas are represented as enjoying heaven indefinitely without aiming at Nirvana. In fact, the Tibetan idea is, that these Buddhas and saints only descend in their corporeal emanations upon earth, much like the avatars of the Hindu gods, being incorporate in a succession of saints. Naturally they are much reverenced, as they are believed to raise their worshippers to the blissful heaven where they abide. Thus did Buddhism give promise of heavens which were attainable, and throw into the background the far-distant Nirvana.

Solitary Buddhas.

In the third century three Bodhi-satvas were worshipped in Northern India besides Maitreya. At first protectors of Buddha, they were gradually credited with the function of watching over all Buddhists. The first, Avalokitesvara, the lord that looks down (with pity), is in Tibet regarded as a sort of supreme spirit, who, while remaining ever in heaven, becomes incarnated in successive Grand Lamas. He presides over the temporal well-being of all human beings, ghosts, and animal spirits. He is termed "God of mercy," "Lord of the world," etc., and is prayed to very frequently in bodily danger or disease, as well as for relief from future re-birth. He is generally depicted with several faces and arms, the former pyramidally placed in three tiers, two hands folded in adoration of Buddha, and two others holding the lotus and the wheel. Often he greatly resembles Vishnu. Vajra-pani (the thunderbolt-handed) is a sort of Buddhist Siva, controlling and destroying evil spirits; while Manjusri (he of glorious beauty) is possibly a deification of the Brahman who introduced Buddhism into Nepal.

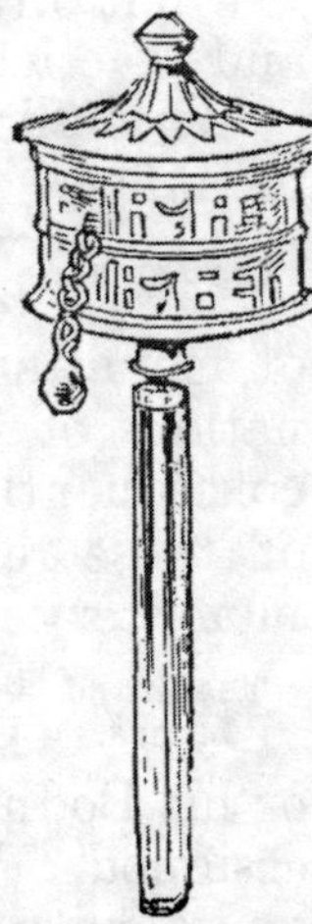

TIBETAN PRAYER WHEEL.

The Dhyani-Buddhas.

Later still a new mystical worship arose, worshipping the Dhyani-Buddhas, or Buddhas existing in the higher worlds of abstract meditation, corresponding to the earthly Buddhas and representing them. Each of these was supposed to give off a Dhyani Bodhi-satva, to preside over and protect Buddhism between the death of one Buddha and the coming of the next; and before long, the Dhyani-Buddha corresponding to Gautama, namely Amitabha (diffuser of infinite light), was worshipped as a personal god. Some of the Nepalese Buddhists developed a still more advanced theory of a primordial or Adi-Buddha, the source of all things, out of whom the Dhyani-Buddhas proceeded, and corresponding to the Hindu supreme Brahma. But neither Adi-Buddha nor Amitabha were regarded as creators of the world out of nothing.

Buddhist heavens.

The elaborate descriptions of the twenty-six successive Buddhist heavens, in which many of the Hindu gods were fabled to dwell and reign, we cannot reproduce. Six are inhabited by beings still liable to sensuous desires; sixteen by those in successive stages of abstract meditation, called the worlds of the

Brahma gods, and Brahma rules there, but yet is greatly inferior to Buddha. All these gods have to pass into a new form of existence after vast periods of time. Finally, there are four heavens of formless beings. All their mythology, though departing enormously from primitive Buddhism, does not violate the view that Buddhist Arhats (saints) and Buddhas are ranked above all the popular divinities. We need not enlarge upon other additions to Buddhism from Hinduism, and also from popular beliefs in demons, spirits of animals, nature spirits, sorcery, and magic. These additions are abundant, and rise but little, if at all, above the corresponding ideas and practices among savage races.

We shall not detail the inferior gradations of the Tibetan monkhood, but pass on at once to the superior monks, who are rightfully termed Lamas, or superior teachers, and are, like European abbots, heads of monasteries. Some of these are believed to be incarnations of deceased saints and Bodhi-satvas; they are consequently termed Avatara Lamas. The lowest grade of these represents a saint or the founder of a great monastery; the second grade is a living emanation of a Bodhi-satva; while the highest or Grand Lama is an incarnation of a supreme Buddha or his Bodhi-satva; to them a wide range of authority is assigned. There is also a female hierarchy in the convents, with its female avatars.

The Lamas.

The Grand Lamas.

To understand the Tibetan system, we must sketch in brief its history. The first monasteries were founded at Lhassa in honour of two princesses, wives of the Tibetan king who introduced Buddhism. In the eighth century the translation of the enlarged (Maha-yana) canon of Buddhist scriptures into Tibetan was begun. It extended to 108 volumes (forming the Kanjur), and was followed by 225 volumes of commentaries and general literature, known as the Tanjur. After several fluctuations, in the latter part of the eleventh century Buddhism again revived, under the influence of Atisha from Kashmir and Brom Ton, a Tibetan. Many monasteries were founded in that and

History of Tibetan Buddhism.

the next centuries, those at Sakya and Raseng being the most important. Raseng, founded by Brom Ton in 1058, was devoted to the strict rules of Buddhism (the yellow sect); Sakya was more lax, and became the headquarters of the red sect, many of whom were married before becoming monks. In the thirteenth century the power of the Mongols spread over Tibet. Kublai Khan adopted Buddhism and greatly favoured the Tibet monks. Already great authority had gathered round the chiefs of the Sakya and the Raseng monasteries, and Kublai exerted his authority to appoint the nephew of the ruler of the Sakya monastery to succeed his uncle, and made him a tributary ruler over Tibet. In return for his authority, he and his successors were required to crown the Mongol emperors. This first Grand Avatara Lama, known as Phuspa Lama, devised the Mongol alphabet, started a revision of the Tibetan Buddhist texts, which prepared the way for their translation into Mongolian, and founded many monasteries. When the Ming dynasty supplanted the Mongols in China, they continued to favour the Tibetan Lamas, but raised three other chief Lamas to similar rank. At the end of the fourteenth century there arose a reformer, Tsong Khapa, who, after studying the originals of the Buddhist scriptures in Tibet, raised again the standard of orthodoxy, and gathered round him many thousand monks of the strict yellow sect; he built and became the first head of a great monastery at Galdan, and his followers built others. He wrote many books, restored celibacy, abolished many superstitious forms of worship, and renewed the practice of retirement for meditation at a fixed season, which had not been kept up in Tibet owing to its lack of a rainy season. After his death in 1419 (since celebrated at the Feast of Lamps, as his ascension to heaven), he was reverenced as an incarnation of Amitabha, Manju-sri, or Vajra-pani, and his image is still seen in temples of the yellow sect, with those of the Dalai and Panchen Lamas on the right and left. Since his time (though it cannot be precisely traced) there has arisen the practice of discovering each new

The Mongol emperors.

The Dalai and Panchen Lamas.

incarnation in an infant, probably to avoid discussions and competition. At any rate, at present there are two Grand Lamas: one the Dalai or Ocean Lama, at Lhassa, the other the Tashi or Panchen Lama at Tashi Lunpo, not far from the British Indian frontier. The former is believed to be an incarnation of the Dhyani-Bodhi-satva Avalokitesvara, the latter of his father or Dhyani-Buddha, Amitabha; but the Dalai Lama is by far the most powerful, or rather his representative, an elected chief Lama who attends to business, while the Dalai himself is supposed to be lost in divine meditation, and receives the reverence and worship due to his character and origin. There appear to have been various modes of keeping up the succession, viz., by the dying Lama stating in what family he would again become incarnate, or by consulting sacred books and soothsayers, or by the Panchen Lama interpreting the traditions and discovering the new Dalai Lama, and *vice versâ.* Now-a-days the Chinese court has a predominant influence in choosing new Grand Lamas. Yet all the forms of divination, signs, choice by lot, etc., are gone through; and similar proceedings take place in the election of all Lamas in whom saints are supposed to be incarnated. The same is the case in various Mongolian monasteries. When the choice has been made, the child is brought before a great assembly of the monks, and is expected to recognise clothes, books, etc., belonging to the deceased Lama, and to answer questions as to his former life as Lama. Among the chief Lamas may be mentioned those of Galdan (where the body of Tsong Khapa is said to be still visible poised in the air, and uncorrupt), Kurun in Mongolia, Kuku in Tartary, the Dharma-rajah of Bhutan, and the Grand Lama of Peking. The Dharma-rajah of Bhutan, belonging to the Red sect, has for his titles: "Chief of the realm, Defender of the Faith, Equal to Sarasvati in learning, Chief of all the Buddhas, Head-expounder of the Shastras, Caster out of devils, Most learned in the holy laws, an Avatar of God, Absolver of sins, and Head of the best of all religions."

Succession of Grand Lamas.

While in many parts of northern Buddhistic countries

the monasteries are small buildings near or combined with a chapel or temple, in Tibet, Mongolia, and Ladak there are many immense monasteries

Great monasteries.

BUDDHIST MONASTERY IN TIBET.

or Lamasseries, often in retired and lofty situations, but also aggregated about great centres such as Lhassa and Tashi Lunpo. About 500,000 monks owe allegiance to these two capitals, and there are at least thirty large monasteries in and near Lhassa. Potala, on the north-west of Lhassa, has been the abode of all the Dalai Lamas since the fifth, Navang Lobsang (1617–1682), who rebuilt it. This great building, four storeys high, on a commanding height, has in or connected with it ten thousand rooms for monks. Everywhere are statues of Buddha and other saints, and varied offerings of the pious, who throng to Lhassa to pay their worship to the Grand Lama, with gifts of gold, silver, and copper. The great building is surmounted by a cupola overlaid with gold.

The Vatican of Buddhism.

Thomas Manning is the only Englishman who has ever seen a Dalai Lama; this was on the 17th December, 1811. He described him as a cheerful, intelligent child of seven. Mr. Sarat Chandra Das, C.I.E., saw the present Dalai Lama in 1882. The interview was conducted with impressive silence and dignity by the high officials. Consecrated water coloured yellow with saffron was sprinkled on the company; incense, great lamps, and a yellow hat with five points (denoting the five Dhyani-Buddhas) are important elements in the ceremonial, which is not complete without all sharing tea with the Lama from a golden teapot, preceded by a grace in proper Buddhist form, and concluding thus: "Never even for a moment losing sight of the three Holies (Buddha, the Law, and the Order); always offer reverence to the Tri-ratnas (or three jewels); let the blessings of the three be upon us." Consecrated rice, touched by the Grand Lama, was distributed to the faithful. The sacred youth sat all through the ceremony cross-legged on a throne-like altar with wooden lions on either side.

Interview with Grand Lama.

It is said that Lhassa almost vies with Benares and Mecca as a place of pilgrimage, Potala, the Vatican of Buddhism, being the great resort; and the rice, the pills of blessing, the scraps of silk, and the prayer-papers or flags which the Grand Lama has consecrated, are treasured for life.

Tashi Lunpo, with its great monastery of the Panchen

Lama, has been much more frequently visited by Europeans. This monastery is much more varied, consisting of several hundred distinct houses, surrounded by pinnacled gilded temples and topes. It is, however, in connection with the oldest monastery—Labrang in Lhassa—that the greatest temple of Buddhism in Tibet is to be found. It is three storeys high, with a portico and colonnade of huge wooden pillars. Opposite the entrance are the usual great statues of the four great kings; beyond is a long oblong hall, like a basilica, with rows of columns dividing it into three longitudinal divisions, with two transepts. The walls contain no windows, but across the central division or nave is stretched transparent oil-cloth, which is the only mode of admission of daylight to the building. A row of small chapels flanks each side of the long building. In the transepts are seats for the monks, and beyond the second is a sanctuary with an altar for offerings; at the extreme west end, in a special recess, is a grand altar with many steps, and on the summit is the revered gilt image of Gautama Buddha, respecting the origin of which various stories are told. On the upper steps of the altar are many images of deified saints; and the temple contains very many images and pictures of Buddha, saints and deities, as well as relics. In front of this altar are lofty thrones for the Dalai and Panchen Lamas, flanked by smaller ones for the other Avatar Lamas; seats of less dignity are provided for the heads of monasteries and higher orders of monks in the western transept. Five thousand oil lamps give light, and the muttering of the chief Buddhist formula goes on continually. Tibetan temples are usually much smaller than this; the chief features are altars with images of Buddha and the Bodhisatvas, bowls for offerings, bells, etc.

Tashi Lunpo.

The Tibetan Buddhists have outdone every other race in one respect; that is, in praying by machinery. Impressed with the importance of accumulating religious merit as a means of shortening their stay in lower forms of life, and accelerating their entrance to heaven, they not only orally repeat multitudes of

Praying by machinery.

times the "jewel" formula, which has acquired such vogue among them, but they get it repeated by turning machines or extending flags to the wind, in or on which the sacred formula is written. This formula consists merely of the sentence, "Om mani padme Hum." The first syllable is the Hindu sacred syllable; the next two words mean, "the Jewel in the Lotus," an allusion, it is said, to Avalo-kitesvara as the patron of Tibet appearing from or seated on a Lotus. The last syllable is regarded by some as an Amen. The whole formula is thought by Sir Monier-Williams to have some relation to Hindu Siva-worship, and, he says, "no other prayer used by human beings in any quarter of the globe is repeated so often. Every Tibetan believes it to be a panacea for all evil, a compendium of all knowledge, a treasury of all wisdom, a summary of all religion." Each of its syllables is believed to influence one of the six courses or stages of transmigration through which all must pass, diminishing his stay in them, or in time abolishing it altogether.

Prayer cylinders.

The favourite prayer cylinders are of metal, having the mystic invocation engraved on the outside, while the cavity is filled with paper in rolls, on which it is written as many times as possible. This cylinder can be made to revolve on a handle, and is whirled in the hand, or rotated by a chain or string. "All day long," says Capt. Gill in "The River of Golden Sand," "not only the Lamas, but the people may be seen muttering the universal prayer, and twisting their cylinders, invariably in the same direction with the hands of a clock. One or more great cylinders, inscribed with this sentence, stand at the entrance to every house in Tibet; and a member of the household or a guest who passes is always expected to give the cylinder a twist for the welfare of the establishment. At almost every rivulet the eye is arrested by a little building that is at first mistaken for a water mill, but which on close inspection is found to contain a cylinder, turning by the force of the stream, and ceaselessly sending up pious ejaculations to heaven; for every turn of a cylinder on which the prayer is written is supposed to convey an invocation to the deity. Sometimes enormous barns are filled with these cylinders, gorgeously painted, and with the prayer repeated on them many times; and at every turn and every step in Tibet this sentence is forced upon the traveller's notice in some form or another."

Prayer walls and flags.

Another variety of praying ingenuity is the erection of long walls inscribed with any number of this and other invocations, by which travellers who walk in the proper direction gain the credit of so many

EMBLEM OF DHARMA (THE LAW), AT SANCHI (BUDDHIST).

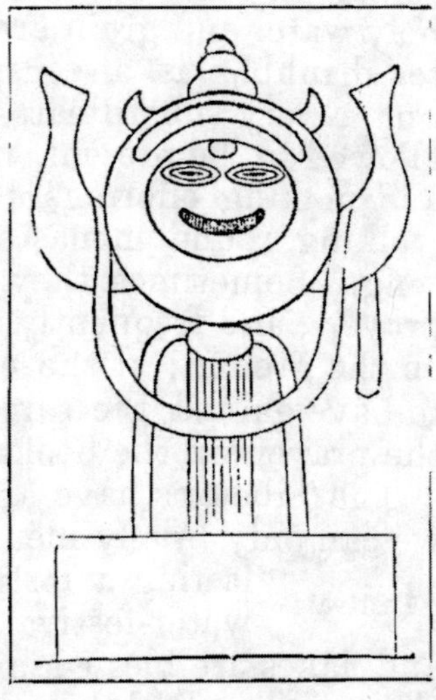

EMBLEM OF DHARMA, TEMPLE OF JAGANNATH, PURI.

repetitions. Praying-flags, with prayers and symbols, extended by every wind, praying drums which frighten away evil spirits, bells which have the same function, or which call the attention of the deities or saints, armlets with sacred sentences or relics inside, and various other objects, are among the "properties" greatly used in Tibetan Buddhism, while the rosary for counting the number of repetitions of prayer is a more familiar object in Tibet than even in Roman Catholic countries.

The monks of the Tibetan monasteries meet in their

temple or chapel three times a day for worship: at sunrise, midday, and sunset. They are summoned by a loud conch-shell trumpet, and enter in procession. A bell gives the signal to commence repeating or chanting prayer formulas, passages of the Law, litanies, etc., often with noisy musical accompaniments. The ritual is varied by each monk repeating a sentence in turn, the recital of the praises and titles of honour of Buddha or one of the Bodhi-satvas. When one of the Grand Lamas is present, the service is very elaborate. Incense and perfumes are burnt, and at times holy water and grain are distributed. In some ceremonies tea-drinking is a conspicuous element. Laymen play but a very subordinate part in these services. They are allowed to be present, repeating prayers and invocations and making offerings; they may also acquire merit by walking round monasteries, temples, etc., without stopping. Sometimes they carry loads of books containing prayers, and frequently prostrate themselves at full length on the ground; at the end of their journey they are held to have gained the same merit as if they had recited all the prayers in the books they carried.

Daily worship of monks.

The Tibetans have a number of special festivals which we can only briefly mention. The new year's celebration, lasting a fortnight, is a sort of carnival; at the water-festival in August or September, rivers and lakes are blessed, and the people bathe to wash away their sins. Buddha's birthday and the anniversary of his death are very important days; on the latter, every monastery and temple, and every house in Lhassa is darkened with the burning of incense. The festival of lamps, the ascent of Tsong Khapa to heaven; and days of spirit-hunting and performances of religious dramas, are among the diversified holidays of Tibet. Periods of fasting, especially before the great festivals, are observed by the devout. Of course these are more observed by the monks of the yellow sect. One of these periods of fasting lasts four days, during which the monks confess their faults and meditate on the evils of demerit. On the third day no food whatever is taken,

Festivals.

Fasts.

THE CALL TO WORSHIP IN A BUDDHIST MONASTERY.

and not even the saliva must be swallowed; not a word is spoken, and each monk is engaged without intermission in silent prayer and confession. Many monks keep the four holy days of each month as fast days.

The Papal domain of Buddhism.

Tibet, then, is the Papal domain of Buddhism. Some lamasseries are enormously rich. They own half the country, constantly receive legacies, and even grow rich by usury. No taxes are paid by them, and their own lands are attended to by large numbers of slaves. Many of the monks do not keep their vows of celibacy, and the common people are said in their hearts to detest the Lamas for their oppression. Whether this is generally true or not, every rational mind will agree that Tibetan Buddhism is by no means an unmixed good.

CHINESE BUDDHISM.

The influence of Buddhism in China is still great, though not as extensive as formerly, owing to the loss of the patronage of the emperors; but it exists in a considerably modified form. "The worship of Pu-sah," says Dr. Beal, "in the houses of the rich and poor, is hardly recognised as Buddhist in its origin; and, indeed, the very term Pu-sah, which is the Chinese form of Bodhisatva, is explained as of native origin, and signifying 'universal benevolence,' whilst the objects of Buddhist worship, such as the Goddess of Mercy and the Queen of Heaven, have been placed among the number of their genii." Also the images of Pu-sah are to be found in the houses of many officials and others who would deny that they were Buddhists.

Introduction of Buddhism to China.

Chinese Buddhism dates from A.D. 61, when the Emperor Ming-ti is said to have had a dream in which he saw a golden figure of a god hovering over his palace. He inquired of one of his ministers what this could mean, and was told that a divine person named Buddha had been born in the West, and that his dream was probably connected with him. The emperor in consequence sent a mission to India to obtain books and news concerning this person. They returned in A.D. 67, with two Buddhist monks, together with various books, pictures, and relics. The emperor listened to them readily, and had a temple built for them in his capital Loyang (now Honan-fu). The narrative of these events includes various miracles worked by the Buddhists in proof of their religion.

Chinese life of Buddha.

The short life of Buddha which these priests introduced and translated into Chinese is of special interest, for, as we have seen, no separate life of Buddha exists in the southern canon. In the Chinese life he is generally termed Sakyamuni, the Sakya sage, and his proper name, Gautama, is scarcely mentioned. This title, Sakyamuni, seems to have been more acceptable to the northern Buddhists, because of the belief that the name Sakya was like that of a prominent Central Asian people, the Sacæ or Scythians; and this name has been adopted as the title of the Chinese Buddhists (Shih-kian or Shih-tsen).

Mythical details.

It would be most interesting, if we had space, to give an account of the life of Buddha as depicted in Chinese books. Previous Buddhas, appearing through enormously long ages, are named; and the Buddha of the present age (Sakyamuni) is said to have gone through a number of stages of elevation in previous ages. At last, in the age immediately before the present one, Sakya became a Bodhi-satva, was born in the Tushita heaven, and finally descended to earth on a white elephant with six tusks. The narratives which follow, while explicable as consistent with the life we have already given, are overlaid with much exaggeration and myth. The life is arranged so as to explain the origin and scenes of the very numerous books of the northern canon. Thus at one time Sakya is instructing the Bodhi-satvas; at another he is in the heavens of the Hindu gods, teaching Indra, Yama, etc. All this serves as a scene for the development of the Bodhi-satva mythology. After long abstinence and meditation, and severe temptation by the king of the Maras, Sakyamuni became a perfect Buddha (*i.e.*, in Chinese phrase, from being Pu-sa became Fo). In order to convey the truth to men simply, and as they could receive it, he assumed the guise of an ascetic, preached the four primary truths, established the order of monks, and sent them out to propagate his doctrine. He is afterwards said to have subdued a fierce snake and to have made him take the vows of the order; to have resisted the fiercest temptations of the king of the Maras, and to have gone to the Tushita heaven to instruct his mother Maya. Then followed the reception of his son Rahula and other boys as novices, the admission of women, the establishment of discipline, etc. Sakya is said to have gone to Ceylon himself, to have visited the middle heavens, to have secured the gods (devas) as protectors of his doctrine, to have sent Visvakarma and fifteen daughters of devas to be the patrons of China. He instituted the daily service and ordained honour for his books. In his last days he gave forth his most perfect works, "The Lotus of the Good Law" and "Nirvana," intended to make his disciples long for higher attainments. This was his meaning, say the Chinese Buddhist authors, when he said, "I am not to be destroyed, but shall be constantly on the mountain of instruction." Buddha, entering Nirvana, is not dead, but lives in his teaching. Before his death he is said to have had presented to him images of himself of gold and sandal-wood, which he consecrated, giving his disciples in charge to them. At this time also he forbade the eating of animal food. His death and cremation were attended by marvels too numerous to mention.

Buddhist patriarchs.

In the Chinese records we are introduced to a long series of Buddhist patriarchs, the successive chiefs and defenders of Buddhist law and discipline, each selected by the last patriarch, the first being Maha Kashiapa, appointed by Buddha. A patriarch, says Dr. Edkins, is represented as "one who does not look at evil and dislike it; nor does he, when he sees that which is good, make a strong effort to attain it. He does not put wisdom aside and approach folly; nor does he fling away delusion and aim at comprehending truth. Yet he has an acquaintance with great truths which is beyond being measured, and he penetrates into Buddha's mind to a depth that cannot be fathomed." Such an one had magical powers, could fly through the air, go into trances, and penetrate men's thoughts. Nevertheless he lived poorly, and was meanly clad. Thirty-three of these are named, including five Chinese patriarchs, and their biography is given.

The Buddhist books translated.

From the foundation of Chinese Buddhism a succession of western Buddhist monks and learned men came to China and undertook great labours of translation and preaching to propagate their doctrines. In the fourth century the Chinese were entering the Order by permission of a Chow prince, many pagodas were erected in Loyang, and considerable monasteries were built in North China. Many of the Buddhist teachers professed to work miracles, and certainly dealt in magic. Chinese Buddhist pilgrims visited India and other Buddhist countries, and brought back accounts of marvels they had seen (as, for instance, Fa-hien and Huen-siang). Early in the fifth century Kumarajiva, an Indian Buddhist, assisted by eight hundred priests, produced a new translation of the Buddhist books into Chinese, extending to three hundred volumes.

Opposition of Confucianists.

After this time the rulers of China became for a time hostile to Buddhism; but this was soon reversed, and there was much intercourse between Buddhist princes in India and China. Monasteries and temples multiplied, and magic and wonders, as fostered by the books of the Greater Vehicle, overlaid the original faith. At various times Chinese emperors, followed by their people, combined more or less of Confucianism and Taoism with Buddhism, and seldom prohibited any of them. At various periods the Confucianists sought to put down the Buddhists, to make the monks and nuns marry, etc., and decrees were promulgated against them; and sometimes their property was confiscated and they were compelled to return to secular life. Side by side with religious changes, Hindu Buddhists introduced many improvements in Chinese orthography, science, and literature.

The twenty-eighth Indian Buddhist patriarch, Bodhidharma, visited China in the sixth century, and died there. He exalted meditation at the expense of reading and book knowledge, allowing no merit either to these or to the building of temples. In his view true merit consisted in "purity and enlightenment, depth and completeness, and in being wrapped in thought while surrounded by vacancy and stillness." His influence in China, where he died, was powerful enough to make his followers a distinct sect of contemplatists, as contrasted with the ascetics and the ordinary temple-monks. His sect gradually became the most influential; and it appears to have distinctly weakened the looking for a future life and retribution, by exalting self-reform as to be brought about solely by inward contemplation. Not long after his death a monk of Tien-tai, named Chi-kai, invented a system which combined contemplation with image-worship, and it gradually gained great popularity, his books being after some centuries reckoned among the classics of Chinese Buddhism.

Bodhidharma.

The history of Chinese Buddhism in the middle ages presents a continual series of assaults by Confucianists, alternate persecutions and support by emperors, and frequent interference. Certain temples were destroyed and others exalted; certain monasteries and temples were transferred from one kind of worship to another, from one sect of Buddhists to another; and all the time the emperors did not ostensibly become Buddhists. The Mongol emperors, however, especially Kublai Khan, became decided Buddhists, and used the Chinese imperial temples for Buddhist worship. Towards the end of the thirteenth century a census stated that there were over 42,000 Buddhist temples and 213,000 monks in China, which implies a very great number of lay adherents. After the fall of the Mongols some restrictions were gradually imposed on the Buddhists; and the Sacred Edict, issued in 1662, and still read periodically in public, blames them for fixing their attention on their individual minds alone, and for inventing baseless tales about future happiness and misery. Thus Buddhism is officially dis-

The Mongol emperors.

Modern discouragements.

countenanced, although in Mongolia and Tibet the Chinese encourage and pay deference to it; and in China itself the worship and festivals continue to be very largely attended, although the building of new temples has to a large extent fallen off.

Chinese Buddhism at the present day is so extensive

TWO OF THE GUARDIANS OF BUDDHA. KUSHAN MONASTERY, NEAR FOO-CHOW.

Present state.

and varied that it is only possible to glance at its leading features. In many ways it occupies much the same standpoint as in Tibet; and the Chinese monk takes refuge in Buddha, the Law, and the Order, like his Singhalese brother. The worship of Buddha still remains, in a considerably materialised form; but image-worship is by no means held to be essential by instructed Buddhists, though it is allowed by them for the ignorant and weak. But added to this worship is that of a great number of associated and inferior beings, making Chinese Buddhism at present practically a complex polytheism. Its public attitude may be gathered from an account of the temples and services.

Looking south, like so many Chinese buildings, the temples of the Chinese Buddhists consist of a series of halls, the vestibule being guarded by the same four great kings mentioned at p. 213, carved in wood, and dressed and equipped with various symbols, such as a sword, an umbrella, a snake, or some other object with a well-defined significance to Orientals. They give all kinds of blessings to true Buddhists, and withdraw their favour from kings and nations which neglect the truth. Maitreya (Mi-li Fo) also appears in the same entrance-hall; sometimes even Confucius has an image here, as protector of the Buddhist religion.

Temples.

The great hall opening from the entrance-hall contains the images of Buddha, the Six Bodhi-satvas, Ananda, and many saints, in various symbolical attitudes, Wen-shu and Pu-hien often being placed right and left of Buddha, while Kwan-yin is behind them looking northward. Sometimes Buddha is alone in front, and the other three are in a row behind him. Kwan-yin appears in numerous forms in pictures and sculptures; in one he is represented by a female figure presenting an infant to mothers praying for children. Other halls may be added to the principal ones, containing statues, sculptured scenes, and pictures. The large central hall, according to Dr. Edkins, is intended to symbolise Buddha giving instruction to an assembly of disciples, while the leading idea of the entrance-hall is to show the powerful protection by celestial beings which Buddhists enjoy. All this is in agreement with the narratives in the "Greater Vehicle." There may be many subordinate chapels, dedicated to Bodhi-satvas and other beings of Buddhist, Hindu, and Chinese mythology. The images

Images in the halls.

of the Pu-sa or Bodhi-satvas stand when in the presence of Buddha, but sit when in their own shrines. Even the Taoist images are admitted into the all-comprehending Buddhist temples, as well as those of celebrated Chinese Buddhists.

In North China, especially at Pekin, it is customary, whether the images are of brass, iron, wood, or clay, to make them with internal organs as complete as possible, according to Chinese notions, which are not very correct; but the heads are always empty. Surrounding the abdominal organs is a large piece of silk covered with prayers or charms, while within it are bags containing small pieces of gold, silver, and pearls, and the five chief kinds of grain; but many of these valuables have been stolen from the images.

Realism of images.

While the more intellectual Buddhists explain their temples and images as purely symbolical, and their offerings, bowings, etc., as expressing reverential reception of Buddha's teaching, the common people regard the images as deities, and pray to them for deliverance from sickness, sufferings, childlessness, poverty, etc. Kwan-yin is very exclusively worshipped, being commonly known as the goddess of mercy, who hears the cries of men. This worship is always associated with that of Amitabha (O-me-to), the father of Kwan-yin, and they are believed to dwell in the happy (western) land of Sukhavati. Those born in this paradise have only unmixed joys, of which gorgeous descriptions are given. This heaven has taken a strong hold of the imagination of Chinese Buddhists, and they will repeat the name "Amita Buddh" incessantly, while counting their beads. It is possible, and is strongly held by some, that some of the ideas of this worship, especially of the Litany of Kwan-yin, were derived from Persian, Arab, and Jewish sources. It is a wide-spread belief that Kwan-yin, moved by infinite compassion, has promised to become manifest in all the innumerable worlds, to save their inhabitants. He also visited all the hells for this purpose: and detailed accounts of his visits and their beneficial results are given. There are special elaborate

Kwan-yin.

services in which Kwan-yin is worshipped and invoked, while at the same time Buddha and the other Bodhisatvas are duly honoured. One prayer runs thus: "May the all-seeing and all-powerful Kwan-yin, in virtue of her vow, come hither to us as we recite the sentences and remove from us the three obstacles (of impure thought, word, and deed)." Professor Beal gives the following translation from the Chinese of the confession or "act of faith" in Kwan-yin:—

> "All hail, good, compassionate Kwan-yin!
> Though I were thrown on the Mountain of Knives,
> They should not hurt me;
> Though cast into the lake of fire,
> It should not burn me;
> Though surrounded by famished ghosts,
> They should not touch me;
> Though exposed to the power of devils,
> They should not reach me;
> Though changed into a beast,
> Yet should I rise to heaven.
> All hail, compassionate Kwan-yin."

Incense is burnt, flowers and food are offered, and invocations are repeated again and again to Kwan-yin and Amitabha, with appropriate readings from the sacred books, some of them in Sanskrit and unintelligible alike to priests and people, but supposed to have a magic effect.

Amitabha. The distinctive worship of Amitabha is practised by many, both in China and Japan; they are called the "pure land" sect, who rely on Amitabha to effect their entrance to the bright paradise. The mere repetition of the name with concentrated and undivided attention is believed to ensure paradise; he is also invoked by the form "Praise to Amita Buddha," and the most extravagant promises are made to those who rightly invoke him. This is the prevailing form of Buddhist worship in many parts of China, and it is very popular owing to its putting out of sight Nirvana and presenting a heaven of conscious happiness and joy to the believer.

At the temple Pi-yun-si, west of Pekin, there is a hall of 500 departed saints, arrayed in six parallel galleries; the figures are of clay, full-sized, and seated. In another

TEMPLE OF FIVE HUNDRED GODS, CANTON.

court are scenes from the imagined future state, all modelled in clay, showing the fate both of the good and the evil. These halls are in addition to the usual elaborate series of halls. Pagodas also form part of this great establishment. Similar halls are numerous in the Tien-tai district.

Halls of 500 saints.

Music is much used in Chinese Buddhist worship, the instruments including drums, small and large bells, cymbals, and various metal forms struck by clappers which have no analogy in western music.

Dr. Edkins admits that while the populace believe in the extravagant details of mythology or magic, the priests in the services still read the old passages from the Buddhist books which teach the nothingness of everything; so that, if fully exposed, the most utter contrasts would be found in any of their services.

One of the most famous Buddhist regions of China is Tien-tai, a cluster of hills 180 miles south-east of Hangcheu. It came into note through Chi-kai, who in the sixth century founded his school of contemplative Buddhism there, imagining its grand natural scenery to be the residence of the great saints of Buddhism, the Arhats or Lohans; indeed, he heard them sing near the remarkable rock bridge over a cataract, and now they are represented by five hundred small stone figures at the side of the bridge. Here Chi-kai developed an elaborate comment on and development of Buddhism, which he called "perfected observation." He explained everything as an embodiment of Buddha, subtly getting rid of all the objects of popular belief. He taught his followers various forms of meditation, which his followers have maintained, while not entirely condemning popular belief, nor going to the extreme of Buddhist agnosticism. At the present day monasteries are to be found five miles apart throughout the Tien-tai hill country.

Tien-tai.

Besides this there are numerous important "schools" of Chinese Buddhism, named from prominent teachers, from whom the present heads of monasteries claim continuous succession. Their doctrines for the most part do not differ widely from one

Schools of Chinese Buddhism.

another, but great importance is attached to minutiæ. The Lin-tsi school was founded by a teacher who died in 868, and had a great reputation for magical powers; it is now very widely spread in China and in Japan. It teaches that Buddha is within the believer if he only be recognised. "What is Buddha? A mind pure and at rest. What is the law? A mind clear and enlightened. What is Tao? In every place absence of impediments and pure enlightenment. These three are one." Discipline is strictly maintained by means of three blows with the hand or with the cane, three successive reproofs, and the alternation of speech with silence. We cannot particularise the other varied schools of Chinese Buddhism, but they are as numerous as the principal dissenting bodies in England.

The Lin-tsi.

The monasteries need not be particularly described, after what we have said of Buddhist monasteries in other countries. They all have a temple or worship-hall attached. Most of the larger establishments own land or other property, but not often sufficient for all expenses, which are met by mendicant expeditions, the offerings of worshippers, and voluntary presents sent to them. The procession of monks walks through the streets to receive alms beating a gong or cymbal at intervals, and often reciting Buddhist formulæ. The monks dress very differently from the Chinese people. In officiating they usually wear yellow garments of silk or cotton, with a wide turn-down collar and huge sleeves; at other times their clothes are mostly of an ashy grey. Their heads are closely shaven two or three times a month, and many have one or more places on the scalp burnt with red-hot coals. Their celibacy appears to be strict, and they do not own any relationships in the outside world, and show very little sociability in their intercourse with the people. They spend much of their time in chanting their sacred books, mostly in a form which represents the sound without the sense of the Hindu or Tibetan originals. Some monasteries keep their large bells constantly tolled day and night, so that the sound never ceases.

Monasteries and monks.

A large monastery has numerous rooms devoted to specific uses, including a library, study, reception-rooms for distinguished guests, and a place for keeping living animals, not for food, but as a work of merit. Sometimes there is a fish-pond full of fine fish which must not be caught or eaten. Special provision is made for cattle, swine, goats, fowls, etc., many being deposited by lay people in fulfilment of a vow, together with money or grain to support them until their death. The monks professedly refuse all animal food, but it is believed that some transgress. On the whole, the mass of the Chinese do not highly reverence the Buddhist monks, because they transgress the principles of filial obedience so deeply rooted among them; but they are nevertheless much employed to conduct private religious ceremonies, whether on behalf of recently deceased persons, those suffering in hells, or the sick and infirm. Frequently the succession of novices in the monasteries is kept up by the purchase of boys from their parents.

BUDDHIST NUN, WITH CAP AND ROSARY.

Within the monastery ranks there are frequently ascetics who for years together have no intercourse with the outside world, but sit in constant silent meditation in their cells, receiving their food through a hole in the door. Usually the bodies of deceased monks are burned in a special cremation-building, the ashes and unconsumed bones being afterwards collected and deposited, in an earthen vessel, in a special room or building of the monastery.

Ascetics.

There are numerous Buddhist nunneries in China, under the especial patronage of Kwan-yin, and while many join them of their own accord, others are bought when young girls. The nuns shave the whole head like the men, do not compress their feet, and wear a very similar costume to the monks. Some learn to read the Buddhist books, and attend upon those who worship at the temples. They also visit the sick and afflicted, and pay special attention to those who place themselves under their spiritual care. Although they have taken a vow of celibacy, the nuns are generally accused of breaking it, as in Tibet; and in some districts the Chinese officials have closed all nunneries for this reason.

Nunneries.

While Buddhism is not ardently believed in by a large proportion of the Chinese, it is undoubtedly regarded with considerable respect; and its formulæ and practices, especially those which are magical, are largely resorted to as a matter of precaution. Words not understood by the people are continually repeated by them with some sort of belief in their efficacy in overcoming evil influences. The workman will burn his paper with the charm written on it before beginning his morning's work; while the man of learning, who professes to despise Buddhism, knows by heart the magical sentences of the Ling-yen-king, or Heart Sutra.

Popular aspect.

The Buddhist calendar includes a very complete set of festivals and processions, though they are not made the occasion for such display as in Burmah. The emperors' and empress's birthday, the anniversaries of emperors' deaths, and the four monthly feasts are, of course, kept. Then there are days for worshipping the devas of the older Hindu mythology, for eclipses of the sun and moon (addressed as Pu-sahs or Bodhi-satvas, the power of Buddha being invoked to deliver them), for sacrifice to the moon, and praying for fine weather or rain. The Deva Wei-to (really the Veda) is invoked as protector, and his birthday is kept, as also the birthdays of three other divine protectors, including the god of war, of Buddha, and each Bodhi-satva, the anniversaries of the death of the chief Chinese Buddhist saints, and of the founder of a monastery, etc. But this list might easily be lengthened.

Buddhist calendar.

Independent of its professors, Buddhism has exerted a great influence in tempering the character of Chinese religion. The discountenancing of sacrifices, the tenderness to animal life, the conception of a spiritual aim in religion, and of self-discipline as of supreme importance, have not been without far-reaching effect on the Chinese. The example of Buddha as beneficently desirous of being born in the world to save it, his patience and self-sacrifice in his successive lives, his teaching of the noble path and the desirability of freedom from the fetters of this life have all tended to elevate the popular faiths. A more doubtful influence of Buddhism has been the popularisation of beliefs in material hells. A great variety of tortures and circumstances of punishment are described, and the demons are represented as delighting in human sufferings. On the one hand it is alleged that the beliefs on the whole have tended to discourage the crimes that are said to be visited with such punishments, on the other, that the popular mind is thereby familiarised with pictures and descriptions of horrible cruelties.

Influence of Buddhism in China.

The tolerance inculcated by Buddhism, too, has had its effect in spreading a considerable indifference to religion in China, while on the other hand it has favoured its own existence. But the extent of mutual concession and accommodation to be found among the Chinese in religious as well as other matters is a very pleasing feature, when it does not signify lifelessness or mere indifference. The Buddhists too deserve credit, for their representations of Buddhas and Bodhi-satvas are pre-eminently merciful, although their objection to suffering as an evil loses sight of its medical and beneficial influence. Buddhism, too, has in China acquired more regard for filial duty than elsewhere.

We may also note how greatly Buddhism has contributed to the artistic and literary development of the Chinese. The pagoda form is theirs especially. It is derived from the Indian tope or dagoba; the base or platform signifies the earth, the semicircular building covering it the air, and the railing above, the heaven; the spire and umbrellas above have been expanded into

TEMPLE OF THE HUNDRED PAGODAS, HONG-KONG.

successive storeys or platforms, representing the successive worlds above the heavens. In many cases, however, the Chinese pagodas have no religious significance, and only relate to the popular geomancy by which luck is determined. Those which contain Buddhist relics are always connected with monasteries. Some are of brick, others of porcelain, others of cast iron. Many are now falling to ruin, and few are now built. Flower cultivation is another artistic feature in China and Japan which has a connection with the Buddhist flower offerings; many beautiful flowers are grown in the temple and monastery gardens for use as offerings and in decorations.

The do-nothing sect. We must not conclude this account of Chinese Buddhism without calling attention to an interesting sect of reformed Buddhists who have spread considerably since the beginning of the sixteenth century in the lower ranks of the Chinese, known as the Wu-wei-kian, or "Do-nothing sect." They oppose all image-worship, but believe in Buddha without worshipping him. They meet in plain buildings with no images, and containing only an ordinary Chinese tablet dedicated to heaven, earth, king, parents and teachers, as signifying the fit objects for reverence. They enjoin the cultivation of virtue by meditation alone, and inward reverence for the all-pervading Buddha, who is within man and in all nature. Their founder, Lo Hwei-neng took the title Lo-tsu (the patriarch Lo); on the anniversaries of his birth and death, the new year, and in the middle of the eighth month, they meet to drink tea and eat bread together. They are strict vegetarians, believing strongly in metempsychosis and the consequent sin of taking animal life. They have no order of monks or of priests. Matter they regard as perishable, and believe that at the end of the world they will be taken to heaven by Kin-mu, the golden mother, whom they regard as the mother of the soul. She is indeed more an object of worship by this sect than Buddha, being regarded as a protectress from calamities and sickness, and from the miseries of the unseen world. So far have the Taoist notions invaded even this pure form of Buddhism.

BUDDHIST CEREMONY, JAPAN.

JAPANESE BUDDHISM.

Buddhism found its way to Japan in the sixth century A.D. both from China and from Corea, but gained no great influence until the ninth, when the priest Kukai, or Kobo Daishi, showed how to adapt Shintoism to Buddhism by asserting that the Shinto deities were transmigrations of the Buddhistic ones. Thus explained, Buddhism gained great ascendency. In the seventeenth century a philosophical awakening took place, under which every man was taught to long for perfection, to believe in successive transmigrations of souls, and to look forward to the perfect reward of absorption into Buddha. A very great number of Buddhist shrines and temples exist, vastly more ornate and wealthy than those of the Shinto, containing images of extraordinary variety for adoration, supporting till lately a numerous priesthood, who took care to attract the people in every possible way, by spectacles, games, lotteries, and even shooting galleries. The recent revolution, however, has been attended with a great spoliation of Buddhism, suppression of temples and monasteries, melting of bells for coinage, etc.; and the religion now only exists on sufferance, and has already put forth renewed efforts to gain spiritual influence over the people.

The Shin-shin.

There are numerous sects, corresponding in the main to those of China, some being contemplative, others mystic, others taking charge of the popular ceremonies. The Shin-shin especially reverence Amitabha as being willing and able to save those who believe in him. No prayers for happiness in the present life are made by them, and they teach that morality is of equal importance with faith. They have many of the finest temples in Japan, and are remarkable for their active missionary work in China and Corea, and for the high standard of education they maintain. The priests are allowed to marry and to eat meat. The creed of the sect, as stated by one of its principal teachers, is as follows:

"Rejecting all religious austerities and other action, giving up all idea of self-power, we rely upon Amita

Buddha with the whole heart for our salvation in the future life, which is the most important thing, believing that at the moment of putting our faith in Amita Buddha our salvation is settled. From that moment invocation of his name is observed as an expression of gratitude and thankfulness for Buddha's mercy. Moreover, being thankful for the reception of this doctrine from the founder and succeeding chief priests whose teachings were so benevolent, and as welcome as light in a dark night, we must also keep the laws which are fixed for our duty during our whole life."

JAIN EMBLEMS.

CHAPTER X.

Jainism.

Jainism and Buddhism—Mahavira—Jain beliefs—Temples at Palitana—Mount Abu—Parasnath—The Yatis.

THE Jains are at the present day an important body of religionists in India, more for their wealth and influence than their numbers. It is said that half the mercantile transactions of India pass through their hands as merchants and bankers, largely in the north and west of India, and in smaller numbers throughout the southern peninsula. Till comparatively recently they were believed to be quite a modern sect of Hindus, at any rate not much more than a thousand years old. But the careful researches of several eminent scholars have led them to the belief

Jainism and Buddhism.

that Jainism is coeval with, if not slightly older than, Buddhism, and took its rise in the same development of Brahman asceticism and reaction from Brahmanical tyranny. We cannot enter into the details of the discussion, but shall simply take this view as supported by the best authority, Prof. Jacobi.

There are some resemblances between Buddhism and Jainism which do not necessarily show that the one is derived from the other, but rather that they took their rise in the same age or during the same intellectual period. Buddhism proved the more adaptable and appealed to more widespread sympathies, and surpassed and overshadowed Jainism; but the latter, less corrupted, and more characterised by charitable actions, has survived in India, while the former is extinct. We find similar titles given to the saints or prophets in both, such as Tathagata, Buddha, Mahavira, Arhat, etc.; but one set of titles is more frequently used by the one, another by the other; and it is noteworthy that the word Tirthankara, describing a prophet of the Jains, is used in the Buddhist scriptures for the founder of an heretical sect. Both lay great stress on not killing living creatures; both worship their prophets and other saints, and have statues of them in their temples; both believe in enormous periods of time previous to the present age. The rejection of the divine authority of the Vedas and of the sway of the Brahmans is also common to the two. There is further almost an identity between the five vows of the Jain ascetics and those of the Buddhist monks: namely not to destroy life, not to lie, not to take that which is not given, to live a life of purity, and to renounce all worldly things (the last being much more comprehensive than the corresponding Buddhist vow); but it appears that the first four were equally the vows of the Brahman ascetics. There are other points in the life of the Jain monks which agree substantially with rules laid down for the Brahman ascetics.

Vardhamana, or Mahavira (his name as a Jain prophet), the great founder of Jainism, figures in their Kalpa Sutra as the twenty-fourth prophet, and appears to have been a younger son of Siddhartha, a Khsatriya noble or chief of Kundagramma, not far from Vesali, already mentioned in our account of Buddhism, and the wife of Siddhartha, was sister of the king of Vesali, and related to the king of Magadha. At the age of twenty-eight Mahavira became an ascetic, and spent twelve years in self-mortification. After that period he became recognised as a prophet and saint, or Tirthankara (meaning conqueror or leader of a school of thought), and spent the remaining thirty years of his life in teaching and in organising his order of ascetics, mostly within the kingdom of Magadha, but also travelling to Sravasti and the foot of the Himalayas. Mahavira is referred to in the Buddhist books under his well-known name Nataputta, as the head of the rival sect of Niganthas, or Jains, and several contemporaries are referred to in the books of both religions. We may put down Mahavira's date as about the fifth and sixth centuries B.C., but the earliest extant works of the Jains do not go beyond the third century, and were not reduced to writing till the fifth or sixth century A.D. It is very doubtful how far Mahavira is indebted to Parsva, his predecessor, according to the Kalpa Sutra, by about two centuries. The lives of the earlier Jains, like those of the predecessors of Gautama, are altogether mythical. Adinath is the earliest of them.

Mahavira.

The life of Mahavira, as related in the Kalpa Sutra, contains but few details, and is very far from having the interest of that of his great contemporary. He is declared to have torn out his hair on entering the ascetic life, to have gone naked for eleven years, and to have abandoned all care of his body. All perfections of circumspect conduct and self-restraint are attributed to him. He at last reached the highest knowledge, unobstructed and full, so as to become omniscient. At his death he became a Buddha, a Mukta (a liberated soul), putting an end to all misery, finally liberated, freed from all pains.

"Mahavira," says Professor Jacobi, "was of the ordinary class of religious men in India. He may be allowed a talent for religious matters, but he possessed not the genius which Buddha undoubtedly had. The Buddha's philosophy forms a system based on a few fundamental ideas, whilst that of Mahavira scarcely forms a system, but is merely a sum of opinions on various subjects." The matter of the Jain works yet translated is so inferior to that of the Buddhist scriptures that we shall not make any extracts from them.

Jain beliefs.

The Jains believe in a Nirvana, consisting in the delivery of the soul from the necessity for transmigration; and they do not look for an absorption of the soul into the universal Soul. In fact they do not teach anything about a supreme deity. Right perception, clear knowledge, followed by supernatural knowledge, leading to omniscience, were the stages of progress to Nirvana. The space occupied by each of the perfected ones who have attained Nirvana is stated to be boundless, increasing according to their desire. Their parts are said to be innumerable, and there is no returning again to a worldly state, and no interruption to that bliss. Their term of existence is infinite, and they exercise themselves in the highest philosophy. Believers must also practise liberality, gentleness, piety, and sorrow for faults, and kindness to animals and even to plants. This last the Jains exhibit in the present day by an extreme unwillingness to injure living creatures. They believe all animals and plants (and even the smallest particles of the elements) have souls, and they spend much money in maintaining hospitals for sick animals. They will not eat in the open air during rain or after dark, for fear of swallowing a fly or insect; they strain water three times before drinking it, and will not walk against the wind for fear that it should blow insects into the mouth. The strict devotees carry a brush to sweep insects out of the way when they sit down, and a mouth-cloth to cover the mouth when they are engaged in prayer. In strictness the Jains disregard Vedas, gods, and caste; but practically they yield considerably to caste regulations, they pay some devotion to many of the Hindu deities and have a numerous list of good and bad spirits of their own, and they appeal to the Vedas as of considerable authority when they support their views. Now-a-days the peculiarity of nakedness is only retained by the ascetics among the Digambaras (sky-clad ones), and then only at meal-times. The Svetambaras, the other sect of the Jains, are white-robed and completely clad. They have no sacrifices, and practise a strict morality. Many of their beliefs are common to Brahman and Buddhist philosophies, such as that re-births are determined by conduct in previous states of existence.

The Jains possess some of the most remarkable places of pilgrimage in India, situated in the midst of most lovely mountain scenery. At Palitana, in Kathiawar, is the temple-covered hill of Satrunjaya, the most sacred of the pilgrim-resorts of the Jains; and Jains from all parts of India desire to erect temples upon it. Many of them are very small buildings only about three feet square, covering impressions of the soles of two feet marked with Jain emblems, and sacred to Mahavira. The larger temples have considerable marble halls with columns and towers, and plenty of openings, unlike Hindu temples; the marble floors have beautiful tesselated patterns. In the shrine, on a pedestal, are large figures of Mahavira, sitting with feet crossed in front, like those of Buddha. Often on the brow and breast are five brilliants, and gold plates adorn many parts of the body. The eyes are of silver overlaid with pieces of grass, and projecting very far, so as to stare very prominently. The larger temples, says Fergusson ("History of Indian Architecture"), "are situated in *tuks*, or separate enclosures, surrounded by high fortified walls; the smaller ones line the silent streets. A few *yatis*, or priests, sleep in the temples, and perform the daily services, and a few attendants are constantly there to keep the place clean or to feed the sacred pigeons, who are the sole denizens of the spot; but there are no human habitations, properly so called, within the walls. The pilgrim or the stranger ascends in the morning, and returns when he has performed his devotions or satisfied his curiosity. He must not eat, or at least must

Temples at Palitana.

not cook his food on the sacred hill, and he must not sleep there. It is a city of the gods, and meant for them only, and not intended for the use of mortals." Some

JAIN TEMPLE OF ADINATH, GWALIOR.

of the temples date from the eleventh century, but the majority have been built in the present century.

Mount Abu, in Rajputana, is another remarkable place

of pilgrimage, and has been termed the Olympus of India. There are five temples, two of which, according to Fergusson ("History of Indian Architecture"), are unrivalled for certain qualities by any temples in India. They are built wholly of white marble, and the more modern of the two was built (between 1197–1247) by the same brothers who erected a triple temple at Girnar; for minute delicacy of carving and beauty of detail it stands almost unrivalled. A simpler yet very elaborate one, erected in the eleventh century, is a typical example of larger Jain temples; it has a central hall terminating in a pyramidal spire-like roof, containing a cross-legged seated figure of the deified saint worshipped, who in this case is Parsva, the predecessor of Mahavira. There is also a large portico surmounted by a dome, and the whole is enclosed in a large courtyard, surrounded by a double colonnade of pillars forming porticos to a range of fifty-five cells, as in Buddhist viharas, but each occupied by a facsimile of the central image, and over the door of each are sculptured scenes from the saint's life. In some Jain temples the image of Mahavira or other saints is repeated in an identical form hundreds of times, each with cells or niches. Remarkable skill and ingenuity have been displayed in the decoration of the columns and other parts of the Jain temples.

Mount Abu.

Parasnath, in Bengal, is the eastern metropolis of the Jains, having been the supposed scene of the entrance into Nirvana of ten of their twenty-four deified saints. In one view of Parasnath there are to be seen three tiers of temples rising one above another, in dazzling white stone, with fifteen shining domes, each with bright brass pinnacles. In style these temples differ from those in the West or South, and are partly derived from Hindu temples and partly from Mahometan mosques. There are no priests to perform ceremonies for the pilgrims; each performs his devotion according to his own views. They have to pay toll to the priestly order before entering, and to leave some contribution to the repairs of the buildings. Extreme cleanliness being one

Parasnath.

of the Jain principles, it is carried out perfectly in the temples, producing an effect of surpassing beauty. "On entering the centre and holy chamber," says one of the few European visitors who have gained admission, "it is impossible to avoid being impressed with the simple beauty of the place. The pavement is composed of fine slabs of blue-veined marble; and on a white marble pediment, opposite to the entrance, five very beautiful images of the Jain saints sit in dignity waiting for the prayers of their disciples, which are rendered more deep-toned by the echoing influence of the dome." Pilgrims visit every shrine in the holy place, a work of extreme labour, owing to the number of peaks; and the pilgrimage is completed by a circuit round the base of the group of hills, a distance of something like thirty miles.

The yatis.

The yatis, or ascetics, among the Jains have no absolute rule as to worship, being only devoted to meditation and abstraction from worldly affairs; but they often read the Jain scriptures in the temples, while the ministrants, attendants, etc., in the temples are Brahmans. The Jains fast and specially devote themselves to religious duties during a part of the rainy season (the Buddhist Vassa). At its commencement they are accustomed to confess their sins to an ascetic and obtain absolution for them. The Svetambaras are the broader of the two sects, taking their meals clothed and decorating their images, and allowing that women may attain Nirvana, which the Digambaras deny.

[On Jainism see "Sacred Books of the East," vol. xxii.; "Imperial Gazetteer of India;" "Statistical Account of Bengal;" "Encyclopædia Britannica," Art. Jain.]

CHAPTER XI.

Zoroaster and the Zend-Avesta.

The Avesta—Zend and Pahlavi—The Magi of the Bible—The Greeks and the Magi—Modern study by Europeans—Zoroaster—A real personage—His life in Eastern Iran—His date—Mythical developments—Marvels and miracles—Contrary opinions—The doctrines of Zoroaster—Ormuzd and Ahriman—Dualism—Importance attached to thoughts—Relation to early Aryan religion—Comparison with Vedic religion—Ahura—Zoroaster and the settled agriculturists—Attributes of Ormuzd—The name of Ormuzd —Lofty conception of the Deity—The Amesha-Spentas—The Yazatas or spiritual genii—Mithra—Vayu—Sraosha—The soul of the bull—The powers of evil—Ahriman—The daevas and druj—The Yatus, Drvants, etc.—Zoroaster magnified—The universal conflict—The Fravashis—Immortality—Future rewards and punishments—The final dissolution and renovation.

The Avesta.

THE Zend-Avesta[1] is the popular name of the great religious book or collection of books of the Parsees, a wealthy and influential body of Indian residents (numbering over 70,000) whose ancestral home was Persia, but who after the seventh century, when the Persians were overthrown by the Mohametans, took refuge in Western India and the peninsula of Guzerat. Only a few thousand descendants of the old people still keep up the ancestral worship in Persia itself, in Yezd and its neighbourhood. Properly speaking, the old collection of books is the *Avesta*, Zend (or "interpretation") being the name of the translation and commentary on it

[1] See "Sacred Books of the East," vols. iv., v., xviii., xxiii., xxiv., xxxi. "Encyclopædia Britannica," ninth ed., articles "Persia," "Pahlavi," "Parsees," "Zend-Avesta," "Zoroaster." "Avesta," translated with commentary by Prof. de Harlez, second ed. Paris, 1881. "Civilisation of the Eastern Iranians," by Prof. Geiger, translated into English by D. P. Dastur; London: Henry Frowde, 1886. (G.)

in the Pahlavi or early Persian language. Nor is "Zend" strictly a correct term for the language of the Avesta; both the book and the language in which it is written are properly called Avesta, and there is no other book remaining in the language. But the language of the Avesta is very generally termed Zend, since that name has long gained currency. This language was that of north-eastern Iran in its wide sense, and was akin to Sanskrit. From it or a closely allied form the Iranian or Persian family of languages is derived.

Zend and Pahlavi.

Considering how much was known by the ancient Hebrews and Greeks about the Zoroastrian religion, it is a surprising fact that little more than a century ago Sir William Jones rejected the Avesta as a modern rhapsody. The priests of this religion were the Magi or "wise men" of the Old and New Testaments, located in "the East" among the Chaldæans and Persians, and viewed by the Israelites chiefly as astrologers, diviners, and interpreters of dreams. In Daniel xx. we read that the prophet and his associates were reckoned "ten times wiser than all the magicians and astrologers." How deeply this view of them impressed itself, we see in the fact that from their Greek name "magoi" is derived our generic term for all professors of enchantment and preternatural powers. Daniel is represented as interceding for the Magi when condemned to death by Nebuchadnezzar, and was himself appointed Master of the Magi; again and again after this we find that one common ground was recognised between the religions, both hating idolatry and acknowledging the "God of Heaven." The "wise men (Magi) from the east" of Matthew ii. may not have been from Persia, but the mention of them implies the high position they held and the respect paid to their persons and doings. Later references to Magi in the New Testament imply what was the fact, that large numbers of impostors had become distributed through the Roman empire, among whom may be mentioned Simon Magus and Elymas.

The Magi of the Bible.

The Greeks early knew about the Magi through Herodotus and other travellers and historians; and Aristotle and other philosophers wrote about the Persian religion in lost books. The Magi appear to have recommended the destruction of the Greek temples in Xerxes' invasion. After the Greek conquest of Persia the name of the Magi represented a hated system of divination, and the religion of a conquered foe. Both Plato and Xenophon, however, speak of the Magi with respect. Philo, the great Alexandrian philosopher describes them as men who gave themselves to the worship of nature, and the contemplation of the Divine perfections, and as being worthy to be the counsellors of kings. Much literature was put forth in Greece as being the oracles of Zoroaster, but having very faint traces of his system. Throughout the middle ages, however, no real knowledge of the ancient Persian religion existed in Europe. Gradually after the Renaissance the old knowledge was re-collected; and travellers in Persia and India gathered the beliefs of the Parsees and described their practices. Thomas Hyde, an Oxford professor, in 1700 published the first accurate description of modern Parseeism; and in 1723 Richard Cobbe brought to England a copy of the Vendidad, which was hung up by an iron chain in the Bodleian library, a treasure which nobody could read. More than thirty years later, Duperron, a young Frenchman, after years of persuasion and investigation, obtained from the Parsees of Surat both their books and the means of translating them, and in 1764 brought to Paris the whole of the Zend-Avesta; in 1771 he published the first European translation. But it was loudly asserted that the Avesta was a forgery and a late concoction; and it was not till the Pahlavi inscriptions of the first Sassanian emperors had been deciphered by De Sacy, and they in turn led to the reading of the Persian cuneiform inscriptions by Burnouf, Lassen, and Rawlinson, that it was proved beyond doubt that the Avesta was written in a still more ancient language. Zend, as it is usually called, is apparently derived from a common source with Sanskrit; and its grammatical forms remind one of Greek and Latin as well as of the language of the Vedas.

The Greeks and the Magi.

Modern study by Europeans.

ZOROASTER.

So much scepticism has been displayed as to the Avesta that it is scarcely surprising to find that many have doubted the existence of any person corresponding to Zoroaster or Zarathushtra (in modern Persian, Zardusht), although they might in some cases admit that he was a mythological personage developed out of some man. But it requires very cogent proof to upset the unanimous voice of classical antiquity, which speaks of Zoroaster as a real person and the founder of the Persian religion. The period when he lived and the details of his life must be admitted to be doubtful; and his name is not mentioned in any cuneiform inscription yet deciphered. No doubt the Zoroaster of the later parts of the Avesta and of the Zend is largely mythical, and of these myths we must later give some account. But the Zoroaster of the gathas or hymns contained in the Yasna appears as a man, trusting in the Divine Being whom he worships, facing fierce opposition from without, crippled at times by the faintheartedness of his supporters, sometimes suffering from inward doubts and struggles, and again exulting in secure confidence. And it is less marvellous to believe in these sentiments as having proceeded from a man who was the founder of a religion than to believe they were invented long afterwards in the successful days of the religion, when it was beginning to decay. But, as in the case of Buddha and also of the early history of Buddha, these old Aryans had no notion of writing biographies. All we have from them is incidental information, which may be even more reliable, when sifted, than details professing to be biographical would have been in that age.

Zoroaster a real personage.

Although his birthplace is uncertain, Zoroaster's active life and teaching may safely be placed in Eastern Iran, possibly in Bactria. The later parts of the Avesta describe him as teaching during the reign of Vishtaspa, the same word as is rendered Hystaspes by the Greeks; but there is reason to believe this king belonged to a much earlier period than Hystaspes,

His life in Eastern Iran.

the father of Darius. This king was evidently the patron and friend of the great religious teacher; and his influence greatly contributed to Zoroaster's success. Two brothers, Frashaoshtra and Jamaspa, the latter a minister of the king, were among Zoroaster's prominent supporters; indeed he married their sister Hvovi. Like some other religious leaders, Zoroaster derived much aid from his relatives and their followers; and he appears to have had a family of sons and daughters. The Avesta does not speak of his death; but in the late Shah-Nama, or book of Turanian kings (13th century), it is related that he was murdered at the altar in the storming of Balk by the Turanian conquerors. Almost the only means that we have of indicating Zoroaster's date is the fact that when Cyrus reigned, in the 6th century B.C., the Magian religion was firmly established in Western Iran. Various conjectures assign him dates between 1000 and 1400 B.C.

His date.

Turning now to the view of Zoroaster given by the later parts of the Avesta, it is easy to see that he became invested with marvellous powers, nothing less than supernatural, and was in fact made part of the Magian mythology. He is described as smiting fiends chiefly with his prayers, driving away Ahriman the evil spirit with huge stones which he had received from Ormuzd, the supreme and good god. At his birth the floods and trees rejoiced. Ormuzd is even represented as sacrificing to a spring, and praying that Zoroaster may be brought to think and speak and do according to his law. Zoroaster in fact becomes the supporter of Ormuzd, and drives away Ahriman and the fiends that try to kill him. He is a godlike champion, who kills the powers of evil with the word of truth or the sacred spell. At some far-off period a posthumous son will be born to him who will come from the region of the dawn to free the world from death and decay, and under his rule the dead will rise and immortality commence.

Mythical developments.

Still later, in the Bundahish we have more details and marvels about Zoroaster, and from it a legendary history of the great teacher may be compiled. During his early life a whole series of marvels occurred, mostly protecting his life from danger. His early life was blameless, but it was only after he attained the age of thirty that his mission commenced. He appears to have emigrated from his native country to Iran proper, with a few followers, and miracles were worked in his progress. The spirit Vohu-mano ("the good mind") introduces him to Ormuzd, the supreme Being; he asks permission to put questions to Him, inquiring which of God's creatures is best, and receiving the answer, "He is the best who is pure of heart;" and then receives instruction as to the names and duties of angels and the nature of the evil spirit Ahriman. Various miraculous signs are shown to him. He sees a fiery mountain and is commanded to pass through the fire, but is not hurt thereby. Molten metal is poured into his breast without his feeling pain; and these wonders are explained to him as having a mystic meaning. He then received the Avesta from Ormuzd and was commanded to proclaim it at the court of King Vishtaspa. This belief in the communication between Zoroaster and Ormuzd runs through the whole Avesta. In every important matter he questions Ormuzd and receives a precise answer from him. Various statements are made that these revelations took place upon a mountain, which afterwards burst out into flames. When he at last presented himself at court, the king's wise men endeavoured to refute him, but were compelled to own that he had beaten them in argument; finally the king accepted the Avesta, after the prophet had been accused as a sorcerer and had proved his mission by miracles. The king at last did nothing without consulting Zoroaster, and erected the first fire-temple.

Marvels and miracles.

Having treated Zoroaster as having been a real historical personage, round whom many mythical or exaggerated narratives have collected, we will quote a few sentences showing the contrary opinion held by not a few scholars: "All the features in Zarathushtra point to a god: that the god may have grown up from a

Contrary opinions.

man, that pre-existent mythic elements may have gathered around the name of a man, born on earth, and by-and-by surrounded the human face with the aureole of a god, may of course be maintained, but only on condition that one may distinctly express what was the real work of Zoroaster. That he raised a new religion against the Vedic religion, and cast down into hell the gods of older days can no longer be maintained, since the gods, the ideas, and the worship of Mazdeism (*i.e.*, Zoroastrianism) are shown to emanate directly from the old religion, and have nothing more of a reaction against it than Zend has against Sanskrit." (Darmesteter, S.E., vol. iv.)

THE DOCTRINES OF ZOROASTER.

The most special feature of Zoroaster's teaching is the dualistic principle, according to which Ahura Mazda (Ormuzd), the good spirit, is constantly antagonised by Angra Mainyu (Ahriman), the evil spirit, who is the originator of everything evil. The latter is to be ultimately expelled from the world, and man must take an active part in the struggle, his conduct being regulated by the code revealed to Zoroaster by Ormuzd. Ormuzd and Ahriman are believed to have been co-existent, and opposed in the earliest period known to the Gathas; but the ultimate triumph of Ormuzd indicates essential if latent inferiority in Ahriman. It must not be taken that other spirits were not believed in by Zoroaster; but as far as one can judge, his special teaching relates to the supremacy and greatness of Ormuzd and his final victory.

Ormuzd and Ahriman.

Dualism.

As regards conduct in this world, Zoroaster enforces the doctrine that no one can occupy a position of indifference; he must be either on the side of good or of evil. The only proper course was to choose the good, and to follow it in thought, word, and deed. This was announced clearly in the first gatha; and we must concede to Zoroaster the great merit of seeing the importance of the thoughts, and tracing evil to that source. When we remember how

Importance attached to thoughts.

few of the hymns of the Rig-Veda refer to sin or its expiation, and how slight are the traces of feelings of guilt, and the necessity for obtaining forgiveness for it from the Deity, it will be seen that the Avesta contains distinctly an advanced teaching.

Relation to early Aryan religion.

Whatever may have been Zoroaster's contribution to the religious progress of his race, such a religion as his could only become accepted where there was already a large basis of positive belief, even if that belief were erroneous; and as there can be no doubt that the Iranians were derived from the same stock as the Aryan Hindus, we must compare their early religion with the features found existing in the Avesta, in default of any document recording what was the state of belief upon which Zoroaster began to work. And this study leads to most interesting results.

Comparison with Vedic religion.

The general name for a god in the earlier portions of the Rig-Veda is *deva* (bright); in the Avesta the evil spirits are called *daeva*, essentially the same word; while in the later Rig-Veda the name means exclusively a good spirit, a beneficent god. In contrast to this, we find the use of an alternative name to *deva* in the earlier parts of the Rig-Veda, namely *asura*. This is the same word as *ahura* in the Avesta, forming part of the name Ormuzd (Ahura Mazda) and limited to a good sense. Yet in the later Rig-Veda and in Brahmanism the same name is exclusively applied to evil spirits. We have not space to trace fully how this divergence was concomitant in India with the deposition of Varuna from the supreme place among the gods and the rise of Indra; but it may be inferred from the Avesta that in Zoroaster's time the people of Iran were divided between two distinct and contrasted forms of belief—the wilder unsettled nomads who believed in the devas, the original spirits of the Ayran race, and who ill-treated and sacrificed cattle; while the more settled people believed in the ahuras, the patrons of cattle, and elevated the care of cattle into a sacred function.

Ahuras.

Zoroaster therefore appeared as a champion of the

belief of the settled peoples, and added the epithet Mazda, the wise, to the name of the chief god whom they already believed in. He identified the old devas, still believed in by the nomads, with powers of evil, false gods, devils. These, he taught, were all different manifestations or helpers of a predominant evil principle, often called Druj, or deception, and less frequently Angra Mainyu, or Ahriman. This is but a concentration and development of the early Aryan belief in a conflict between the powers of nature, some benefiting and others injuring mankind.

Zoroaster and the settled agriculturists.

The frequent brief address to Ormuzd in the Vendidad is "the most blissful spirit, creator of the material world, thou Holy One," or more fully, "I venerate the Creator, Ahura Mazda, the brilliant, radiant, greatest, best, most beautiful, mightiest, wisest, best-formed, most exalted through holiness, giving profusely, granting much bliss, who created us, who prepares us, who maintains us, the most blissful spirit." Dr. Geiger lays stress on the spiritual view which is given of Ormuzd, and says that he is not represented as having any visible form, except where the sun (Mithra) is spoken of as "the body and the eye of Mazda." Anthropomorphism is rare as applied to the Supreme Being in the Avesta: and Geiger looks upon all the passages as symbolical, which speak of wives and relatives of Ormuzd. But we cannot be blind to the extreme probability that such relationships would be looked upon as real by the general mass of the people, however definitely the leaders may have regarded them as symbolical.

Attributes of Ormuzd.

Great importance is evidently attached to the "name" of Ormuzd, and it is interesting to compare it with the "name" of Jehovah as treated in the Old Testament Scriptures, and the 99 names of Allah in the Koran. These names, as given in the Ormuzd Yast, are "the One of whom questions are asked, the Herd-giver, the Strong One, Perfect Holiness, Creator of all good things, Understanding, Knowledge, Well-being, and the Producer of well-being, Ahura (the Lord), the most Beneficent, He in whom there is no harm, the Un-

The name of Ormuzd.

conquerable, He who makes the true account (that is of good works and sins), the All-Seeing, the Healer, Mazda (the All-wise)." He is represented in the gathas as not to be deceived, and as looking upon everything as a warder with eyes radiant with holiness. How high is the conception of the deity reached in the gathas may be seen from the following extract from one of them (Yasna 44):—

"That I ask of Thee, tell me the right, O Ahura!
Who was the father of the pure creatures at the beginning?
Who has created the way of the sun, of the stars?
Who but Thou made it that the moon waxes and wanes?
This, O Mazda, and other things I long to know.
Who upholds the earth and the clouds above,
That they fall not? Who made the water and the plants?
Who gave their swiftness to the winds and the clouds?
Who is, O Mazda, the creator of the pious mind?
Who, working good, has made light as well as darkness?
Who, working good, has made sleep and wakefulness?
Who made the dawn, the mid-days, and the evenings?"

There is no doubt that Ormuzd is believed to have existed before any material thing, and to have called the world into existence by his will. He is specially mentioned as the creator of the holy mind, of religious truth, and of the prayers and offerings. Fire is also a special creation of Ormuzd, the importance of which we shall see later. Being omniscient and infallible, he rewards the good and punishes the evil both in this world and the next. Thus we read in the gathas:—

"Whosoever in righteousness shows to me
The genuine good actions, to me who am Zarathushtra:
Him they (the divine beings) grant as a reward the next world,
Which is more desirable than all others.
That hast thou said to me, Mazda, thou who knowest best."

The impious are thus threatened: "Whoso brings about that the pious man is defrauded, his dwelling is finally for a long time in darkness, and vile food and irony shall fall to his lot. Towards this region, O ye vicious, your souls will conduct you on account of your actions."

There have not been wanting those who see in the resemblances between this conception of the supreme Deity and that of the Jews a proof that the one was derived from the other; but the view that they are distinct and unrelated finds warm advocacy. Thus Dr. Geiger says: "In this sublime conception of the Avesta, Ahura Mazda undoubtedly stands far above the deities of the Vedic pantheon. Only the Jehovah of the ancient Jews may be compared to him. But however obvious the similarity between the God of Israel and the god of the Mazdeans may be, still I reject entirely the assumption that the Avesta people have borrowed from the Jews. Upon the Iranian soil a narrowly-confined nation has, independently and of itself, attained that high conception of God, which, with the exception of the Jews, was never attained by any Aryan, Semitic, or Turanian tribe." (G.) To another student, Professor Geldner, Ormuzd appears as the idealised figure of an oriental king. To Professor Darmesteter he is the developed idea of the old Aryan "Heaven-God," and many features betray his former sky nature. Thus "he is white, bright, seen afar, and his body is the greatest and fairest of all bodies; he has the sun for his eye, the rivers above for his spouses, the fire of lightning for his son; he wears the heaven as a star-spangled garment; he dwells in the infinite luminous space."

Lofty conception of the Deity.

The sevenfold arrangement of the Vedic gods which was sometimes made, and from which were developed the twelve adityas, was seen also in the Iranian religion, and it is a question whether it did not exist very early, Ormuzd becoming the most prominent and finally the supreme. In some parts of the Avesta mention is made of seven Amesha-Spentas (the blissful immortals), of whom Ahura Mazda is chief. The names of the others are (1) Vohu-mano, the good mind, (2) Asha-vahishta, the best holiness, (3) Khshathra-varya, the desirable sovereignty, (4) Spenta-Armati, moderate thinking and humble sense, (5) Harvatat, well-being, happiness, health, (6) Amertal, long life, immortality. The abstract meanings of these names render it difficult

The Amesha-Spentas.

to understand them, but there is no doubt that they are invoked in the Avesta as real beings who can answer prayer. We find them very definitely associated with particular functions: Vohu-mano protects herds, Asha is the genius of fire, Khshathra has the care of metals, Spenta-Armati is the guardian of the earth, while the last two protect the waters and plants. We may here indicate with some reserve Geiger's explanation of the abstract meaning of some of the Amesha-Spentas, as connected with these practical functions. Vohu-mano, the good mind, is the protector of herds because the people who accepted the Zoroastrian doctrine, and consequently were of good mind, were the cattle-rearers, as opposed to the nomads. Vohu-mano came also to be regarded as the guardian of all living beings. The connection of Asha, purity, with fire, is evident, fire being the symbol of purity. Armati (the Vedic goddess Aramati) is the protector of the earth, regarded as "the humble suffering one which bears all, nourishes all, and sustains all. In the Rig-Veda Aramati is devotion, or the genius of devotion. By the Indian commentator Sayana, Armati is regarded as wisdom, but he also defines the same word twice as the 'earth.'" Harvatat, health, is the master of water, for the waters dispense health. Amertal, long life and immortality, is the genius of plants, which dispel sickness and death, especially the Haoma (Indian Soma) plant, which gives health and long keeps up the vital powers. The white Haoma gives immortality. Fire is spoken of as the son of Ormuzd, and Armati as his daughter. In one place (Yast xix.) we find all invoked as sons of Ormuzd: "I invoke the glory of the Amesha-Spentas, who all seven have one and the same thinking, one and the same doing, one and the same father and lord, Ahura Mazda."

Another subject of great interest is the part played by the *yazatas*, sometimes characterised as angels or spiritual genii presiding over elements or over abstract ideas. Mr. Dastur says: "In the abstract, anything that is excellent and worthy of praise in the moral and material universe and that glorifies the wisdom of the

Deity is a yazata." (G. p. xxiv.) Mithra is one of the most significant of these, because he can be identified with Mitra, the Vedic god of the heavenly light, closely associated with Varuna. Mithra was believed to see and therefore know everything, and became the witness of truth and the preserver of oaths and good faith; consequently he punishes those who break their promises. He is also the lord of wide pastures and the prince of the countries. The tenth yast contains many hymns to Mithra, from which the following extracts are made (S. E. xxiii.).

The yazatas, or spiritual genii.

Mithra.

"Ahura Mazda spake unto Spitama Zarathushtra, saying: 'Verily, when I created Mithra, the lord of wide pastures, O Spitama, I created him as worthy of sacrifice, as worthy of prayer as myself, Ahura Mazda. The ruffian who lies unto Mithra (or who breaks the contract) brings death unto the whole country, injuring as much the faithful world as a hundred evil-doers could do. Break not the contract, O Spitama, neither the one that thou hadst entered into with one of the unfaithful, nor the one that thou hadst entered into with one of the faithful, who is one of thy own faith. For Mithra stands for both the faithful and the unfaithful.'"

"We sacrifice unto Mithra, the lord of wide pastures, who is truth-speaking, a chief in assemblies, with a thousand ears, well-shapen, with ten thousand eyes, high, with full knowledge, strong, sleepless, and ever awake.

"Who upholds the columns of the lofty house and makes its pillars solid; who gives herds of oxen and male children to that house in which he has been satisfied; he breaks to pieces those in which he has been offended."

On behalf of Mithra, loud claims are put forth for a sacrifice, invoking him in his own name. He is prayed to for riches, strength, and victory, good conscience and bliss, wisdom and the knowledge that gives happiness. In one place he is a warlike, courageous youth, who drives in a chariot with four white horses through the heavens, and also into battle; who becomes a yazata of war. See the account of Mithraism, later, p. 276.

Vayu, another Vedic deity, is the storm yazata in the Avesta, and is appealed to by Ormuzd to grant him power to smite Ahriman. He is invoked as a strong warlike helper in every danger. Among other important yazatas are that of Fire, the messenger of the gods, sent down as lightning and sun-fire to the earth; that of the waters, Ardvisura Anahita, Tistrya the rain-bestower, Verethragna the fiend smiter, and the Sun and Moon, etc. Many of these are identical in name and epithets with Vedic gods or spirits, and in reading the yasts we seem to hear again the strains of the Rig-Veda.

Vayu.

"He who offers up a sacrifice unto the undying, shining, swift-horsed sun, to withstand darkness, to withstand the daevas born of darkness, to withstand the robbers and bandits, to withstand death that creeps in unseen, offers it up to Ahura Mazda, offers it up to the Amesha-Spentas, offers it up to his own soul.

"We sacrifice unto Tistrya, the bright and glorious star, for whom long the standing waters, and the running spring-waters, the stream-waters and the rain-waters:

"When will the bright and glorious Tistrya rise up for us? When will the springs with a flow and overflow of waters, thick as a horse's shoulder, run to the beautiful places and fields, and to the pastures, even to the roots of the plants, that they may grow with a powerful growth?"

The spirit or god Sraosha must also be mentioned; his name signifies obedience, especially to the Holy Word. He it was who first tied together the *baresma*, the consecrated sacrificial branches; he first sang the sacred hymns; three times a day he descends on the world to smite Ahriman. Hence he has been termed the priest-god; the holy prayers are the weapons with which he smites. He requires a man to rise early that he may perform the due rites; he pities the poor and needy, and guards the sanctity of the covenants. Again Ashi or piety, moral order, the daughter

Sraosha.

of Ormuzd and sister of Sraosha, Mithra and others, bestows the human intellect, defends matrimony, and cares actively for the house. She confers power and riches, and gives beauty to maidens.

The soul of the bull. Another spirit is named Geush-urvan, "Soul of the Bull"; in the gathas we find this spirit complaining before Ormuzd of the oppressions and dangers inflicted on him by enemies. Besides those named, many other spirits are invoked, such as the holy doctrine, the Holy Word, the genius of justice, etc. Here we see how prone Zoroastrianism was to personify abstract ideas, just as the Vedic religion personified material objects or forces.

The powers of evil. We now come to the obverse side of the picture—the powers of evil, and their relations to Ormuzd and the forces of goodness. It has already been stated how prominently the Avesta asserts dualism in the government of the world; but there are not wanting those who consider that Zoroastrianism is not more dualistic than Christianity, and point to the fact that no attempt is made to account for the origin of either spirit, while the temporary character of the power of the evil one is distinctly asserted. (West, S. E., vol. xviii.) Haug says that Zoroaster held the grand idea of the unity and indivisibility of the supreme Being, and sought to reconcile the existence of imperfections and evils with the goodness and justice of God by supposing two primeval causes which, though different, were united. But it is surely simpler to take the plain statements of the gathas, that two powerful beings opposed and counteracted each other, but that the good Being is the stronger and will ultimately conquer, as expressing the essence of the creed of Zoroaster. If one reads the gathas naturally, without prepossessions, it will appear that Ahriman is imagined to have existed from the beginning.

Ahriman. Ahriman, the prince of the demons, is the opposite and counterpart of Ormuzd in all characters. He dwells in infinite darkness, and is all darkness, falsehood and wickedness, and around him all evil spirits collect. Any good man is his enemy, and he is represented as being enraged at the birth of Zoroaster. The evil spirits are the daevas, (devas) male, and the druj (female). There are six principal evil spirits corresponding to the Amesha-Spenta: thus (1) Akomano, evil mind; (2) Andra (Indra), destructive fire; (3) Saru, the tyrant, opposed the first three of the Amesha-Spentas.

The daevas and druj.

The first section of the Vendidad exhibits in detail the way in which Ahriman counterworked the beneficent creation of Ormuzd. His first creation was the serpent in the river, and winter, followed by the cattle-fly, corn-carrying ants, the mosquito, demon-nymphs and wizards, etc.; and also the sinful lusts, unbelief, pride, unnatural sins, the burying and burning of corpses, the oppression of foreign rulers, and excessive heat, each following a beneficial creation of Ormuzd. Ahriman was also represented as the killer of the first bull, the poisoner of plants, the causer of smoke, of sin, and of death.

Some of the associate spirits of evil can be identified with Vedic spirits; such are the Yatus, wizard demons. The Pairikas are demon-nymphs who keep off the rain-floods. The Drvants or Dregvants are head-long-running fiends. The Varenya daevas are the fiends in the heavens. Bushyasta sends people to sleep at dawn, and makes them forget to say their prayers. We cannot go into the details relating to all these.

The Yatus, Drvants, etc.

We must note how in the Yasts Zoroaster appears as the typical and best human being, who first antagonised Ahriman. Thus, we read in Yast 13, "We worship the piety and the Fravashi (see p. 262) spirit of the holy Zarathushtra, who first thought, spoke, and did what is good, who was the first priest, the first warrior, the first plougher of the ground, who first knew and taught; who first possessed the bull, and holiness, the word and obedience to the word, and dominion, and all the good things made by Mazda; who first in the material world proclaimed the word that destroys the daevas, the law of Ahura; who was strong, giving all the good things of life, the first bearer of the law among the nations; for whom the Amesha-Spentas longed, in one

Zoroaster magnified.

accord with the sun, in the fulness of faith of a devoted heart; they longed for him, as the lord and master of the world, as the praiser of the most great, most good, and most fair Asha; in whose birth and growth the waters and the plants rejoiced; and whose birth and growth all the creatures of the good creations cried out, "Hail!" (S.E. vol. xxiii.) Here we see, as if in process, the deification of a human being.

The universal conflict. The conflict between good and evil was represented as universal in its extent. Every power or being or material thing was engaged on one side or the other. All animals and plants belong to one or the other, or are forced into their service. Sometimes the gods and fiends are seen under the guise of dogs, snakes, otters, frogs, etc.; and it was held a crime to kill the creatures of Ormuzd, while a man might atone for evil by killing the creatures of Ahriman. Darmesteter, speculating on this aspect of the Avesta, says, "Persia was on the brink of zoolatry."

The good and the wicked. Of course mankind were shared between Ormuzd and Ahriman. The servant of Ahriman and of Asha (fire) offers sacrifice to them with libations of haoma juice (the Vedic Soma), the great healing and invigorating plant, which when drunk by the faithful benefits the gods; sacrifices of consecrated meat and libations of holy water. He aids Ormuzd and the holy spirits by every good thought, word, and deed, and by increasing the number of and protecting the creatures of Ormuzd. The priest, or Atharvan, who drives away fiends and diseases by his spells: the warrior who destroys the impious, the husbandman who produces good harvests, are all workers for Ormuzd, and those who do the contrary, for Ahriman. The former will have a seat near Ormuzd in heaven, and at the end of time the dead will rise and live happily on the earth, which will then be free from all evil.

The Fravashis. In this connection we may note the belief in the existence of a spirit (*Fravashi*) distinct from the body originally, separated from it by death, and believed to be simply the spirit of ancestors; but this developed into a belief in Fravashis as the immortal principle or counterpart of any being, whether gods, animals, plants, or physical objects. They are spoken of in Yast xiii. as "the awful and overpowering Fravashis," bringing help and joy to the faithful, helping in the maintenance of all creations. Because of the help they give in the perpetual conflict between good and evil, the Fravashis are worshipped and invoked on all occasions. They are praised as "the mightiest of drivers, the lightest of those driving forwards, the slowest of the retiring, the safest of all bridges, the least erring of all weapons and arms, and never turning their backs"; they are correspondingly dreadful to the foe. They are, however, said to ask for help thus: "Who will praise us? Who will offer us a sacrifice? Who will meditate upon us? Who will bless us? Who will receive us with meat and clothes in his hand, and with a prayer worthy of bliss?" High above all other Fravashis is the Fravashi of Ahura Mazda.

Immortality.

There is no doubt that the Avesta teaches the doctrine of immortality, and a coming world which is "better than the good." The idea of a bridge conducting men thither has been common to many religions. The early Avesta represents it as a chinvat bridge, or bridge of retribution, at which justice is administered. The good go to the abode of light and glory where Ormuzd reigns and is praised in hymns. The evil, the false priests, and idol-worshippers go for all eternity to the habitation of the devils, in eternal night, scorned by the demons. Yast xxii. gives a detailed description of the fate of the good and of the evil.

Future rewards and punishments.

A good man's spirit, remaining near the head of the body, tastes during the three nights succeeding the death of the body as much happiness as the whole living world can taste. He passes into the most blissful region and is met by his own conscience in the shape of a beautiful heavenly maiden who recites to him all his good deeds, and then conducts him through the Paradises of Good Thought, Good Worth, Good Deed, and Endless Light. The evil man correspondingly suffers for three nights as much as the whole living world can suffer, and then is brought through a foul region into the hills of Evil Thought, Evil Word, and Evil Deed, and finally into endless darkness. Later this vision is amplified.

The final dissolution and renovation.

In one passage of the gathas we find mention of a final dissolution of creation, when the final distribution of rewards and punishments will take place; but the general tenor of the Avesta is to look for a regeneration of the earth, with a resurrection of the bodies of the dead, to join their souls. Many hold that this view of the resurrection was original in Zoroastrianism, and that it was adopted from the Persians by the Jews. The end of the world is to be preceded by the appearance of three great prophets, all regarded as supernatural sons of Zarathushtra, the last one (Astvat-erta) being named the victorious Saviour, embodied piety, overcoming all torments of men and demons. He is to renew the world, he makes the living immortal and awakens the dead from their sleep, brings death, old age and decay to an end, and grants to the pious eternal life and happiness. One last decisive struggle takes place between the powers of light and darkness, and Astvat-erta, with the aid of the good spirits, vanquishes the demons, and extirpates evil. Then comes the peaceful and happy reign of Ormuzd and all the good, no longer disturbed by any evil-disposed being.

CHAPTER XII.

The Zoroastrian Books—Mithraism.

The Avesta—Country of its origin—Date of the Avesta—The Gathas—People to whom addressed—The Vendidad—The most pleasing and displeasing things—Impurity of corpses—Exposure of dead—Law of contracts and assaults—The Vispered and Yasna—The liturgies—The early rites of Mazdaism—Rise of the Magi—Loss of Zoroastrian books—The Pahlavi texts—The Bundahish—The Shayast la-Shayast—The Dadistan-i-Dinik—The Spirit of Wisdom—Mithraism—Mithraic monuments—Antagonism of Christians—Mithraic ceremonies.

THE AVESTA.

FROM the Avesta itself it appears to be conclusively proved that it originated in Eastern Iran, east of the central desert of Persia, the land of the Syr-Daria, nearly all the places mentioned in it being situated therein, with the exception of Ragha, near its western boundary. Babylon is the only famous western city mentioned. A passage especially noted is this, in which the Aryan country is described as the first created and best land. "As the first of the lands and as the best dwelling-place, I, Ahura-Mazda (Ormuzd), created the Aryana-vaija (the country), situated on the good Datya. Thereupon Angra Mainyu (Ahriman), who is full of death, counter-created the water serpents and a winter produced by the demons." (G.) This Aryan country was very possibly in Upper Ferghana.

Country of its origin.

The Avesta itself testifies to its own date in the following way. It does not mention any town which was famous in the Median and Achemenian period except Ragha; nor does it mention the names of later nations or empires. It only knows Aryans, not Persians, Parthians, or Medes as such. It does not even contain any reference to the battles between the Medes and the Babylonians, still less to the conquests of Alexander the Great. And this is the more significant as it alludes to many external events, battles, inroads of foreigners, the hostility of the Aryans to non-Aryans, and of the settled agriculturists to the nomad tribes. The tribal grouping was in full force, and only specially powerful kings were able to unite the tribes into kingdoms. It is much more natural to regard all this as a sign of great antiquity, especially when coupled with the primitive type of the Avesta language. And it is not safe to dismiss portions of the narrative as purely mythical because all trace of some of the names mentioned has vanished. Herodotus's statement that the Medes were anciently called Aryans, supports this view of the antiquity of the record which deals solely with Aryans, before the Medes had become a distinct people.

Date of the Avesta.

Let us take the gathas, or hymns of the Avesta, contained in the Yasna, and study them for traces of the people among whom they were composed. In them Zoroaster speaks directly. The king Vishtaspa is described as his pious friend in his great work, wishful to announce it; and in many ways the gathas address or speak of contemporary persons and events. The religion itself is in process of formation, and its followers are subject to persecution. No doubt mythology is intermingled; but if everything which contains mythological interpretations or descriptions were adjudged to contain no historical fact, very much more than the Avesta would have to be sacrificed.

The gathas.

One important fact intimating the great age of the gathas, and also showing the connection of the Aryan people they describe with the Aryans of the Rig-Veda, is the high importance attributed to the cow, showing special attention to its breeding and rearing. Thus they were in the pastoral state which succeeds a nomad life, and becoming more settled than mere keepers of sheep and goats, which can be readily transferred from place to place. We are expressly told in the gathas that the cow is the giver of permanent homes, and the especial care of the active labourer, and also leads to the development of agriculture. In the Vendidad, in contrast to this, agriculture has become of equal importance with cattle-breeding. In the gathas antagonism is represented as occurring between the nomads and the agriculturists, and the former oppose the teaching of Zoroaster. In fact, the nomads plundered the settled people then as now, and naturally disliked the moral teacher of their more civilised brethren. We find Zoroaster assigned as the special protector of the cow, and the announcer to man that the cow is created for the industrious and the active. In the later parts of the Avesta we find the religion of Zoroaster firmly established and an order of priests (Atharvans), but the people are still peasants and shepherds, and their daily life is intimately connected with their religion, the annual feasts being specially related to the agricultural and pastoral life. The people do not yet seem to have used salt. Glass, coined money, and iron were unknown; the bronze age still ruled. One passage, which has been alleged to refer to Gautama, and to show the date of the Avesta to be later than his time, is not at all conclusive, and the name is rather an old Iranian form; also the name Gautama occurs in the Rig-Veda. It was, in fact, an early Aryan name.

The people to whom addressed.

The Vendidad is specially the Zoroastrian book of purification; but the first two sections belong to the older literature. The first section at once touches a natural chord by representing Ahura-Mazda (Ormuzd) as telling Zoroaster that he has made every country dear to its own people; were it not so, they would all have come to the Aryan country, which was created best of good lands. The counter-creation of Angra Mainyu (Ahriman) is then described, giving rise to the ten months of winter. Other neighbouring coun-

The Vendidad.

tries were then created, followed by Ahriman's creation of special evils or plagues, including various sins, evils, and insect plagues. In the second section Zoroaster asks Ormuzd who was the first mortal with whom he had conversed; and he replies, "The fair Yima, the great shepherd," who appears to have represented the founder of civilisation. Afterwards he was told that a period of fatal winters was approaching, and he was commanded to gather into a large enclosure all kinds of seeds and grains, and to make a sort of terrestrial paradise. This Yima is compared in some respects with Yama, the ruler of departed spirits, in the Rig-Veda.

The third section gives an enumeration of five things most pleasing and five most displeasing to the earth.

The most pleasing and displeasing things.

These are, (1) the place where one of the faithful with wood for the altar fire, and the sacred bundle of twigs, steps forward praying to Mithra, the lord of wide pastures, and Rama Svastra, the god that gives good pastures to cattle; (2) the place where one of the faithful erects a house for a priest, with wife, children, and herds; (3) the place where one of the faithful cultivates most corn, grass, and fruit; (4) where there is most increase of flocks and herds; (5) and where they yield most manure. The unpleasing places relate to the corpses or other creations of Ahriman, and also the captive wife and children of one of the faithful.

Impurity of corpses.

No man is allowed to carry a corpse alone, and every corpse, if buried, must be disinterred (for exposure) within six months. A large part of the Vendidad relates to the extent of defilement by corpses or portions of dead matter and the means of purification. Throughout all we see the guiding principle that purity, especially of the body, is of prime importance; but impurity is believed to be the work of a demon, which especially inhabits a corpse, and thence passes to those who touch it. Peculiar washings and spells are enjoined in order to expel the impure spirit. Nowhere has this idea of impurity connected with the dead been more elaborately developed. The evil spirit is expelled from the corpse itself by the "four-eyed dog" being brought near and made to look at the dead. In practice this is interpreted as a dog with two spots above the eyes. This may be compared with the four-eyed dogs of the Vedic god Yama, and the three-headed Cerberus, watching at the doors of hell. Wherever the corpse passed, death walked with it, threatening the living; consequently no man or animal might pass that way till the deadly breath had been blown away by the four-eyed dog, the priest aiding with his spells.

Exposure of dead.

Fire, earth, and water being all holy to Zoroastrians, corpses must be kept as far as possible away from them and placed on the highest summits, where there are always corpse-eating dogs and birds, and fastened by the feet and hair lest the bones should be carried away. The bones must afterwards be laid in a building known as the Dokma, or tower of silence. This principle was carried out very thoroughly, partial death and sickness being equally unclean. Everything proceeding from the human body was impure, even parings of nails and cut hair. Sickness was sent by Ahriman, and must be cured by washings and spells. If several healers offered themselves together, one healing with the knife, one with herbs, and one with the holy word or by spells, the latter was to be preferred. Hence the class of priests included the chief doctors.

Law of contracts and assaults.

The fourth section of the Vendidad is occupied with laws about contracts and assaults; the latter are of seven degrees, and guilt is estimated as very greatly increased by each repetition of the offence. Crimes are punished not only by stripes, but in addition by penalties after death. Offences against the gods were punished more heavily than offences against man; and death is the punishment of the man who falsely pretends to cleanse the unclean, and the man who carries a corpse alone, these being special offences against the gods. Repentance only saves the sinner from penalties after death. The burning or burial of the dead, the eating dead matter, and unnatural crimes were inexpiable, apparently punished by death as well as future torments.

The Vispered and Yasna properly form an indivisible part of the Avesta; in fact, they constitute a liturgy. The Vispered, which is very short, contains merely invocations and invitations to Ormuzd and the good genii to be present at the ceremonies about to be performed. The Yasna means literally "offering with prayers," and includes the gathas or hymns, to which we have already referred. These were to be recited by the priests alone (the laity not being present), during the performance of certain religious ceremonies, which in brief were the consecration of holy water, of the sacred twigs or Baresma, and of the juice of the Haoma, and the offering of the draonas, or little round cakes, on which pieces of cooked flesh were placed, and afterwards eaten by the priests. Properly it was the priest's duty to recite the entire Avesta once every twenty-four hours, and principally during the night, this being essential in order that they might keep themselves fit to perform the rites of purification.

The Vispered and Yasna.

The liturgies are not of interest proportionate to their length, and it is difficult to give an idea of their varied character within our limits. Here is a brief extract from the Vispered: "We honour the omniscient spirit Ahura-Mazda. We honour the light of the sun. We honour the sun, the Amesha-Spentas. We honour the perfect Mantras. We honour the brilliant works of purity. We honour the assemblies, of which fire is the cause. We honour pure and benevolent prosperity and intelligence." Again, "Apply your feet, hands, will, Mazdeans, disciples of Zarathustra, to the practice of the good works prescribed by law and justice, to the avoidance of bad actions, contrary to law, and unjust; give to those who lack."

The liturgies.

The Yasna largely consists of lists of those in whose honour the various consecrated objects are offered, or to whose praise the priests are chanting. Thus: "With this Baresma and holy water I honour the pure spirits of the months, pure spirits of the pure world. I honour the new moon, pure spirits of the pure world." Frequently various points in the history or achievements of the spirits are alluded to. Then the features of Ormuzd's rule are spoken of: "Reign undisputed over the waters,

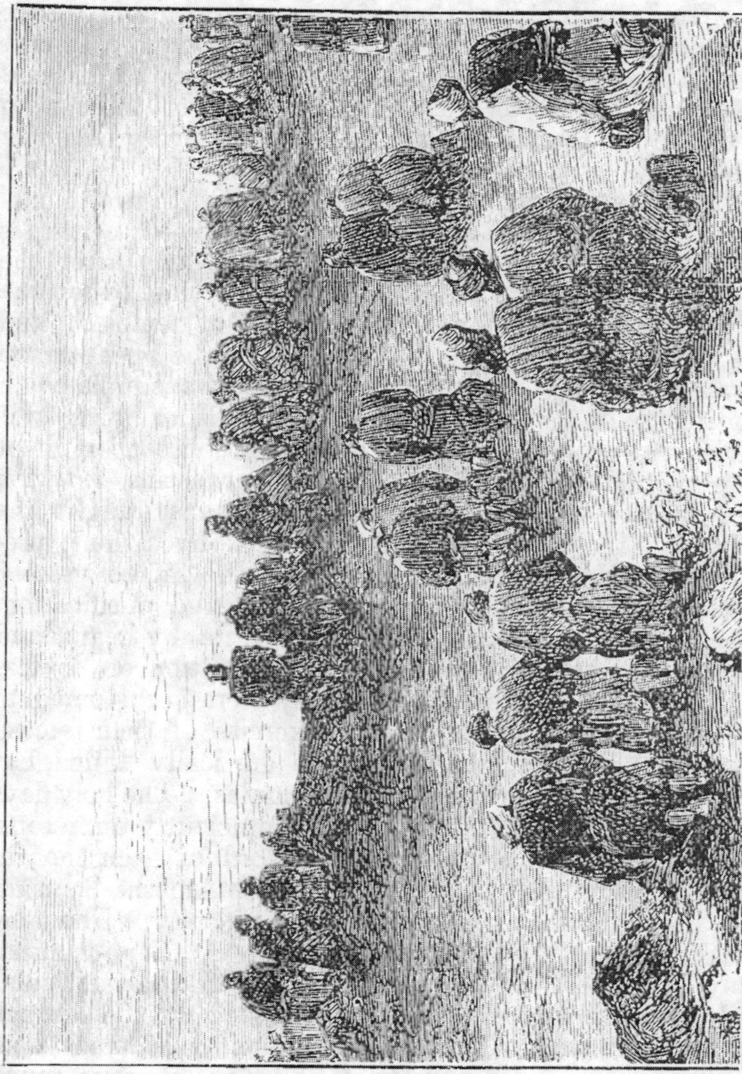

PARSEE SUN-WORSHIP.

over the trees, over all that is good and of pure origin. Make the just man powerful, and the wicked powerless and weak." A long account of the origin and history of Haoma is put into the mouth of Zoroaster, and prayer is offered to him as a person, in extravagant terms. Paradise, health, long life, prosperity, conquest, safety, posterity, etc., are among the gifts besought of Haoma. He is also asked to frustrate the efforts of those who would injure the worshipper, and to bring every calamity upon him.

From these various indications we may picture to ourselves the Zoroastrian religion as practised centuries before the Christian era, and long after the time of Zoroaster. It is to be noted that the Avesta contains no mention of temples; and the sacred fire was kept up on altars in the open air on elevated places, at most surrounded by a simple wall. No image or representation of the gods or genii was made; fire alone was sufficient to symbolise them, kept up perpetually in great stone or copper basins, fed with the choicest wood. The priests (atharvans) taught the holy law, recited the sacred texts and invocations, prepared the Haoma, washed and kept the sacred vessels, and presided at ceremonies of penance and purification. They were expected to know the Avesta by heart, and had charge of the instruction and initiation of novices and students. It appears that they were accustomed to go from place to place in the exercise of their sacred functions; and some of them were medically skilled, but performed many cures by sacred formulas. The holy days which the religion prescribed were sufficiently numerous, including the 1st, 8th, 18th, and 23rd of each month, sacred to Ormuzd, the 3rd and 5th to the Amesha-Spentas, and every day had its special spirit or deity. The new year's festival to Ormuzd, and that of the autumnal equinox to Mithra, were among the principal festivals; and the dead in general were celebrated on the last ten days of the year. The contaminations that made men impure, as we have already detailed them, gave much work to the priests in purification.

The early rites of Mazdaism.

By the time of Darius, Chaldæan and Semitic image-worship had influenced the worshippers of Ormuzd to a limited extent. Darius placed a symbolical picture of the god on his inscriptions; Artaxerxes II.

Rise of the Magi.

erected statues and a temple to Anahita, at Ecbatana. How the Magians became the priests of the Avesta religion we have no clear account. They appear to have been a tribe or caste of the Medes, and probably they were the inheritors of the primitive Aryan tradition, who accepted the Zoroastrian development of it, and acquired great influence in the Persian empire, becoming not only teachers of religion, and priests, but also political administrators and advisers; and they appear to have become combined or amalgamated with the priestly families of old Persia. The Sacred fire was carried before the kings by Magians, and the king's sons were instructed by them in the religion of Zoroaster. It is doubtful whether at this time they occupied themselves with soothsaying, prophecy, the interpretation of dreams, etc.; it is probable that these offices were performed by the Chaldæan priests. The Greek historians represent that no one could sacrifice in Persia without a Magian. They offered sacrifices at high places, first praying to fire (or rather, looking towards the sacred fire). They sacrificed animals, striking them down with a club; but no part of the flesh was set apart for the deity, the soul of the animal only being required. "As far west as Cappadocia," says Strabo, "there were enclosed places, in the midst of which was an altar heaped up with ashes. On this the Magians kept up the unquenchable fire. Each day they went and sang for an hour before the fire, holding in their hands a bundle of twigs." The Magian religion extended even to the cities of Lydia, where Pausanias observed their worship.

The exposure of corpses was but partially practised by the ancient Persians, and may have been restricted to the priests. Certainly the kings were buried: but under the Sassanian monarchy, the dead were exposed according to the modern custom.

There can be little doubt that the Avesta anciently consisted of many more books than we have at present. Various traditions speak of their number (twenty-one) and contents, and the efforts made to preserve them.

Loss of Zoroastrian books. Alexander the Great, in a drunken frolic, burnt the palace at Persepolis, which contained one of the two then existing complete copies of these books, and the other was said to have been taken away by the Greeks. The attempts of the Sassanian kings of Persia to collect and preserve the Zoroastrian books were rendered futile by the destroying fury of the Mohammedans, and those who refused to adopt the faith of the conquerors emigrated to India, and settled chiefly on western shores. They preserved some portions of the Avesta, together with translations, commentaries, and original works in the Pahlavi language and character, which prevailed in Persia from the third to the tenth century A.D.

The Pahlavi texts. In these Pahlavi texts we have much of the middle period of Mazdaism, "with a strange mixture of old and new materials," says Dr. West, "and exhibiting the usual symptom of declining powers, a strong insistence upon complex forms and minute details."

The Bundahish is one of these texts which gives an account of cosmogony and legendary history, describing

The Bundahish. creation under the good and evil influences of Ormuzd and Ahriman, with their conflicts, and coming down to early Persian kings and to Zoroaster, with a brief account of later Persian history. There are many references which indicate that this is a translation with commentary from an Avesta original. The Bahman Yast is a remarkable prophetical book, in which Ormuzd is said to give to Zarathustra a narrative of the future history of his religion.

The Shayast La-Shayast is a work about "the proper and the improper," or laws and customs about sin and

The Shayast. impurity. The nature and degrees of different breaches of propriety, the kinds of good works and those who can or cannot perform them, the mode of atoning for sins, various kinds of worship, and an infinite number of detailed rules are given, showing no elevation of mind, but a pedantic reliance on outward formal purification.

The Dadistan-i-Dinik, by Manuskihar, a high priest of the Parsees, was written in the ninth century, and represents the doctrines and practice of the modern Parsees. The title signifies "Religious Opinions or Decisions." The purpose of the creation of men is defined as "for progress and goodness," which men are bound to promote. Man is bound to glorify and praise the all-good Creator. "A righteous man is the creature by whom is accepted that occupation which is provided for him, and is fully watchful in the world as to his not being deceived by the rapacious fiend." The evil happening to the good in this world to so large an extent is attributed to the demons and evil men; but for this they receive more reward in the spiritual existence, and by it they are kept from evil and improper actions. Explanations are given as to the exposure of the dead, the knowledge by the soul of the fate of the body, the future of the evil and the good. A brilliant picture is given of heaven, and a very dark one of hell. The sacred thread-girdle is declared to be a sign of the service of the sacred beings, a token of sin ended, and a presage of beneficence. The sacred ceremonial is pleasing to Ormuzd, because it entirely fulfils his commands, and produces propitiation of good spirits, the increase of digestiveness, the growth of plants, the prosperity of the world, and the proper progress of living beings. The proper mode of celebrating the ceremonial is described; but there is little in it that adds to the essentials already described, and nothing that is of a very lofty or original character. Another Pahlavi book, "Opinions of the Spirit of Wisdom," is of interest for its expressing the belief that the "innate wisdom" of Ormuzd, a distinct personality created by Ormuzd, produced both the material and spirit worlds, and can appear in a personal form and give instructions, such as those recorded in the work itself. Another similar book is called by its author "The Doubt-dispelling Explanation," and defends and expounds the dualism of Mazdaism, asserting that other religions can only account for the origin of evil by degrading the character of the supreme Being, or by supposing a corrupting influence to be at work, which is really an evil

The Dadistan-i-Dinik.

The spirit of wisdom.

spirit. He makes references to, and attacks the inconsistencies he finds in Mohammedan, Jewish, Christian, and Manichæan doctrine.

MITHRAISM.

The recurrence of the name of Mithra in the preceding chapters, from page 7 onwards, will already have been noted; and we must now give a brief account of the obscure cultus which has been termed Mithraism, which some assert to have been the most widespread religious system in the Roman empire for some centuries after the rise of Christianity, having been even brought into this country by the Roman soldiery (see J. M. Robertson in "Religious Systems of the World," 1890, pp. 225–248). In the Veda, Mithra is twin-god with Varuna; in Zoroaster, he is lord of wide pastures, created by Ahura-Mazda; he was still lord of the heavenly light, and so became specially the sun-god, god of light and truth, of moral goodness and purity, punishing the Mithra-Druj, 'him who lies to Mithra'; hence also he is a judge in hell. (S.E., iv. xxiii.) Rawlinson says that Darius Hystaspes placed the emblems of Ahura-Mazda and of Mithra in equally conspicuous positions on the sculptured tablet above his tomb (B.C. 485); and his example was followed by later monarchs. The name Mithradates, "given by Mithra," so often borne by Eastern monarchs, is another testimony to the influence of Mithra. He came to be regarded as a sort of intermediate between Ormuzd and Ahriman, a mediator eternally young, preserving mankind from the evil one, and performing a mysterious sacrifice, through which the good will triumph; and in some aspects Mithra was regarded as a female deity, and there are many Mithraic monuments on which the symbols of two deities appear, male and female. The Græco-Roman bas-relief of Mithras slaying a bull, in the British Museum, indicates one form of the symbolism associated with this god, and connected with the idea of sacrifice and purification; and in other associations a ram was slain to Mithra. We learn from Origen that the Mithraic mysteries included a complex represen-

Mithraic monuments.

tation of the movements of the stars and planets, and of the disembodied human soul among them.

Much of the difficulty of comprehending Mithraism really is due to its opposition and proscription by early Christianity, and to the secrecy with which its worship was carried on, largely in caves. There are many remains of Mithraic altars cut out in rocks, and he was even named "Mithras out of the rock." The rites were probably to a large extent derived from those of Zoroastrianism. At the vernal equinox, the deity appears to have been symbolically mourned as dead, a stone image being laid by night on a bier to represent the dead god; and Justin Martyr and Tertullian describe initiation and other ceremonies of the worshippers of Mithra, which they regarded as imitations of the Christian sacraments. We can see in the light of the Greek myth of Persephone, that this was no imitation, but an early and widespread symbolism of the early death of Nature, and the restored life of spring-time. Initiation was an elaborate ordeal, including trial by water, by fire, by cold, by hunger, by thirst, by scourging, etc.; and the worshippers were divided into different grades, called after different birds and other animals. Tertullian says that the soldier of Mithra was offered a crown, which it was his place to refuse, saying Mithra was his crown. Mithraism seems to have had considerable popularity among the later Roman soldiery, and to have been acknowledged by the emperors, so that there are many military inscriptions, "Deo Soli Invic to Mithræ,"—"to the invincible sun-god, Mithra." The most usual representation of him depicts a young man in Oriental costume kneeling with one knee on a prostrate bull, grasping the head and pulling it back with his left hand, while with the right he plunges his sword into its neck. A dog, a snake, and a scorpion drink the blood flowing from the bull, and the sun and moon occupy the two sides of the relief.

Antagonism of Christians.

Mithraic ceremonies.

There is much curious speculation and fact bearing on Mithra-worship, but the study cannot yet be said to be placed on a basis of certainty; and to say that Christianity borrowed largely from Mithraism, is quite unproved.

CHAPTER XIII.

Modern Parseeism.

The Parsees—Their persecutions—Their principles—A Parsee catechism—The priesthood—Devotions of the laity—Festivals—Ceremonial rites—Deathbed forms—The towers of silence—Ceremonies of departed souls—Family life.—Foundation and consecration of towers.

THE PARSEES.

A PEOPLE within a people, like the Jews in England, the Parsees have attained and maintained an influence and wealth far beyond their numerical proportion. Their persistence is in its way as strong a testimony to the power of heredity as any. The people survive by their commercial ability; their religion survives with them, like Judaism with the Jews. Persecution was long their fate, both in Persia and India; the difficulties of their struggle for existence have fixed their striking characteristics in a mould more tenacious of life. May we not say that they have largely preserved a pure faith in one supreme beneficent God, Ormuzd, and believe them when they repudiate the designation fire-worshippers, and reject idolatry in all forms? Fire they revere, fire is the symbol of their god, and they do not treat fire lightly in any circumstances; indeed, they are the only people who universally refrain from tobacco-smoking, as offending their religious principles. But they are equally fixed in the determination not to defile any of the works of Ormuzd, whether earth, water, animals, or plants; and their practices of cleanliness and frequent personal ablution must have contributed

Persecution of the Parsees.

Their principles.

greatly to their maintenance in health. The greatest number of them is to be found in Bombay; they are numerous in Surat, Ahmedabad, and other cities of Gujerat; and they are to be found in many other cities under British Indian rule. Their total number is about 82,000, including 8,000 in Persia (Yezd, etc.). Their name is derived from their original province, Pars, or Fars, from which Persia is named.

The Parsees, or Guebres, of Yezd have still thirty-four fire temples great and small, but possess very few books; and till lately were in a very degraded condition and in great poverty, being most unjustly treated by their Mahometan neighbours; their condition has, however, been mitigated by the persistent efforts of the Parsees of Bombay and of the British ministry in Persia. At Baku, on the Caspian, they still have fire temples.

A Parsee catechism.

Till recently the pure faith was only preserved by a few of the Parsee priests; and the average priest was little but a reciter of portions of the sacred books and formulas by rote, without understanding the language in which they were written. Of late years a catechism of instruction has been prepared for the instruction of Parsee children, from which we learn that they are taught that there is one God, Ormuzd, and that Zartusht (Zoroaster) is his true prophet; that the religion of the Avesta was communicated to him by God, and that it is true beyond doubt; that God is good, and that good deeds are enjoined. All evil and wickedness are strictly forbidden. Morality is confined within three words, pure-thought, pure-word, pure-deed; truth is particularly enjoined. Evil deeds will bring punishment after death in hell, and judgment is believed to take place on the fourth day after death, determining whether the deceased goes to heaven or hell. But a future resurrection is held out as certain, when God only can save any one. It is also enjoined upon believers that they turn their face towards some luminous object while engaged in prayer and worship, which must be of frequent occurrence in the day. Angels are believed in, who aid mankind in various ways, and superintend various parts of creation. Prayers are addressed to these spirits. Prayer is made that the evil may become virtuous and be pardoned by the mercy of Ormuzd. There is no propitiation of the evil spirits, or prayer to them.

The priesthood is handed down by inheritance from father to son, although priests may become laymen. The high priests, or dasturs, are the especial religious authorities, imposing penances and declaring doctrine. The ordinary priests, or mobeds, and the lower priests, or herbads, complete the religious orders of the Parsees. They have a council, or Panchyat, composed of six dasturs and twelve mobeds, which settles all the joint affairs of the Parsee community. At present the condition of the Parsee priesthood is one of progress; two colleges, representing the two sects of the Parsees (marked by comparatively unimportant differences), have been established, under able teachers; and learned works of considerable value bearing on the history and ancient texts of their religion have been produced by Parsees who have studied at German universities and write English with fluency. The Parsee community does not make offerings to the priests and to the temples the chief or only meritorious work; but its charitable institutions are numerous, and a Parsee beggar is unknown.

The priesthood.

As to the devotional practices of the laity, a man who is very religious will say prayers many times a day, albeit in the Avesta language, which he does not understand. Prayer may be said on rising from sleep, after bathing, and after every operation of life, before and after meals, and before going to bed. Among the strangest and most repulsive of Parsee practices, to western notion, is the habit of rubbing nirang (cow's urine) over face and hands, as a specific against devas or evil spirits, a prayer or incantation being recited at the same time. Devotions at the Parsee fire altars are quite optional, and they may be performed at any time by the worshippers, who usually give something to the priests. There is, however, a considerable attendance at the festivals, about once a week, and at special seasons, such as the six days' festival in

Devotions of the laity.

Festivals.

the middle of winter, celebrating the six periods of creation, that at the spring equinox in honour of agriculture, that to Mithra, etc. On the tenth day of the eighth month there is a festival to Fravardin, who presides over the souls of the departed, when special ceremonies for the

FIRE TEMPLE OF PARSEES, BAKU

dead are performed, the towers of silence are visited, and prayers said for them in the small temples in the grounds; these are in addition to annual celebrations for the dead in each house. New Year's Day is both a day of religious festival and social intercourse, when the fire-temples are visited and prayers said, looking towards the altar of sacred fire. Visits to friends, with ceremonial hand-joining, follow, and alms are given to the poor.

The Parsee infant, born on a ground floor, to which he is again brought as soon as he is dead, has his nativity cast on the seventh day by a Brahman or Parsee astrologer-priest; at seven years old he is purified with nirang, and invested with the sacred girdle of seventy-two threads, representing the seventy-two chapters of the Yasna. As the priest blesses the child, he throws upon its head portions of fruits, spices, and perfumes. This is the ceremony of the *kusti*. Marriages are carefully arranged by the astrologer, but are celebrated with a religious ceremony, in which the couple are tied together by a silken cord gradually wound round them, while a benediction is pronounced in Zend and Sanskrit. It is in their funerals that the Parsees are most peculiar. A dying Parsee will be attended by a priest, who repeats to him consolatory texts from the Avesta, gives him the sacred Haoma juice to drink, and prays for the forgiveness of his sins. The body is then taken to a ground-floor room from which everything has been removed, laid upon stones, washed in warm water, dressed in clean white clothes, and laid upon an iron bier. The priest, in the presence of the corpse, gives an exhortation to the relatives to live pure and holy lives, so that they may meet the deceased again in paradise. This exhortation consists of the first gatha of Zoroaster. A dog is brought in to look at the deceased, this being known as the *sag-did* or dog's gaze. This used to be looked upon as a means of judging, by the dog's instinct, whether life was really extinct; but it is now explained as securing the passage of the soul over the Chinvat bridge, over which only the pious pass to heaven. The carriage of the body to the towers of silence is committed to a special class of Parsees called Nessusalar, or unclean, from the work they perform. The towers of silence in Bombay are constructed on the top of Malabar Hill, a great home of vultures. Built of stone, they rise about twenty-five

Ceremonial rites.

Deathbed forms.

The towers of silence.

feet, with only a small entrance below. On arrival at the appointed tower, prayers are said at the neighbouring fire-altar. The body is then exposed on a stone platform within the tower, so that all fluids pass into a well, into which also the bones left by the vultures are swept. During the three days after death a priest constantly prays before a burning fire, fed with sandal-wood near the spot where the dead body was laid, the soul not being believed to leave this world during that period. On the fourth day after death there is a further ceremony for the soul of the departed. Contributions to charities are made in memory of the deceased, and successive annual, *muktad*, or ceremonies of departed souls, keep them in remembrance.

Ceremonies of departed souls.

The well-to-do perform a ceremony every day of the first year after a death; and the last ten days of their year are specially set apart for the muktad. One of the rooms of the house is specially cleaned and set apart, and every morning choice flowers and fruits are placed there, and prayers are offered in it by the relatives, not only for the dead but for themselves for forgiveness of their past sins.

Parsees keep their heads covered day and night, having imbibed an idea that it is sinful to be uncovered. Parsee women occupy a much higher position than among Hindus and Mohammedans; and in recent years women have been admitted to meals in common with the men. The family life, especially of the well-to-do, has much in it that is admirable. The education of women has made great progress among them in recent years. Much superstition still exists about the significance of particular days, every day having some special thing for which it is best suited; some days for beginning a journey, others for choosing a new house, others for soliciting a bride, etc.

Family life.

The largest tower of silence in Bombay is about ninety feet in diameter, or 300 feet in circumference, the outer (circular) walls being built of very hard stone, faced with white plaster. Inside the tower is a circular platform extending to its full circumference, formed of large stone slabs, divided into three rows of exposed receptacles for

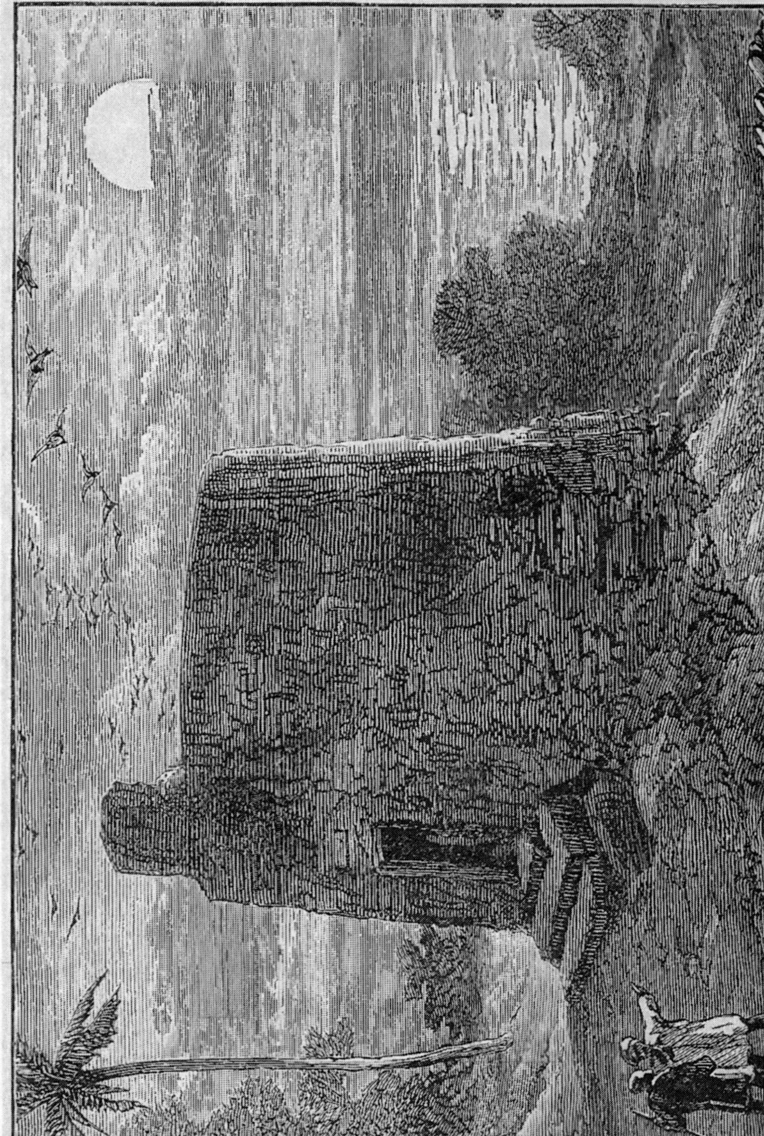

TOWER OF SILENCE, MALABAR HILL, BOMBAY.

the bodies of the dead, diminishing towards the interior, the exterior row being used for men, the middle for women, and the inner for children. Each receptacle is separated from the others by ridges about an inch high; and channels are cut for the purpose of conveying all liquids into a deep hollow, or well, in the centre of the tower. "When the corpse has been completely stripped of its flesh by the vultures, which is generally accomplished within one hour at the outside, and when the bones of the denuded skeleton are perfectly dried up by the powerful heat of a tropical sun, they are thrown into this pit, where they crumble into dust." There are also four drains leading from the pit to the exterior, opening into four wells. "At the mouth of each drain charcoal and sandstones are placed for purifying the fluid before it enters the ground, thus observing one of the tenets of the Zoroastrian religion, that "the mother earth shall not be defiled." The wells have a permeable bottom, which is covered with sand to a height of five or seven feet.

Foundation and consecration of towers.

The foundation-laying and the consecration of a new tower is an occasion of great ceremony. After the ground has been marked out and limited with a thread carried round a large number of nails arranged in a circle, prayers are offered to Sraosha, the guardian deity of the souls of the dead, to Ormuzd, and to Spenta Armati, the guardian deity of earth, to departed souls, and to the seven Amesha-Spentas. These prayers, acknowledging that it is wrong to contaminate the earth with the bodies of the dead, pray that the enclosed space, and no more, may be occupied for depositing the bodies of departed souls. At the consecration of a dokhma, a trench is dug all round it, and then in the centre of the tower two priests perform the Yasna and Vendidad prayers and ceremonies in honour of Sraosha for three consecutive mornings and nights. On the fourth morning there is a prayer in honour of Ormuzd; and afterwards there are similar prayers to those at the foundation. Other services outside the tower follow, during and after which thousands of Parsees visit the tower, which is afterwards closed to everybody. Sometimes the towers are erected by public subscription, but private persons frequently bear the sole expense, it being considered a specially meritorious act to build one.

Thus, in the midst of antagonistic creeds, persists the religion associated with the name of Zoroaster, a standing revelation to us of the ideas and worship of long-distant ages. Reverence and worship for the great Ormuzd, the supreme Being, principally typified by the wondrous fire, dread of the evil spirit and anxiety to avoid the evils he can bring, and practical charity chiefly characterise this most interesting survival from the past. Learned modern Parsees maintain and teach that invocations to spirits other than the supreme God do not belong to the religion as originally established by Zoroaster, and that they may all be dispensed with, retaining the belief in one God and in purity of thought, word, and deed. They hold also that all their ritual and ceremonies may be altered according to the spiritual state and needs of the community.

[For the best account of the modern Parsees and their present religious state, see "History of the Parsees," by Dosabhai Framji Karaka, C.S.I., late member of the Bombay Legislative Council. Macmillan, 1884.]

INDEX.